Economic and Financial Aspects of Social Security

First Published in 1960, *Economic and Financial Aspects of Social Security* presents an important intervention by Professor J. Henry Richardson, an experienced authority on social security. Specially valuable is the chapter which considers what proportion of national income can be afforded for social security and also that on the alternatives of financing by accumulating large funds or by 'pay-as-you-go' methods. The author directs particular attention to age and retirement and urges that both social security systems and industrial organization should be so devised as to give encouragement and facilities for older people to continue working as long as they are fit. He also discusses remedies for poverty arising from sickness and large families with low incomes. The value of social security as a factor in economic security and in the redistribution of income, safeguards against inflation, and the problem of saving today for consumption in the future are also examined. This book is an essential read for scholars and researchers of political economy, labour economics and economics in general.

T0382719

Economic and Financial Aspects of Social Security

An International Survey

J. Henry Richardson

Routledge
Taylor & Francis Group

First published in 1960
by George Allen & Unwin Ltd.

This edition first published in 2022 by Routledge
2 Park Square, Milton Park, Abingdon, Oxon, OX14 4RN

and by Routledge
605 Third Avenue, New York, NY 10017

Routledge is an imprint of the Taylor & Francis Group, an informa business

© John Henry Richardson 1960

Publisher's Note
The publisher has gone to great lengths to ensure the quality of this reprint but points out that some imperfections in the original copies may be apparent.

Disclaimer
The publisher has made every effort to trace copyright holders and welcomes correspondence from those they have been unable to contact.

A Library of Congress record exists under LCCN:

ISBN: 978-1-032-18441-8 (hbk)
ISBN: 978-1-003-25454-6 (ebk)
ISBN: 978-1-032-18443-2 (pbk)

Book DOI 10.4324/9781003254546

ECONOMIC AND FINANCIAL ASPECTS OF SOCIAL SECURITY

An International Survey

BY

J. HENRY RICHARDSON

Cassidy Research Visiting Professor 1956-7
School of Social Work
University of Toronto

Formerly Pro-Vice-Chancellor
and Professor of Industrial Relations
University of Leeds

Ruskin House

GEORGE ALLEN & UNWIN LTD

MUSEUM STREET LONDON

FIRST PUBLISHED IN 1960.
SECOND IMPRESSION 1961

PRINTED IN GREAT BRITAIN
BY PHOTOLITHO
in 10 *on* 11 *pt Times type*
BY UNWIN BROTHERS LIMITED
WOKING AND LONDON

THE HARRY M. CASSIDY MEMORIAL RESEARCH FUND

The Cassidy Memorial Research Fund was established in 1952 to commemorate the pioneer work of the late Harry M. Cassidy, Director of the School of Social Work, University of Toronto, 1945-51. In particular, it is intended to further Harry Cassidy's conviction that the policies of social welfare and practices of social work need to be based on objective study and research. It is an essential principle of research that the results should be published and available for study and use. For this reason, the Fund sponsors publication of the results of research work when it is satisfied that the work has been thoroughly done and the material is of intrinsic value. Publication under the sponsorship of the Fund does not imply responsibility for the content of the work, or agreement with the opinions expressed: these are properly the responsibility of the authors.

PREFACE

Social security is a major feature of public social policy today. From tentative beginnings in a few countries in the early decades of the present century it has rapidly become a big factor in the lives of many millions of people throughout the world. My interest in it began in the 1920's while I was engaged in research into international comparisons of wages and standards of living as a member of the staff of the International Labour Office. These studies showed clearly that if a major concern of workers is about their weekly wages, a second one almost equally vital is security for themselves and their wives and children, including provision for their maintenance during sickness, disablement from accidents, unemployment, and the years of retirement.

No one could live through the depression years of the 1930's without recognising the need for comprehensive programmes of social security. Millions of skilled, competent able-bodied workers lost their jobs through no fault of their own, and they and their families suffered severe hardship and privation. As Professor of Industrial Relations in the University of Leeds I had opportunities to study conditions at first hand in severely depressed areas in Britain. However, Britain was fortunate in having organized a widespread system of unemployment insurance, and the benefits paid to the unemployed not only mitigated their hardships, but provided purchasing power which was one of the factors that made the depression somewhat less severe in Britain than in the United States, Canada and Germany.

In a visit to the United States during the depression years, where at one time as many as sixteen million workers were unemployed, I was able to see something of the chaos that resulted from the lack of an adequate system of social security. Hastily improvised relief works were started and assistance was given, but there was wide recognition that a more permanent system was necessary. This led to the adoption of the New Deal Social Security Act, 1935, which, with amendments, brought into being the Old-Age, Survivors, and Disability Insurance Program, laid a foundation for unemployment insurance and allowed for federal grants-in-aid to states for assistance to the aged, dependent children and the blind and for the development of measures to help disabled persons. This represents a great advance though it leaves a number of gaps.

When I visited Australia in 1938 a comprehensive programme of social security was under active discussion in Parliament, and was subsequently adopted. The tour also included New Zealand, where the Social Security Act, 1938, provided the first complete co-ordinated social security system in any country. Later, in 1946, the United Kingdom also instituted a comprehensive system.

After the Second World War, as a member in the United Kingdom of the Colonial Labour Advisory Committee of the Secretary of State for the Colonies, I had opportunities to consider problems of social security in the underdeveloped territories of the British Commonwealth to which the Committee gave special attention in order to give guidance in the formulating of policy in these areas. In this period I was adviser on social security to the governments of British Guiana, Barbados, Bermuda and Venezuela. Visits to Burma, India and West Africa also enabled me to study the relation between wages and the social security needs of workers in the early stages of industrialization in these countries, where conditions differ so greatly from those in the advanced countries of the West.

This experience in representative countries with low as well as high standards of living and a wide variety of political and social traditions, provided a useful basis for considering the fundamental aspects of social security and the extent to which one country can draw on the experience of others or must work out a quite different system of its own. In a short chapter on social security included in my book, *An Introduction to the Study of Industrial Relations* (1954), I wrote: 'Social security is a subject big enough to require a volume or even several volumes to itself.' At that time I wanted to write more extensively on the subject but saw no early opportunity of doing so. However, soon afterwards I was awarded the Cassidy Research Visiting Professorship for the year 1956-7 in the School of Social Work, University of Toronto, to study economic and financial aspects of social security. This award provided welcome facilities to concentrate on the subject and gave me freedom from teaching, university administration and committee work.

During the year at Toronto valuable assistance was given by Professor Charles E. Hendry, Director of the School of Social Work, Professor John S. Morgan, Mrs Florence Strakhovsky, Research Secretary of the Cassidy Memorial Research Fund, and by other members of the staff of the School with whom I worked in continuous co-operation. Visits were made to Ottawa, Washington and New York for consultations with officers in federal government departments, with authorities in schools of social work and with business men, trade unionists and others interested in social security. Contacts were made with the provincial departments of health and welfare in Ontario, Manitoba, Saskatchewan, Alberta and British Columbia, whose deputy ministers and their colleagues were most helpful; there were also opportunities to discuss problems and policies with university people, members of the medical profession, hospital administrators and representative leaders in industry, agriculture and labour. Particular mention must be made of the valuable information supplied by the Ministry of Pensions and National Insurance in Great Britain, the Social Security Division of the International Labour Office and by members of the staff of the United Nations.

Special thanks for information and suggestions are due to Mr George F. Davidson, Deputy Minister of Welfare in the Canadian Department of National Health and Welfare, to his colleague, Dr Joseph W. Willard, Director of the Research and Statistics Division of the Department, and to Mr Richard E. G. Davis, Executive Director of the Canadian Welfare Council. Mr J. G. Bisson, Chief Commissioner of the Unemployment Insurance Commission, and his colleagues, Mr R. J. Tallon and Mr C. A. L. Murchison, kindly gave a detailed account of the problems and policies of the Commission.

In Toronto much useful information was made available by Mr James S. Band, Deputy Minister of Public Welfare for the province of Ontario, Dr J. T. Phair, Deputy Minister of Health, Mr E. E. Sparrow, Chairman of the Ontario Workmen's Compensation Board, and I had valuable discussions with Mr W. M. Anderson, President of the North American Life Assurance Company, and with Professor Malcolm G. Taylor of the Department of Political Economy, University of Toronto.

In the United States valuable help was given by Commissioner Charles I. Schottland of the United States Department of Health, Education, and Welfare, Social Security Administration, and by his colleagues, Mr Robert J. Myers, Chief Actuary, Mrs Ida C. Merriam, Director of Research, and Mr Robert M. Ball, Deputy Director. I benefited greatly from discussions with Dr Eveline M. Burns of the New York School of Social Work, Columbia University, with Dr Wilbur J. Cohen, Professor of Public Welfare Administration, School of Social Work, University of Michigan, and with Dr Victor Howery, Director of the School of Social Work, University of Washington, Seattle, who together with Mr W. G. Dixon, Director of the School of Social Work, University of British Columbia, assisted me in my work when on the Pacific Coast. During 1955-6, as Visiting Professor of Economics at the University of California, I also had opportunities to study standards of living and social security problems in the rapidly expanding economy of the Pacific region, and during 1957-8, when I was Visiting Professor at the New York State School of Industrial and Labor Relations, Cornell University, the discussions I had with members of the faculty were of great assistance.

The economic and financial aspects of social security constitute a very large subject of study, and in writing this book I have had to select what I considered to be the most significant aspects. The book is, therefore, a personal evaluation based on comparative analysis. My intention, however, has not been to present firm conclusions, but to open questions for discussion. Discussion is vital at the present stage of the evolution of social security if the issues are to be clarified, if the available resources are to be put to their best use and if the right blend of public responsibility, voluntary effort and individual responsibility is to be found.

J.H.R.

CONTENTS

		page
PREFACE		9

I   INTRODUCTION   15
*Social Security in Primitive Communities—The
Need for a Comprehensive Social Security Pro-
gramme in an Industrial Society—Social Security
Still Piecemeal and Incomplete—Some Basic Issues*

II   DEFINITION AND SCOPE   27
The Content of Social Security—Scope and Method

III   BASIC POLICIES AND PRINCIPLES   36
*The State and the Individual—Variable or Uniform
Flat Rate Benefits—Contributions—Public Assist-
ance—Benefits in Cash—Need for Co-ordination*

IV   SOCIAL INSURANCE   55
*Comparison with Private Insurance—Changes Nec-
essitated by Inflation—Contributions and Tax-
ation—Contributions by Workers—Contributions by
Employers—Contributions by Public Authorities—
Distribution of Costs*

V   ACCUMULATION OF FUNDS *versus*
'PAY-AS-YOU-GO' FINANCING   69
*Private Saving—Governmental Social Security
Financing—Investment of Social Security Funds—
Present Saving and Future Resources—Effects of
Inflation—Growth in Productivity—Productive In-
vestment of Funds*

VI   PROPORTION OF SOCIAL SECURITY
PAYMENTS TO NATIONAL INCOME   85
*International Comparisons—Hypothetical Expendi-
tures—Distribution of Social Security Expenditures*

VII   AGE AND RETIREMENT   98
*Chronological and Biological Age—Productivity and
Wages—The Effects of Labour-Saving Machinery—
Decisions on Retirement—The Problem of Pro-
motion—The Efficiency of the Aged—Provision for
Old Age—Age for Social Security Pensions—Rates
of Benefit—Methods of Financing—Provident
Funds—Pooled Contributions—Special or Ear-
marked Taxes—General Taxes—The Canadian
System—Occupational Pensions—Welfare Services
for the Aged*

VIII FAMILY ALLOWANCES 139
The Evolution of Family Allowances—The Wage Dilemma—State Allowances—Income Tax Allowances for Children—Economic and Social Value

IX HEALTH 156
Priorities—Cash Income Insurance—Medical Care—Medical Care in the United States and Canada—Some Medical Professional Problems—Some Financial Considerations

X OTHER CONTINGENCIES 182
Unemployment Insurance—Workmen's Compensation — Long-Term Disability — Widows and Orphans—Maternity—General

XI SOME ECONOMIC CONSIDERATIONS 211
Underdeveloped Countries—Social Security as a Factor in Economic Stability—The Redistribution of Income—Inflation—Federal, Regional and Local Responsibilities—International Standards and Relative Costs

XII CONCLUSIONS 233

SELECTED REFERENCES 247

INDEX 256

CHAPTER I

INTRODUCTION

Comprehensive measures of social security are a recent development. Although social insurance was introduced in Germany in the 1880's, extensive application was impracticable during the nineteenth century because laissez-faire doctrines were still dominant and poverty was widely regarded as the result of the incompetence, thriftlessness and vices of the poor. In earlier centuries before the growth of modern industry, the problems of insecurity were different and the solutions adopted were simpler than in the complex, economically interrelated communities of today.

Apart from poor relief, which is now outmoded except in the more rationally administered form of public assistance, extensive systems of social security are a feature essentially of the present century. In some advanced countries, including the United States and Canada, they began only in the 1930's or 1940's and much is still piecemeal and unco-ordinated. In many underdeveloped countries the 1950's were still years of limited tentative experiments and there was much discussion in these countries about priorities and the limitations imposed by their poverty, low standards of productivity and dearth of trained administrative personnel.

In all countries the principles and methods of social security are under continuous active discussion, changes are frequent and nowhere has a final pattern evolved. In many countries there are gaps in the social security scheme and substantial numbers of people are not effectively protected. In underdeveloped countries these gaps are often due to lack of resources, while in some wealthy advanced countries public opinion is not yet ready for comprehensive coverage. There is, therefore, scope for much research into basic principles, trends of evolution and the proportions of national income which countries can afford to spend on social security in relation to the many other claims on their resources, including capital for investment to increase productivity and raise standards of living.

SOCIAL SECURITY IN PRIMITIVE COMMUNITIES

Social security problems in primitive communities, whether in former periods or in underdeveloped countries today, differ greatly from those in communities where modern industrial conditions are established. Wars, including tribal conflicts and raids, were in earlier times a cause of insecurity, destruction, poverty and distress. Destruction of life and property by natural forces, such as earthquakes and floods, was in some ways more serious than it is today, as means of transportation and communication were so limited that people might be dying of hunger in one locality when resources which could have saved them were available only a few hundred miles away. Today the news of disasters flashes round the world within minutes or hours, and relief is rapidly mobilised. Yet communities in earlier times had their systems of social security. The most famous and extensive was that organised in Egypt by Joseph, who accumulated vast reserves in the seven years of plenty and spread their distribution over the seven lean years, thereby establishing an effective relation between saving and spending and avoiding wide fluctuations in standards of living. Most early communities were predominantly agricultural, and seasonal variations in output were regularly adjusted by storage so that supplies of food would not fluctuate too widely from plenty to scarcity; nevertheless, in poor years privation was often severe.

Whereas in a wage economy the insecurity of a family's income is caused principally by unemployment of all kinds, including seasonal unemployment, nowadays in a rural economy of small holders and peasant cultivators insecurity is caused not only by unfavourable weather and other causes of bad harvests, but also by fluctuations in agricultural prices, particularly where crops are sold for cash in world markets. In the inter-war years, the unstable standards of living of peasant cocoa farmers in the Gold Coast and of workers in rubber plantations in Malaya were the result of big changes in prices. Protection against these risks may take the form of marketing schemes and of insurance against losses in crops and livestock. Emergency relief on a national or international scale is needed when local communities are the victims of disasters, caused by the forces of nature, which are too serious for them to meet.

Some causes of insecurity were often less drastic in earlier times than they are today. Children began to earn their keep at an early age, and large families were usually an economic asset. Sick people and victims of accidents who were temporarily unable to work were provided with food and other necessaries by members of their families, by neighbours in the village who knew them well, by monastic or other religious institutions or by the local lord of the manor. Invalids, widows, orphans and the aged were similarly sustained. Local communities and tribes were knit together for mutual support and security.

Such neighbourliness is indeed a most valuable feature of human relations today as well as in earlier times, but so often nowadays in big urban centres people do not know those who live near them, and frequent movement prevents them from establishing those close associations and friendly relations which strengthen the foundations of security through direct mutual aid. In the feudal system, with all its drawbacks and restrictions, each individual had his established place and continuity of relationships and responsibilities; the coming of the industrial age not only broke the hampering chains of feudalism but destroyed the security it had provided.

THE NEED FOR A COMPREHENSIVE SOCIAL SECURITY PROGRAMME IN AN INDUSTRIAL SOCIETY

In the past, industry has borne only a part of the real costs of production. It has paid for the raw materials used, for machinery and factory buildings and the wages of its workpeople, but it has not adequately covered the social costs of industry. During the nineteenth century, when there was little state intervention and trade unions were too weak adequately to protect the workers, the road along which industry advanced was strewn with human derelicts. Victims of industrial accidents received little or no compensation, workers whose health was broken by injurious industrial processes were left to fend for themselves and the aged were dependent in the last resort on the harsh humiliations of poor relief and the grim institutional accommodation of the workhouse.[1]

Though industry depended on a large labour force, workers were dismissed with little or no notice whenever trade was slack, and were left to face poverty from loss of wages until industry wanted them back again. This treatment would be meted out even to men with long service, and scarcely a thought was given to their future or what would happen to the families dependent upon them. Industrial progress was often rapid but many people fell by the way-

---

[1] The social costs of industry cannot be reckoned solely in terms of the direct costs to the workers. Air pollution, the destruction of amenities and many other consequences of industrial development represent costs which industry has neglected to meet. A review of these wider aspects is given by K. William Kapp in *The Social Costs of Private Enterprise* (Cambridge, Mass., 1950).

B

side. Some argued that the unemployed man had only himself to blame if he went down, but it is now recognised that usually he was the victim of a system which he did not understand, and that the answer to his problem was for the community to organise ways of helping him to find another job and to provide systematically for his needs until he could maintain himself again. Only recently has attention been directed to the responsibility of employers so to plan and organise their work and labour force that redundancy is reduced to a minimum, and to pay appropriate compensation to workers with considerable service if they are dismissed because of lack of work. The growing attention being given in some industries to a guaranteed annual wage and to severance pay based on length of service is linked with the idea of giving the worker some security against seasonal and other lay-offs, and of making employers responsible for minimising unemployment from such causes.

Nowadays, technological developments, automation and electronic controls are accelerating the pace of industrial change. They generally represent substantial immediate and long-term advantages to the community, although some people will lose because, for example, their former skills are no longer wanted. There are also uncertainties about the effects of atomic devices on the health of the community. However, attitudes today contrast with those in the nineteenth century: governments are now more alive to the necessity of regulating industry to prevent injury to human welfare, trade unions in many countries are strong and alert in protecting the workers and leading industrialists recognise that it is good business to satisfy the reasonable claims of those they employ.

Contrasts between agricultural and industrial economies, and the greater anxieties and insecurities of the latter, are forcefully expressed by Professor Charles E. Hendry in an article in which he refers to the early farm immigrants to Canada, who were called 'settlers' and lived in 'settlements'.[2] These terms suggest security, and mutual aid and neighbourliness in times of difficulty. Apart from their exposure to the vagaries of the weather, the workers on the land had a feeling of self-sufficiency and a sense of security. With the coming of industrialisation a cash economy replaces a crop economy, mobility of labour is a necessity, workers become dependent on the manoeuvres of high finance and economic policy and their services may become unwanted because of the invention

[2] "Age of Anxiety", *Canadian Welfare* (Ottawa: Canadian Welfare Council), September 15, 1955, pp. 143-51. Professor Hendry is Director of the School of Social Work, University of Toronto.

of labour-saving machines. 'Unemployment becomes an even greater threat than the ominous shadows of a sky darkened by the approach of a hail storm across prairies ripe with wheat.' The worker is faced with uncertainties and insecurities, and is inevitably anxious about his future and that of his family. Fortunately, the productivity of modern industry provides resources sufficient to establish new forms of security.

This book is concerned essentially with security provided by the state. However, state provision is closely related to private provision by individual thrift, voluntary insurance and schemes for workpeople organised as 'fringe' benefits associated with their employment. One of the fundamental problems of social security is to determine what should be the extent of the state's responsibilities and what should be borne by individuals and private groups. Another problem is to determine how much a country can afford to spend on social security, remembering, however, that much of the expenditure pays for itself in the better health and greater efficiency of the population. Writing about Britain during the Second World War, Professor Cassidy with great insight said that the social services 'instead of being a luxury, or a sop to the conscience of the wealthy, or a desirable but costly charity, or an irresistible political demand of organized labour, are actually an indispensable element in the full mobilization of the nation.'[3] What was true of these services in time of war is equally valid in time of peace, and social security can make a big contribution to increasing the efficiency of production. Britain did not curtail her systems of social security during the war, but indeed expanded them, and it was in the war years that the still more comprehensive post-war scheme was planned.

The economic and humanitarian value of social security has been increasingly recognised, and many countries spend on it from 5 to 15 per cent of their national income. The size of this expenditure is mainly accounted for by measures taken during the second quarter

[3] Harry M. Cassidy, *Social Security and Reconstruction in Canada* (Toronto, 1943), p. 2. A somewhat similar view was expressed in a report on a co-ordinated policy regarding family levels of living that was submitted to the United Nations by a group of experts under the chairmanship of Dr George F. Davidson, Deputy Minister of Welfare in the Canadian Department of National Health and Welfare. The group was convened jointly by the United Nations and the International Labour Organisation. They said : 'Instead of treating social policy as a housemaid whose function is to tidy up human suffering and insecurity left in the wake of economic development, social objectives should be "built-in" on an equal footing with economic objectives into comprehensive social economic planning' (United Nations document E/CN. 5/321, February 28, 1957, Appendix)

of the present century in recognition of the value of social security. Among the items of national expenditure, social security comes second only to defence, itself in the widest sense a form of social security, and if substantial progress could be made in removing international tensions and in reducing expenditure on armaments, social security and education would become the most important items of public expenditure.

The cost of social security is a fair and reasonable charge on the community to cover the inevitable insecurities of life, some of which, particularly unemployment, are consequences of industrialisation and specialisation in modern production. In terms of human capital, it somewhat resembles the cost which employers bear to offset the depreciation of machinery, buildings and other material capital. Often employers would fully cover the depreciation of material capital, but neglected human capital. For each human being, life is whole and indivisible, and somehow, from the output of industry, resources must be pooled and spread to provide comprehensively for maintenance, not only by adequate wages during working years but by assistance for the periods when earnings cease and for the children who will be the next generation of workers.

Social security for all was one of the objectives of the Atlantic Charter, which included among its purposes the assurance that people in all lands may 'live out their lives in freedom from fear and want'. Yet some of the leading signatories of the Charter still have considerable gaps in their systems of social security, and, in consequence, many people have not been given assurance of freedom from want.[4] Although for some people, and in some circumstances, fear and insecurity may be spurs to action, generally these are evils, and freedom from them is essential if the best work is to be done. Some few may stagnate because of security, but for the great majority basic security is necessary for attaining the highest standards of efficiency. Without such security, freedom itself is endangered.

From the beginning of the present century, some countries began

---

[4] The Canadian Prime Minister, Mr W. L. Mackenzie King, speaking at the annual convention of the American Federation of Labor in Toronto on October 9, 1942, said, 'The era of freedom will be achieved only as social security and human welfare become the main concern of men and nations.' They include 'useful employment for all who are willing to work, standards of nutrition and housing adequate to ensure the health of the whole population, social insurance against privations resulting from unemployment, accident, death of the breadwinner, ill health, and old age.' King, *Labour and the War* (Canada and the War Series, Ottawa, 1942).

to see the need to introduce better methods than poor relief to cope with the insecurities which were largely caused by industrialisation, and particularly by the mobility of labour, the wage economy, a more individual form of society and the breakdown of traditional simple methods of provision by tribes and rural communities. There was a growing recognition that social welfare ought to be a responsibility of government. In consequence, social insurance has evolved as the most effective form of security. The impact of modern industry was rapid, almost revolutionary. In many countries, however, it was not until the distresses and chaos caused by the depression of the 1930's that a substantial advance in the provision of security was made. Necessity compelled action.[5]

SOCIAL SECURITY STILL PIECEMEAL AND INCOMPLETE

In all countries, social insurance began piecemeal, either for special groups of workers or for particular risks, but the general trend has been to widen its scope by including more industries, and agricultural workers, farmers, domestic servants and self-employed people (who were excluded from the earlier schemes), and by covering more risks. Yet, substantial gaps often remain.

It is to be expected that there should be gaps in the social security schemes of underdeveloped countries; they lack resources, and only small proportions of the population living in industrial urban centres have become insecure because they no longer benefit from the traditional rural and tribal methods of provision. The leaving of gaps is, however, more surprising in some wealthy, highly industrial countries. In the United States, for example, though comprehensive provision is made for old age and short-term unemployment, there is a lack of sickness insurance, medical care (including

[5] In Canada, as recently as 1944, although it is true that there were old age pensions under a Dominion-provincial scheme, they were paid only after a means test, as were also benefits for widows and orphans financed by nearly all provincial governments. According to the Department of Finance, *Report on the Administration of Old Age Pensions* (Ottawa, 1941), p. 10, half the Canadians over seventy years of age were then in receipt of old age pensions based on a means test. Many in the other half must have been in need but did not apply for assistance, while others, no doubt, had quite low standards of living even if they could not have qualified for a means test pension. After the war, in order to provide better standards of social security and to establish systems which would be of value if depressions were experienced again, the federal government introduced comprehensive measures to provide old age pensions and family allowances without means tests.

hospital accommodation), and provision for children in large families of low-paid workers.

The existence of gaps is due to a variety of factors, and these vary from country to country in accordance with special conditions and traditions. Sometimes a gap is merely temporary, and is progressively filled as experience is gained and methods are evolved for meeting administrative difficulties. A good illustration is provided by the Old-Age, Survivors, and Disability Insurance Program in the United States, the scope of which has been widened until it is almost comprehensive. It now includes self-employed persons, domestic servants, agricultural workers, widows and orphans, people over fifty years of age suffering from total permanent disability and others who were excluded in the early stages.

Some gaps remain because of the opposition of vested interests. Many members of the medical profession may strongly resist the establishment of public health services, and insurance companies may oppose some forms of social insurance because they fear their business might suffer. Such vested interests emphasise the value of voluntary insurance and point out that the number of people who protect themselves in this way is increasing.

Each country has its own attitude to social security, and this affects both scope and methods. In Canada and the United States, for example, in the prosperous years after the war, special emphasis has been placed on free enterprise and industrial economic expansion, and in some fields this emphasis has led to undue reliance on voluntary insurance and individual responsibility. If private measures were to become sufficiently widespread, comprehensive and reasonable in cost so as to provide adequate protection for almost the whole population, then various extensive state schemes would be unnecessary, and the needs of small residues of people who, for one reason or another, were not protected by private insurance could be met by public assistance. There would be no need to set up an elaborate system of social insurance for this small minority. Evidence, however, shows that large numbers of people in the poorer sections of the population are not properly protected by voluntary insurance. Many of them may have some insurance, but not nearly enough, so that figures showing the number of people enrolled in voluntary insurance schemes are not a reliable index of adequate protection. Some people take a chance that they will escape the risks, and do not insure partly because their incomes are low and other immediate demands seem more pressing. Thus they may spend more money than they should on hire purchase or instalment buying which presuppose high degrees of security, and particularly freedom fro ι unemployment and sickness. Then there are some who cannot protect themselves or can do so only at high cost because they are regarded as bad risks by insurance companies. The state can include them because they are a relatively small number whose risks can be merged with the smaller risks of the rest of the population. Only by compulsory contributory insurance can people be protected against their failure voluntarily to cover the risks they run, whether their failure is due to carelessness, ignorance or even deliberate choice. It would seem that the state should make basic provision, and that private schemes should provide supplementary benefits, including benefits at higher standards than those which the state should provide.

Sometimes gaps remain because social security measures may involve the transfer of resources from the wealthier sections of the population to the poorer, and the wealthy oppose increased taxation for this purpose. Another reason is that political opinion may be unfavourable because the potential beneficiaries may not be willing to pay increased contributions for social security, preferring to have the money to spend on other things. They do not feel the need keenly enough to be willing to pay the bill. Then again, in countries with federal systems of government, there are often gaps because some aspects of social security are the responsibility of the provinces or states, and in some of them public opinion does not support more adequate schemes.

As already indicated, gaps in social security systems are often due to lack of resources, though this is more true in poor than in rich countries. Like all other claimants to limited national resources, social security must take its place in the queue. By the interplay of political forces, priorities and allocations are arranged, but these change from time to time within a country and are not the same in different countries. In a poor country the claims for food, shelter and other necessaries, and the amounts required for capital development to raise future standards of living are so great that only meagre measures of social security can be attempted.

Before social security was introduced, provision against many of the risks which it now covers was made somehow, but often quite inadequately and with much hardship. For example, provision had to be made either by the families themselves or by voluntary charitable organisations for all the needs of children, for the sick and for the aged. When, therefore, the state undertakes to make provision, the cost is not an entirely new charge on the community. A substantial part of it is a redistribution of the burden to where it can be borne better and more systematically. The cost, apart from administrative expenditure, represents an additional charge only if the state makes provision at higher standards than before and if it fills gaps not previously covered. If the cost is greater, the provision is better.

A noteworthy trend since the Second World War is the growing emphasis on preventive measures, rehabilitation and other services with a similar purpose. In earlier periods less attention was given to such measures and services than to cash benefits. Cash benefits are often easier to arrange than large-scale preventive measures or services to individuals, whether in the form of rehabilitation of the sick or the victims of accidents, or in the form of provision for the welfare of orphans, aged people and others. Both cash benefits and services are necessary. This twofold need was neatly expressed in a publication by the Japanese Ministry of Health and Welfare which said that cash benefits and services were like the two wheels of a cart. In Britain and other countries during the depression years of the 1930's cash benefits were paid to great armies of unemployed, but insufficient effort was made to promote employment. It was argued that to pay insurance or assistance benefits was the least expensive way of dealing with unemployment, and there was not enough recognition of the injury caused by idleness, of the advantage gained by expenditure on public works in multiplying employment greatly beyond those directly engaged on such works and of the permanent value to the country of the works themselves.

SOME BASIC ISSUES

When social security policy is under consideration in any country, many questions are inevitably raised. For example, how much can the country afford for social security? Which needs claim priority? Should the necessary funds be obtained from the general revenues, from special taxes or from workers' and employers' contributions? Can a 'pay-as-you go' system of finance be arranged or must large funds be accumulated, especially for pensions? Should benefits be distributed largely according to need on the basis of a means test, or should the main emphasis be on social insurance and benefits be paid at specified rates without a means test? Should benefits be linked with wage rates so that skilled, highly-paid workers will get bigger benefits than unskilled workers, or should the community provide flat rate basic benefits alike for all, leaving better paid people to make by voluntary means whatever additional provision they wish? To what extent are voluntary methods and private savings effective in providing economic security? To what extent does social security make a country's economy more stable by providing a basic income for individuals? Do social security systems contribute to economic progress and productivity, or do they weaken incentive, reduce the mobility of labour and make adjustments to changes in economic conditions more difficult? These questions indicate some of the many social security problems which are still the subject of controversy.

In the chapters that follow, the definition and scope of social security are considered and various basic principles and policies are outlined. The significance of social insurance is discussed and accounts are given of the relative merits of accumulating funds or using the 'pay-as-you-go' method of financing. Attention is then directed to the proportion of national income spent on social security, use being made of information available for a number of countries. In considering what proportions of the national income may be required in varying conditions to provide the essentials of social security and how the available resources are best distributed between the various claims upon them, it is recognised that the proportions may vary widely. The variations will depend on such factors as the risks covered and the number of potential beneficiaries. Even if these are comprehensively defined, there can be variations because of greater or less liberality in fixing scales of benefit, and because of fluctuations in the number of beneficiaries, particularly in the numbers of unemployed in years of boom and of depression. Except under strictly defined conditions, the proportions of the national income required for social security can be estimated only within wide limits.[6]

There are then chapters on old age and retirement, family allowances and medical care, which are the most costly items in a comprehensive system of social security and the subject of lively political debate in several countries at the present time. A further chapter deals with other social security contingencies, including unemploy-

[6] In years of severe depression, e.g. in the 1930's, a heavy outlay is needed for the maintenance of the unemployed by contrast with the much smaller outlay required in boom years, e.g. the prosperity enjoyed by many countries in the first decade after the Second World War. In the United States, for example, the cost of public assistance and work programmes for the relief of unemployment in 1934-5, which was a year of great unemployment, amounted to almost 6 per cent of gross national product, whereas in 1954-5, when unemployment was low, the cost was less than 1 per cent.

ment, industrial accidents, disability and the death of breadwinners.

Special emphasis is laid on the economic and financial aspects of these problems. No detailed descriptive account is given of the social security system of any one country, but in discussing the main problems, illustrations are drawn from the policies, practices and experience of different countries, particularly Britain, Canada, the United States, Australia and New Zealand. References are made to the special conditions and needs of underdeveloped countries.

No claim is made that the problems of social security are answered in this volume. The questions are considered, information resulting from practical experience is presented and tentative conclusions are outlined. Answers will become increasingly definite and a firmer foundation for decisions on policy will be provided as more experience is gained and more information becomes available.[7]

---

[7] Such studies as those made by the International Labour Office into the costs of social security in various countries, their relation to national income, the sources of revenue and the distribution of benefits for different purposes will provide increasingly valuable information in showing trends as the period covered by the surveys lengthens.

CHAPTER II

DEFINITION AND SCOPE

The essential purpose of social security is to ensure 'freedom from want' by collective or community provision for those people who, because of misfortune, are temporarily or permanently without sufficient resources for their subsistence and essential health services. With the best will in the world it is often impossible for individuals to meet the risks of life unaided, or even with the help of relatives and friends. A young worker with a wife and children may be totally and permanently disabled by an accident long before he could be expected to have saved enough to provide for his maintenance and that of his dependants. Many low-paid workers, after they have met the current necessaries of life for themselves and their families, have little or nothing left for savings or voluntary insurance and are unable to make provision for their old age and other risks. Therefore, to quote from a publication of the International Labour Office, 'as the State is an association of citizens which exists for the sake of their general well-being, it is a proper function of the State to promote social security.[1]

People who are in want or are likely to suffer poverty are mainly those with small means, and social security systems are primarily concerned with them. People who enjoy good and stable incomes are generally able to cover most of the risks of life from their own savings, including their voluntary insurance, and when a social security system pays benefits to such people it has gone beyond its basic function. This function is exceeded when, as in Britain, Canada and other countries, universal old age pensions and family allowances are paid to the rich as well as the poor. There may be good reasons, including administrative convenience, for this procedure, but such systems involve a wider conception of the purposes of social security.

Social security systems, being the responsibility of the state, are established by legislation which entitle specified categories of persons in specified contingencies to receive benefits. The systems are usually administered by departments of the state, such as the

[1] *Approaches to Social Security* (Geneva, 1942), p. 83.

Ministry of Pensions and National Insurance in Great Britain, or by autonomous institutions acting for the state, such as the Unemployment Insurance Commission of Canada and the Social Security Institutes of various Latin American and other countries. Workmen's compensation for industrial accidents and occupational diseases is defined by legislation, but in many countries employers may cover their liabilities by insuring them with private insurance companies which do most of the administration. In other countries, compensation for industrial injuries is administered by the same government department that deals with other aspects of social security, or by an autonomous body, for example the Workmen's Compensation Board of the Province of Ontario, which collects contributions from employers, adjudicates claims in order to avoid expensive litigation and arranges for medical care and rehabilitation.

Viewed broadly, most state activities are closely linked with social security. This is true, for example, of military defence and the prevention of civil strife. Police forces and the administration of justice provide security of life, limb and property against criminals. For purposes of specialised study such activities must, however, be excluded from the field of social security. Education is excluded, as it is a social service rather than a form of social security and does not provide protection against the risks of life in quite the same sense. It is, however, intimately related to social security in so far as it enables people more easily to hold their jobs and to adapt themselves to new occupations in periods, such as the present, of rapid economic and technological change. Also outside social security but associated with it is government action to maintain high levels of employment by controlling credit and by budgetary and other measures of economic policy. More generally, comprehensive policies to eliminate such causes of insecurity as unemployment, disease, inadequate housing and illiteracy are vital elements in a constructive welfare programme, and are intimately linked with, but distinct from social security.

Farm relief programmes present difficulties of classification. Where they help individuals who are faced with privation because their crops have failed or because they are unable to sell their produce owing to lack of demand, they are measures of social security similar to unemployment insurance or unemployment assistance benefits for industrial workers who have lost their jobs. Mainly outside social security, however, are farm price maintenance programmes applied by governments for economic or political reasons. Although it is a relatively small item in national economies, the relief of distress or famine caused by floods, earthquakes, droughts and other natural catastrophies is considered to be a form of social security, but large-scale capital works for flood control or irrigation are not.

Food subsidies, rationing and price control are generally excluded, as their main purposes are different from those of social security. Wage subsidies to low-paid workers are also outside social security; the problems of such workers are better solved by minimum wage systems.

Individuals may voluntarily make provision by savings, payments to private profit-making insurance companies or to mutual benefit associations, and business corporations may operate sickness, superannuation and other schemes for their employees in accordance with collective agreements or otherwise. These are not forms of social security, however, as they are independent of legislative requirements. If participation in the business schemes is voluntary, they are no different from other ways of private saving, and if it is compulsory they are among the conditions of employment and are designed to provide security for workpeople without the intervention of the state. However, private schemes operated by employers should be included in social security if they are accepted by the government as providing the workers with benefits at least equivalent to those of the government's scheme and if the employers concerned are consequently allowed to 'contract out' of the government's scheme.[2] These private schemes are subject to review and they must comply with the standards set by legislation if they are to retain the privilege of private operation.

More difficult to decide are pension and sickness schemes for civil servants and other government employees. Except that the benefits they provide are paid out of government funds, such schemes are similar to those operated by private businesses for their employees. They should therefore usually be excluded, as they are among the

[2] In the Convention concerning Minimum Standards of Social Security that was adopted by the International Labour Conference in 1952, article 6 provides that, in certain parts of the Convention in so far as they relate to medical care, a member country may, for purposes of ratification, take account of protection effected by means of insurance which, although not made compulsory by national laws or regulations, is supervised by the public authorities or is administered in accordance with prescribed standards by joint operation of employers and workers and applies to a substantial proportion of persons whose earnings do not exceed those of skilled manual male employees.

conditions of employment and the benefits are in a sense deferred wages or salaries. The position is similar for the special benefit schemes for workpeople in nationalised industries, including, in various countries, railway work, mining, postal service and public utilities. These schemes may make substantial provision for security, but should be regarded as supplementary to but outside the general social security system of the country, unless the industries are authorised to contract out of the general system because they provide at least equivalent benefits. It would certainly be anomalous and inconsistent to include, for example, benefit schemes for employees of the Canadian National Railways because it is nationally owned and to exclude similar schemes for employees of the Canadian Pacific Railways because it is privately owned. Veterans' pensions and other benefits for war victims and their dependants are in a class by themselves outside the main field of social security, though for some purposes, payments to veterans and social security must be considered together, particularly if without such payments the costs of maintaining the veterans would have to be borne by social security funds.

THE CONTENT OF SOCIAL SECURITY

What then is included? If the purpose of social security is to ensure by public measures the maintenance of incomes sufficient for the subsistence, health and decency of persons who are unable to make adequate provision for themselves and their dependants because their earnings have ceased, were never sufficient or have been seriously reduced, generally by causes over which they have little or no control, an examination of those causes will give the answer.[3] This involves a consideration of the main causes of poverty. They include interruption or cessation of earnings because of sickness, unemployment, old age or the death of the breadwinner of a family. Similar to sickness in their effect on income are occupational diseases, injury from accidents, invalidity and prolonged sickness or incapacity, including blindness.

The insufficiency of low wages to maintain large families is another major cause of poverty. This differs from the previous causes, because even if there is no interruption of employment,

---

[3] When assistance is given to people whose lack of resources is the result of their own conduct it is usually accompanied by stringent conditions or remedial disciplines to prevent recurrence. Though the individual may be responsible for his poverty he is kept from starvation.

earnings are not enough to enable families with many children to meet standards of health and decency. Then there are families whose incomes are ordinarily sufficient but who suffer poverty and incur debt because of occasional expenses which are exceptionally heavy. These include costs of medical care, surgical treatment and hospitalisation, especially during serious illnesses. They are always a heavy burden, but are greatest when the breadwinner's earnings cease because he is too ill to work. In such circumstances people with low incomes need both cash for their maintenance and either free or subsidised service or cash to cover the whole or a substantial part of the costs of medical treatment. Other considerable expenses outside regularly continuing costs are incurred by births and deaths.[4]

In considering health services a distinction must be drawn between medical care needed by individuals when they are sick or the victims of accidents, and public health services rendered to the whole community in such forms as good water supply and sanitation. Social security is concerned with measures for the benefit of individuals who are in need, and logically medical care for them should be included and general health services should be excluded from social security. This is admittedly an artificial and unsatisfactory distinction. Preventive medicine has come to be regarded as more widely effective than treatment that is confined to the sick, and a good water supply, for example, may give much greater security against typhoid and other water-borne diseases than medical attention given when people become sick from drinking contaminated water. By spending more on these preventive measures, on vaccination or inoculation against smallpox, diphtheria and other diseases, and on campaigns to eliminate such insect-borne diseases as malaria and yellow fever, substantial economies may be made in the cost of maintenance benefits and of services to cure those who are sick. Prevention and cure are so closely linked together that in practice it is often impossible to separate the costs incurred for the direct benefit of individuals from those for the provision of general public health services. Wherever practicable, however, they should be separated.

A committee of experts convened by the International Labour Office classified the causes which necessitate social security provision as (a) physical risks—sickness, invalidity, old age, maternity, accidents, death; (b) economic risks—involuntary unemployment; (c) the economic burden of large families. All three lead to the need for cash benefits, while the physical risks also involve medical care in various forms.

Housing and health are also connected, and poor and over-crowded houses are a cause of much sickness. However, housing schemes by public authorities go beyond the purposes of social security and, like education, are properly excluded.

Most definitions are arbitrary and involve borderline or over-lapping items. No logical definition would be altogether clear-cut. Moreover, in the various countries, social security has not in practice been based on logic but on political expediency and administrative convenience. Consequently, some agencies perform functions which are partly within the field of social security and partly outside. Nor is information always sufficient to distinguish between the two, and for this reason it is difficult to compare social security costs in different countries. However, this review is sufficient to indicate the main items that are clearly within social security, some that are marginal or overlapping and some that are outside.

SCOPE AND METHOD

From the foregoing, the main field of social security may be sum-marised as maintenance, under conditions defined by legislation, provided for people and their dependants who are in need be-cause of sickness, unemployment or old age, or who are incapaci-tated for work by injuries, long-term illness or permanent invalidity, together with benefits for large families and for widows and orphans; and grants for the costs of birth and burial. Social security includes the provision, free or subject to small charges, of compre-hensive medical care (including hospitalisation, surgical treatment, prescribed pharmaceutical supplies, artificial limbs and surgical appliances), especially for individuals in the wage-earning and other low income groups. It should provide for the rehabilitation of people who are sick or have been disabled as a result of accidents, and for the retraining in new occupations of people whose former skills and experience are no longer in demand because of changing processes and techniques. Such programmes are designed to bring interrup-tion of earnings to an end as soon as possible by restoring people to gainful employment and making them economically independent again.

The range of application of social security schemes, the risks covered, the methods adopted and the magnitude and duration of benefits vary widely. In Britain and New Zealand, the schemes now in operation apply to all citizens and cover virtually all risks, although in the early stages of the evolution of social security the schemes were more restricted, as they still are in other countries. Many schemes apply only to wage earners on the ground that their incomes are relatively low, and that, as a class, they include substantial numbers likely at some time or other to be seriously short of income for their maintenance. Not infrequently, schemes are limited to employees and others whose wage, salary or income is below a specified level, it being assumed that people who are better off should be able to provide for themselves.[5] Schemes which include contributions by employers are frequently restricted to employees and their dependants, though self-employed persons can be brought in if they pay the equivalent of the amount contributed by both employers and employees. Social assistance schemes usually have a wider coverage than many contributory insurance schemes though they are not necessarily universal, for in some schemes relief is not granted to able-bodied persons, who are expected to fend for themselves.

Not infrequently specified categories of persons, for example agricultural workers, domestic servants and the self-employed, are excluded from contributory insurance schemes, the reason usually being practical administrative difficulties.[6] For similar reasons some schemes are restricted to urban centres or to one region, usually around the capital city. For example, the sickness and accident insurance schemes in Venezuela were at first applied only in the Federal District and neighbouring municipalities and to port workers in La Guaira, and a similar scheme in Burma was at first limited to the Rangoon area. The purpose in both cases was to gain experience and train the administrative personnel, and the systems were then progressively extended to other regions. Certain schemes have been established for specific industries, for example mining and railways. Again, some schemes provide insurance only against sickness and accidents while others cover more or all of the main risks.

It is of interest to note that the International Labour Conference of 1952, in adopting the Draft Convention concerning Minimum Standards of Social Security, included provisions that required countries ratifying the Convention to apply defined social security measures so as to protect not less than 50 per cent of all employees, or economically active persons constituting not less than 20 per

[5] In some schemes, employees with higher incomes are not excluded but contributions and benefits are subject to a specified ceiling.
[6] Those excluded from social insurance schemes are usually covered by social assistance.

C

cent of all residents.[7] Ratification therefore involves the application of social security measures to substantial numbers of people.

The financial soundness of contributory insurance schemes is guarded in various ways. The duration of sickness and unemployment benefits, for example, is often limited to three or six months. Moreover, not only non-contributors but also those who fail to make a specified minimum of contributions are denied benefits, and people who have paid less than a defined number of contributions may have their benefits reduced.

In typical insurance schemes both employers and workpeople contribute, and the state may also do so. For some risks the whole cost is borne by the employers. Thus workmen's compensation is generally financed solely by employers. Again, in the United States, unemployment benefits are financed by a pay-roll tax on employers. Benefits may be in cash or in kind: usually in cash for the maintenance of income, and in kind for medical care services and institutional care of the aged, infirm and orphans; the provision of milk and vitamins, free or at subsidised prices for infants and school children are also in kind.

Social security systems involve a transfer of resources. In countries where the disparity of wealth and incomes is great and schemes are financed mainly by progressive taxation, resources are transferred from the rich to the poor. Where, however, the range of wealth and incomes is relatively narrow, or where schemes are financed largely by the contributions of workers and employers, resources are transferred mainly from the more fortunate who suffer little from sickness, unemployment and other contingencies to the less fortunate in the same class of people.

The flat rates for benefits granted without a means test are not necessarily fixed at the level of subsistence: the benefits may be regarded as a supplement to other resources. Thus in Britain, the National Insurance benefits paid without a means test are somewhat less than the benefits, including allowances for rent, that are paid under public assistance after a means test to people without resources. In Canada the old age pensions (paid to people of seventy years of age and over) and the family allowances are considered to be an addition to other resources, and are generally not large enough

---

[7] Countries whose economy and medical facilities are insufficiently developed may take advantage of specified temporary exceptions, which include a provision that social security schemes shall apply to prescribed classes of employees constituting not less than 50 per cent of all employees in industrial workplaces where twenty or more persons are employed.

for subsistence according to Canadian standards. If such benefits were to be made sufficient for subsistence, they would have to be increased with every appreciable rise in the cost of living, whereas they are often left unchanged for years during which, in inflationary periods, their purchasing power falls substantially.

In this chapter, social security is defined so as to separate measures required and usually operated by the state from all other measures. From the standpoint of the welfare of members of the community, the primary consideration is that basic security should be somehow provided. The extent to which it is provided by private voluntary measures varies considerably from country to country, and for that reason the problem of attempting to define the scope of social security and to evaluate the proportion of the national income necessary for state schemes of basic security is complicated. In the United States, for example, as will be seen later, the proportion of the national income spent on social security measures required by legislation is less than in many other countries. Part of the reason may be that voluntary schemes are highly developed, with correspondingly less need for government action. Already in 1949 in the United States, contributions to voluntary schemes of sickness insurance totalled $1,585.5 million and benefits paid amounted to $1,066.4 million; pension systems established by business corporations covered more than five million workers.[8] Since then, these private measures have grown substantially, though large numbers of people are still inadequately protected and need social security.

It must be repeated that when a social security scheme is introduced or extended and contributions or taxes are collected to finance it, the whole of the cost is not a new charge on the community. Much of the cost had already been borne privately or publicly in other ways. Thus, if an old age pension scheme with fixed benefits paid without a means test is adopted, there will be a substantial reduction in the cost of public assistance for aged people who previously had to apply for relief. Also, some part of the burden of maintaining aged relatives, previously borne by individual citizens often at considerable hardship to themselves and their children, will be transferred to the pension scheme. Only to the extent that the benefits provided by social security schemes are greater than those which had been provided privately will the cost to the community be increased.

[8] Eveline M. Burns, *Social Security and Public Policy* (New York, 1956).

CHAPTER III

BASIC POLICIES AND PRINCIPLES

As already indicated, the essential purpose of social security is to ensure by collective action that the members of a community shall be protected against undue hardship and privation, and also provided with health services when their own resources are insufficient to maintain them and their dependants at a standard recognised by the community as the minimum below which no one should fall. It is almost universally accepted on humanitarian grounds that the resources of the community should be used to prevent any person from falling below subsistence level, and that this purpose can be achieved mainly by the method of providing him with cash for his maintenance and with various health services. These provisions may be regarded as basic social security.

Many social security schemes provide cash and other benefits for people whose resources are above the minimum, as has been mentioned above. This is done, for example, in Canada, where old age pensions and family allowances are paid to wealthy and poor people alike. The payment of such benefits is explained as being easy to administer, particularly as there is no need to apply a means test, which is disliked and requires highly trained staff, or as democratic, since everyone is treated alike. The same practice is followed in insurance schemes which pay benefits at the same rates whether people are in need or not, by contrast with assistance schemes which provide people with different benefits according to their individual needs. Usually, however, a high proportion of the people who receive these benefits are in the relatively low income group, and, bearing in mind that there are substantial advantages in equality of treatment, such systems are properly included in social security, as are social insurance systems in which benefits vary with wages instead of being at uniform flat rates.

Though the main purpose of social security benefits is to give some protection to people whose incomes are insufficient for their subsistence, they also have both economic and social advantages. The efficiency of the people who receive the benefits would deteriorate if no such assistance were available for them. The benefits do not usually reduce the will to work because they are generally much below what most workers can earn. Moreover, many benefits are paid only when workers are unable to work or when no suitable work is available for them, and the benefits cease when workers become fit to work or when jobs can be found. The system has safeguards to prevent serious malingering, and any loss of self-reliance from this cause among a minority is greatly offset by the removal of the fear of extreme privation from large numbers of people.

Partly as a consequence of the greater economic opportunities in Canada and the United States and of the spirit of the pioneering days, the emphasis on individual responsibility is appreciably stronger there than in Britain and other European countries. Indeed, it was not until the great depression of the 1930's, when at times a quarter of the working population were without jobs, that the need for comprehensive measures of social security began to win wide support in North America. Until then, provision by the community was mainly limited to public assistance at meagre levels for those who, after being subjected to a severe means test, were found to be in dire need.

THE STATE AND THE INDIVIDUAL

There is inevitably a wide range of opinion as to the degree to which the state should relieve individuals of the responsibility for the protection of themselves and their dependants against the risks of life. It is therefore an obligation of any author in this field to make explicit his own views on this general question. In this book, the view is taken that the state should only do for people those things which they cannot do for themselves either individually or by voluntary methods, or which the state can do very much more efficiently. Even things which individuals or voluntary organisations can do somewhat less effectively than the state should usually be left to them because their operations are more flexible and promote independence, initiative and self-reliance. The onus on those who support compulsory state systems should be to prove the substantial superiority of such systems over private voluntary arrangements. Social security, except for the aged and infirm, should be regarded not as an end in itself but as a means of promoting individual initiative and self-reliance. As Abraham Lincoln once said, 'You cannot help men permanently by doing for them what they could and should do for themselves.'

As a corollary, it follows that, for economically advanced countries with fairly high standards of living, the greater the productivity per head and the higher the standards of living, the more will people be able to provide for their own needs and the less will they be dependent on social security, provided the national income is reasonably well distributed among the various sections of the population. Therefore, with the growth of productivity, a smaller proportion of the national income should be required for social security, unless the role of social security is broadened from providing basic standards for the lower income groups to ensuring security at better standards for those with higher incomes, an extension which would be likely if insecurity were to increase as incomes and standards of living rose. Yet, most people who are better off are more able to provide security for themselves and should be less dependent on the community. Another factor is that, as countries become richer, preventive health measures and better housing will be likely to reduce sickness rates, while economic measures may be increasingly successful in maintaining high employment and, therefore, in keeping down the social security costs of unemployment.

This conclusion that, if standards of living rise, a lower proportion of the national income may in the long run be needed for social security seems contrary to the expectation of many people that the wealthier a country becomes, the higher the standards of social security it should provide. Yet, it is consistent with a basic principle of social security that people should not depend on the state to do for them what they can do for themselves. It is true that, as the standards of living of a country rise, so will the minimum levels considered necessary for subsistence and for health and decency. But there is no inconsistency between spending a smaller proportion of the national income on social security as productivity rises, and at the same time increasing the standards of benefit for those in need. The country would be able to provide these higher standards by using a smaller fraction of its greater productivity. The *amount* spent on social security will rise, but the increase will depend in part upon the extent to which increases in standards of benefit are offset by reductions in the number of people in need. The amount would tend to rise in periods of inflation.

A few illustrations may be given. A frequent attitude to old age pensions is that as a country becomes richer, the pensionable age should be reduced from seventy to sixty-five or even to sixty years of age. Yet, as will be discussed more fully in the chapter on Age and Retirement, the higher the standard of living of the people rises, the more easily will they be able to provide for their old age by voluntary saving, private insurance and other means, and the smaller the number of people in need at the earlier ages. Moreover, except in periods of severe unemployment, there are advantages both to the country and to the individual in encouraging older people to continue in productive work as long as possible, and with rising standards of health and greater expectation of life, the age at which effective work is practicable can be raised. If a low pensionable age is fixed, some people will be compelled to cease work as they reach that age and others will tend to do so voluntarily.

Again, as standards of living rise, family allowances are less needed by small families, and systems could reasonably be amended to provide for the payment of allowances only for the third and each subsequent dependent child in a family. Persons who became unemployed or sick could be expected to have resources sufficient to provide for themselves for short periods; therefore, the waiting period for cash benefits which is now set at three days in various countries could be extended to a week or more.[1] Also, as incomes rise, people could pay larger direct contributions towards the cost of their medical care. Such changes would increase individual reliance and responsibility, and the savings effected would make it possible either to release funds for other more urgent social security needs or to reduce taxes.

The conclusion that the proportion spent on social security should fall as the national income increases is valid for most economically advanced countries with fairly high standards of living, but not for primitive countries with rural economies. In such countries, many of the economic risks of life are met in a simple, natural way by mutual help by members of the family or tribe. When, however, primitive countries become more industrialised and have greater numbers of their people living in cities and towns, the customary method of support tends to break down, and must be replaced by various forms of social security. Therefore, although the national income may be increasing, the proportion required for social security will also grow.

VARIABLE OR UNIFORM FLAT RATE BENEFITS

Social security systems may provide either variable or uniform flat rate benefits, and the practices differ from country to country and from one division of social security to another. The differences

---

[1] In some countries, e.g. Denmark and Norway, the waiting period for sickness benefits is six days.

are determined by the purposes for which the systems are designed, and these are largely formed by the political and social traditions and doctrines in each country.

Three main systems may be distinguished, and it will be seen that they serve somewhat different purposes. The first, which uses a means test and varies the benefits according to individual needs, is designed to provide only for the subsistence of the poor. In many countries, this is the successor of the former poor law system transformed to accord with current social attitudes. The payments, known as public or social assistance, are made only to the poor, who must prove their need. The system is non-contributory and the funds required are provided from the ordinary public revenues.

A second system is the payment of benefits as a right, without a means test, to employed people in defined categories when they encounter specified contingencies. Often the system applies to all workpeople or to workpeople in defined occupations whose wages do not exceed a given amount. In some ways, the purpose is similar to that of public assistance, as it is assumed that a great majority of the workers whose wages are below the stipulated level will be in need when they become sick, unemployed or are no longer able to work because of disability or old age. Some of the workers will not be in need, but any economies which could be effected by using a means test to exclude them are outweighed by social and administrative advantages. The system can also be extended to self-employed people. The benefits may be financed from general revenues, special taxes, contributions by employers, contributions by workers or by a combination of these in varying proportions.

The benefits may be set at the same rate for skilled workers with high wages as for unskilled workers, or they may vary with wages, as, for example, in the United States Unemployment Insurance and Old-Age, Survivors, and Disability Insurance. Often, where benefits vary with wages, a wage ceiling is fixed and contributions and benefits are paid only in respect of wages below the ceiling. There is, thus, a maximum rate of benefit, and people who wish to have additional protection are expected to provide it themselves, the assumption being that they can do so from their own resources without help from the state. Where the benefits vary with wages, the system is financed by contributions of employers or of workers, or by their joint contributions, to which the state may add subsidies. If benefits are paid at a flat rate, a contributory system may be applied as in Britain, or benefits may be financed from general revenues or from special taxes.

A third system provides benefits to all members of the community, irrespective of their income or status, provided they satisfy
residential and a few other specified requirements. Here, benefits
may be paid to many who could provide for themselves. It represents a greater departure than the second system from the principle
that the state should not do for people what they are able to do for
themselves. The general application of National Insurance to the
whole population of Britain, and the Canadian federal system of
old age pensions and children's allowances are examples. Such comprehensive schemes are more suitable for countries in which, because of progressive taxation, redistributive policies and other
factors, the disparities in the incomes of a major part of the population are moderate than in countries where they are wide. The fact
that the wealthier sections of the population pay high taxes can be
used as an argument in favour of comprehensive social security, as
the benefits they receive are small in relation to the taxes they pay.
Comprehensive systems usually provide uniform benefits, although
benefits could be varied in relation to different categories of income.
The systems can be financed from ordinary public revenues or special
taxes, in which case variable benefits would be impracticable, or
by contributory insurance which would enable variable benefits to
be paid.

The alternatives—flat rate and variable benefits—raise basic issues
of principle. If flat rate benefits usually related to the standards of
income of unskilled and other low income groups are paid, the state
treats alike all the people who are included in the system. It can, by
this method, meet basic or subsistence needs, leaving to people
with higher incomes the responsibility of making supplementary
provision for themselves. But many skilled workers and other well-
paid people also suffer from insecurity. When they are working,
their standards of living are adjusted to their incomes, and if their
incomes cease, they find it difficult to adapt themselves to the
standards which a flat rate benefit would provide. Many people in
middle income groups are becoming increasingly concerned about
the insecurities of modern society, and there has been growing
support among them for a broadening of the role of social security
to provide these groups with benefits related to their standards of
living.

In Britain, where social insurance has hitherto provided flat rate
benefits, the increase in the number of private undertakings with
additional benefits, most of which are at rates varying with the
wages of the workers, has led to demands that such private plans

should be regulated by the state, correlated with National Insurance, and extended to large sections of the population not covered by these plans. Where a large part of the money from which benefits are paid comes from the general revenues of the state, the arguments in favour of flat rates of benefit are strong, but where a contributory system provides most or all of the funds, the benefits can be either at flat or at variable rates. In the social insurance systems of the United States, which are financed by employers or jointly by employers and employees, the benefits vary with the wages of the beneficiaries.

From the first introduction of social insurance in the United States in 1935, strong preference has been shown for benefits to be related to wages, and opinion seems widespread that this policy is superior to that of providing flat rate benefits, though there is some support for the latter. This attitude is in accordance with tradition. Emphasis is placed on the individual, whose efforts and rewards should be linked together; men of greater skill and higher earnings should become entitled to better benefits than men of less skill and lower earnings. Similarly, benefits should be higher for those who have a good record of employment and continuity of earnings than for those who have had many interruptions because of sickness, unemployment and other causes. Benefits differentiated by wages are also supported as compensation for loss of earnings. Alternatively, the argument that benefits are, in effect, deferred wages, lends weight to wage-determined benefits. It is also recognised that skilled workpeople with high earnings enjoy a better standard of living when working than unskilled workers and, therefore, it seems reasonable that social insurance, which is designed to help them when they are not earning, should provide benefits in proportion to their usual living standards. A rate of benefit which would be substantial for an unskilled worker would be meagre for a skilled man whose wages had been twice as high. The system should be related to individual circumstances.

What is controversial in the United States and in other countries which apply this system is the limits within which the system should operate. Usually the maximum benefits obtainable are fixed, and this set amount may be either high or low. Failure adequately to raise the ceiling to allow for inflation has resulted in a narrowing of the range of benefits, and an increasing proportion of workers with high wages are at the maximum rate of benefit which has become a much smaller percentage of their wages than was originally intended. In some countries with wage-differentiated benefits, the system is operated so as to be more favourable to workers at the lower end of the wage scale than to the better-paid workers.

Where contributions and benefits are determined by wages, social objections can be raised against the paying of proportionate contributions by the state, which would be providing more for highly paid workers than for the others. A flat rate per capita contribution by the state would, however, be appropriate, as also might contributions to subsidise the benefits of the lower-paid workers whose wages are not high enough to enable them to pay sufficiently for adequate minimum benefits. These problems have not arisen in the United States because there the state does not pay contributions to the social insurance funds.

Flat rate benefits are more suitable in countries in which wage differentials between skilled and unskilled workers and between different industries and regions are narrow than in countries where they are wide. In Canada and Australia, various country-wide uniform benefits are paid, and they are especially favourable for recipients in regions where incomes and the cost of living are low, for example, in small ports and rural areas in the eastern provinces of Canada by contrast with such urban centres as Montreal and Toronto and the provinces of the West where the cost of living is high. One argument in support of variable social insurance benefits in the United States is that there are big differences in income per head and standards of living between the richer and poorer parts of the country, and also between different industries and occupations.[2] Pensions or other benefits fixed at amounts appropriate for the richer regions would be much too high for the poorer ones. The converse is similarly true. To divide the country into economic regions with separate flat rate benefits based on the standards of living of each region would raise practical difficulties as well as controversial issues. In some underdeveloped countries with low standards of living, the range between the wages of skilled workers and those of unskilled labourers is often wide, and where the wages

[2] In 1955, for example, average personal annual income per head ranged from $2,513 in Delaware and $2,499 in Connecticut down to $1,062 in Arkansas and $946 in Mississippi. In December 1957, gross weekly earnings in manufacturing industries ranged from $94.07 in California, $92.64 in the state of Washington, $89.25 in Illinois and $88.66 in Delaware down to $58.11 in Arkansas and $57.13 in Mississippi. With such wide differences, a national scale of benefits that were not adjusted to regional incomes and standards of living would be impracticable, as well as unacceptable. Figures from *Statistical Abstract of the United States* (1957) and *Monthly Labor Review*, March 1958.

of the unskilled are near subsistence level, a flat rate of benefit appropriate for them would be too low to provide reasonable security for workpeople with much higher standards of living. In conditions of inflation in any country, a system which relates benefits to wages ensures some compensation for the falling value of money. Perhaps the strongest argument in favour of paying social insurance benefits at uniform flat rates, together with appropriate allowances for dependants, is that people who desire additional protection have the responsibility providing it and can make arrangements to suit their circumstances, while the state has undertaken its main obligation in applying a system that meets the basic requirements of those whose needs are likely to be the greatest.

In the Convention concerning Minimum Standards of Social Security adopted by the International Labour Organisation, the *minimum* sickness and unemployment benefits for a man with a wife and two dependent children are 45 per cent of the standard wage of an ordinary adult male labourer, together with any family allowances.[3] The minimum benefit is 50 per cent for invalidity or for incapacity resulting from injuries incurred at work, and 40 per cent for long-term or permanent invalidity from other causes. For old age pensions, the minimum for man and wife is 40 per cent. Whether these benefits are sufficient for subsistence depends on the levels of unskilled labourers' wages in the different countries. At least, they provide a substantial addition to other resources, including the beneficiaries' own savings and assistance given them by relatives. If such benefits are provided by social insurance systems and should prove inadequate, supplementary payments may be made to meet individual needs by the method of public assistance with a means test.

Where benefits are too small in proportion to wages, they fail to provide adequate security. The wider the gap between benefits and wages, especially if the latter are low, the less the security. It follows that the lower the wages, the smaller the gap, or the higher the proportion of wages which should be paid in benefits. Conversely, the higher the general standards of wages above subsistence level in any country, the wider the gap can be. In its Convention concerning Minimum Standards of Social Security, the International Labour Conference adopted a uniform gap with benefits usually between 40 and 50 per cent of the wages of ordinary unskilled labourers, but because of very real difficulties, did not specify narrower gaps

[3] The benefit would be increased for larger families.

for countries where the wages of such workers are close to subsistence levels.

Since skilled workers' wages are substantially higher than those of unskilled labourers, their social security benefits may be only 25 or 30 per cent of their wages if the rates for an average family are only 40 or 50 per cent of the wages of unskilled labourers. As their ways of living, including rents, hire purchase obligations and other costs are adjusted to their earnings and are on a considerably higher standard than those of labourers, this low proportion will represent severe pressure. Knowing, however, that benefits will be small in relation to their standard of living, they will need to make supplementary provision by voluntary savings, including private insurance.

In countries where the wages of skilled workers are much higher than those of the unskilled, it may be preferable to have two or three rates of benefit instead of a single uniform rate, in order that benefits may be more closely related to earnings. Workers would be classified into grades—skilled, semi-skilled and unskilled—each grade covering an appropriate range of earnings. Contributions and benefits would be the same for all workers within a grade, but would differ between grades. This system is more complex to administer than a system in which uniformity can reasonably be maintained and therefore the number of grades should be kept small. In some countries, the work of administration is increased by having a large number of grades. In Venezuela, for example, six main grades, each with its own rate of contribution and of benefit, are in use. In other systems, the workers are not grouped into wage categories for purposes of social insurance, and the benefits vary, as in the United States, with the wages and contributions of each individual worker.

In various countries, especially those with high standards of living, the beneficiaries and their employers are, in effect, paying for a large part of the benefits received, and this realisation may promote demands for contributions and benefits to be related to wages instead of being at uniform subsistence rates. Flat rate benefits have been challenged in Britain, Sweden and Canada, and proposals for wage-related retirement benefits are under active political discussion; they are supported by the Canadian Labour Congress, and such a scheme was adopted by the British Government in 1959. Pensions are related to wages in West Germany. In Sweden, a compulsory supplementary pensions system related to wages was a major political issue in the 1958 elections, the scheme being supported by the Social Democratic party.

Just as in some countries there was an evolution from means test subsistence benefits (which were paid to the poor mainly out of taxes levied on the wealthier sections of the population) to uniform flat rate benefits on a contributory insurance basis without means tests, so, where standards of living are high and the costs of benefits are met mainly by joint contributions borne by industry and labour, the policy of varying contributions and benefits according to wages may be more extensively applied. The policy would have changed from providing basic or subsistence security to providing differential security.

CONTRIBUTIONS

Benefits should be provided as far as practicable from revenues to which the beneficiaries pay substantial amounts either by special taxes or by social insurance contributions. Any compulsory contribution, including money deducted by employers from workers' wages and paid to the government, is clearly a form of tax. These special social security taxes, which are often poll taxes, are imposed on the 'benefit' principle. They should be related to the whole tax system to ensure that taxation is distributed equitably among the different sections of the population. This will assist in determining the proportions in which the cost should be borne by individuals in the beneficiary classes, by employers and business corporations, and from general revenue. Resources must be transferred from the richer to the poorer sections of the community and, especially where income is distributed fairly evenly among different sections, resources must be transferred between those who escape misfortune and those who are its victims. This problem is discussed in chapter XI.

Special contributions are actually taxes, but if they are directly related to benefits they will be more readily accepted and will have psychological advantages. They take away the stigma of charity and give beneficiaries a feeling that they can draw standard benefits as a right. They may keep in check unreasonable demands for bigger benefits because these would involve bigger contributions, but this check is only effective if the contributions form a substantial part of the total cost. In insurance systems which provide variable benefits, there is usually a close, though not necessarily an exactly proportionate relation between benefits and contributions.

PUBLIC ASSISTANCE

Public assistance is an inevitable and permanent feature of any system of social security. It is designed either to supplement the resources of individuals and their dependants so that they can manage to subsist, or, if they have no resources, to be sufficient for their subsistence. In any community, there will always be some people whose circumstances are such that at times they will be in need of assistance, and no individual provision or collective system of social insurance will be comprehensive and flexible enough to meet all the uncertainties and contingencies that life involves. Social insurance benefits paid as a right are based on community-wide averages, and although they may be adequate for most people, they will be insufficient for some. Such insufficiencies can be met only by consideration of special or individual circumstances, and assistance must be adapted to variable needs. The amount regarded as essential for subsistence differs according to the productivity and standards of living of a country, being higher in rich countries than in poor, and higher now in advanced countries because of their greater productivity than it was a generation or a century ago. Assistance for the needy is the oldest form of social security. It is a natural expression of human sympathy, charity and compassion, an element in all religions, and is based on recognition of mutual interdependence.

If social security should have the merit of certainty, public assistance should have the merit of flexibility. It should, however, be reserved for a residue or minority of people whose needs, because of special circumstances, cannot be met adequately by social insurance or other standard benefit schemes. Moreover, even if it is intelligently administered and free from the harshness of the old poor relief methods, it is still disliked and requires a large and highly trained staff to administer. Its use, therefore, should be kept to a minimum. Whenever substantial numbers of people whose needs are similar are found to be receiving public assistance, consideration should be given to devising ways of removing them from the scope of assistance. In the early stages of a social insurance scheme, however, this may not always be practicable. For example, in providing old age pensions by contributory insurance methods, a minimum period of contribution, which is usually several years, is required to qualify for a pension, and people near the pensionable age when the scheme is started may not be able to qualify; therefore, until the system is fully effective, assistance for those in need must be continued.

In any country where the proportion of public assistance is large and social insurance is practicable, there is a strong case for examining the main items of expenditure to see which of them could be taken over by an insurance or other scheme without a means test. Similarly, where expenditure on public assistance is increasing substantially, the causes should be investigated with the object of replacing assistance by other methods. One cause of increase is inflation which, by reducing the purchasing power especially of uniform rates of social insurance benefits, will tend to force increasing numbers of people to turn to public assistance. Here the remedy is to increase the rates of benefits as the cost of living rises. Another cause of increase in public assistance expenditure is a big rise in unemployment during severe and prolonged depression, with the consequence that many workers exhaust their right to unemployment insurance benefits. Two main measures may be taken. One is to prolong the period of insurance benefit and to raise the percentage of unemployment on which the scheme is based, so that by higher contributions, bigger reserves can be built up in good times.[4] A second measure is for the government to apply its economic resources and controls so as to reduce long unemployment.

Investigations in British Guiana in 1954 showed that on the basis of a severe means test, more than 60 per cent of all people aged sixty-five and over had resources of less than $10.00 (West Indian) a month and were receiving old age assistance pensions at the rate of $5.00 a month in Georgetown (the capital) and $3.50 in other parts of the territory. These pensions were the equivalent of only 15 or 20 per cent of the wages paid to the low   grades of unskilled and semi-skilled male workers.[5]

The high degree of dependence of the aged on poor relief is somewhat similar in Barbados and in many other West Indian territories.[6] Certainly, it is highly undesirable that such large proportions of the population should have nothing better to look forward to in their old age than destitution and dependence on public relief after undergoing a severe means test. The considerable improvement in wages and standards of living in recent years in these territories provides

In Great Britain by June 1934, the Unemployment Insurance Fund had incurred a deficit of £105 million, because the rate of unemployment proved higher than that on which the scheme was based, and because unemployment was prolonged. Subsequently, when prosperity returned, the deficit was replaced by a substantial surplus.

[5] J. Henry Richardson, *Report of Inquiry into Social Security in British Guiana* (Georgetown, British Guiana, April 1954). A West Indian dollar has an exchange value equal to approximately 70 U.S. or Canadian cents, but its purchasing power is higher.

[6] J. Henry Richardson, *Report of Inquiry into Social Security in Barbados* (Bridgetown, Barbados, Aug. 1954).

a basis for a compulsory contributory savings scheme to which employers as well as workers could contribute, which in the future would enable a large part of the population to become independent of public assistance in their old age. The burden of maintaining aged parents, a burden that often means great sacrifice to sons and daughters and their children, would also be relieved by the benefits.

The administration of public assistance today in many countries has been greatly improved, if compared with the methods formerly applied in poor relief systems. In the nineteenth century, and even more recently, the standards of poor relief were meagre, often being limited to what would scarcely keep body and soul together, and the conditions applied were often so harsh that self-respecting people, even though in great need, would do anything possible to avoid the stigma of pauperism unless destitution made them desperate. The underlying assumption was that the poor were responsible for their poverty, and that only thriftless, incompetent people would apply for poor relief. This gave it a bad name among decent people, and strong demands were made for drastic reforms to remove its objectionable features, and also for the adoption of systems of social insurance by which benefits would be paid without humiliating inquisitions into means.

It became increasingly recognised that by the working of the economic system, many self-respecting, self-reliant people may, from no fault of their own, lose their jobs and be unable to provide even a meagre living for themselves and their families. Thus, in a period of severe industrial depression, many workpeople including the skilled, who ordinarily earn high wages and can afford a good standard of living, may be out of work for months at a time and find themselves without resources. They, naturally, resent being treated by poor law officers as if they were degenerate idlers trying to live on public charity. They are only too anxious to be at work and support themselves.

A major change has been to administer the system in a more humane way, and to remove its degrading features. Means tests are now often applied with sympathy and consideration for the difficulties of those in need. Individual circumstances are investigated, but the principles and attitudes adopted are more liberal. Thus, the applicant is not required to use up his small savings or sell or mortgage his home before being granted assistance. Relatives outside the immediate family are increasingly relieved of the obligation to provide maintenance. Scales of payment have often been raised above the earlier pauper pittances so as to provide the minimum

D

for health and decency, and have become more standardised in order to remove uncertainties, arbitrary decisions and variations in grants according to the whims and moods of the administering officers. In New Zealand, though benefits vary with income and therefore with means, the old form of means test is not used. Instead, flat or basic rates of benefit are fixed, for example for sickness, invalidity and old age, but the benefits are reduced by successive amounts for income above specified minima.[7] The British system of public assistance with fixed rates of payment (though with variable amounts for rent to allow for differences in rent in different areas), combined with reductions determined by income, is essentially similar, and its pattern is applied in other countries. Standardisation of benefits in many countries has been extended over wider areas. Instead of separate rates of benefit paid by each parish or local poor law union and varying from one district to another, there are uniform rates of benefit administered regionally or even nationally. In periods of prolonged unemployment, workers who have exhausted their rights to unemployment insurance benefits are enabled to draw public assistance benefits with only a minimum of investigation into their private resources. The effect is that of a smooth transition from insurance to assistance.

In Britain, the United States, Canada and other countries during the second quarter of this century, public assistance has been developed along these lines into a refined and flexible instrument of social welfare policy. Though still basically quite distinct from social insurance, it is now applied in ways which make the two systems less sharply different in practice than they used to be. Many scholars and social welfare practitioners, especially in North America, have come to regard public assistance, now that its objectionable features have been removed, as preferable to the automatic payment of cash benefits for dealing with the social security problems of some groups of people. In particular, it ensures contacts between experienced public officials and the individual beneficiaries which enable the human problems of those in need to be considered and appropriate remedies to be recommended or provided. Cash payments alone could not do this.

Yet, even so, in the United States and Canada the recipients of public assistance still seem to suffer a loss of social status. Also,

[7] Alongside the New Zealand age benefit, which varies with income, there is a superannuation system which pays benefits without a means or income test. This system provides for annual increases in the rates of benefit, and in course of time it will largely replace the age benefits.

whereas in some states and provinces the investigations into individual needs are undertaken by professionally qualified social workers, in others they are done by local officials along with other jobs and, in consequence, there are wide variations in the efficiency with which public assistance is administered and in the amounts of benefit as well as advice and guidance given to applicants. There is still much variation in the categories of people who can receive assistance. As a result of anomalies and gaps, some people get no assistance, though their needs are equally or more real and urgent than those of people who receive aid. Further co-ordination and extensions of scope are required to ensure reasonable equity in the assistance of people whose needs are similar.

The improvements made have reduced considerably the bitter hostility to means tests. Nevertheless, the trend of social opinion is increasingly towards social insurance and other schemes without a means test. Public assistance is regarded as a last resort or a residual system to meet the needs of those not otherwise covered. Assistance, therefore, seems to be a diminishing part of social security.

BENEFITS IN CASH

Unless there are powerful reasons to the contrary, social security benefits should be paid in cash and not in kind. This method of payment leaves the responsibility on individuals and families to distribute their resources in the way they consider best in relation to their needs. Mistakes will be made, and there will be abuses such as spending too much on drink and tobacco and not enough on food and clothing, but the great majority of people will meet their varying needs better by deciding for themselves than if they are spoon-fed by the state.

The main exceptions include infirm aged people without relatives, orphans without relatives or foster parents and people who are mentally defective, all of whom may need institutional accommodation and care. Another benefit that should be made in kind is medical care and hospitalisation, the need for which varies so much between individuals and families that some, even if they had the necessary money, might spend too little on medical care and so undermine their health. This would largely be avoided if health services were free or subsidised so that their cost was low. Provision of milk, orange juice and cod liver oil for children is also not difficult to administer and ensures proper nutrition more effectively than if an equivalent amount of money were given to the families.

Contributions and benefits in cash should be adjusted to changes in the purchasing power of money. During post-war years of inflation, the real value of benefits has fallen considerably in some countries, the loss being one-third or more. Frequent changes in monetary rates of benefit are undesirable, but adjustments should generally be made when real values have altered by 10 to 15 per cent. When monetary rates of benefit are increased, there should be a corresponding increase in contributions; otherwise, more of the cost will be borne by the state. Any deficits resulting from delays in making these adjustments should, however, reasonably be borne by the government because of its responsibility for not maintaining stability of monetary values.

The existence of big financial reserves in a social insurance fund does not in itself justify an increase in cash benefits or a reduction in rates of contribution. In the early years of a contributory old age pension scheme, for example, large reserves may be accumulated, but if the scheme is actuarially sound, these reserves will be needed in later years. To increase the rates of pension in the early years would destroy the financial soundness of the scheme.

NEED FOR CO-ORDINATION

The social security schemes of a country should be co-ordinated in order to remove anomalies and inconsistencies and to fill gaps. Because of the piecemeal growth of social security systems, different principles are applied to different parts of the system. As an illustration, the following passage about British social insurance from the Beveridge Report is relevant. There is 'no real difference between the income needs of persons who are sick and those who are unemployed, but they get different rates of benefit involving different contribution conditions and with meaningless distinctions between persons of different ages. An adult insured man with a wife and two children receives 38s per week should he become unemployed; if after some weeks of unemployment he becomes sick and not available for work, his insurance income falls to 18s. On the other hand a youth of 17 obtains 9s when he is unemployed, but should be become sick his insurance income rises to 12s a week.'[8] It was one of the big contributions of the Beveridge Report that it proposed uniform principles and methods by which many such anomalies could be removed.

[8] Sir William Beveridge, *Social Insurance and Allied Services* (London, 1942), p. 6.

Co-ordination is less difficult in countries with unitary constitutions, than in countries with federal constitutions, such as
Canada and the United States, where legislation and conditions are
not the same in each province or state. Yet reviews of social security
systems are essential from time to time in every country, so that,
to quote again from the Beveridge Report, 'the existing social
services . . . [may] be made at once more beneficial and intelli-
gible to those whom they serve and more economical in their
administration.'

The policies and principles applied in various countries show
almost every possible variety. Part of the reason is that govern-
ment-organised systems of social security, with the exception of
public assistance, are a recent growth and are still in an experimental stage. Often the essential purposes have not been clearly
envisaged. Laws have usually been passed in varying political conditions to deal with specific social and economic situations. Inconsistencies and anomalies have resulted, and although in some
countries comprehensive measures of co-ordination have been
adopted—in Britain after the Second World War along the lines of
the Beveridge Report, and in New Zealand by the Social Security
Act of 1938—they have been few and far between.

Once systems have been in operation for several years and people
have become accustomed to them, any proposed changes involving
reductions of some benefits are likely to encounter powerful political
resistance, even though the resources released would provide .for
more urgent needs or make possible a reduction in taxes. Whenever
the time *is* politically opportune, it would be advantageous to adjust
social security systems so as to bring them into greater harmony
with essential objectives.[9]

It must be emphasised that the application of basic principles
and policies does not imply a uniformity of systems and methods
in all countries. Every country has its own economic conditions
and political and social attitudes and these will determine the
systems and methods most appropriate for it. The methods may
differ considerably from country to country. What is essential, however, is that each country in its own way shall provide basic security
for those in need.

[9] One cause of deviation from basic principles is that measures are sometimes adopted which combine more than one purpose. In Canada, Australia
and New Zealand, for example, some schemes for which the name 'social
security' is used in fact go beyond the purposes of security and include wider
features of political and social democracy.

The policies and principles outlined in this chapter will be regarded by many as controversial. It is hoped that they will provoke controversy. At the present stage in the evolution of social security this is desirable, especially in order to determine the best use of the limited resources available and to ensure the right blend of public responsibility, voluntary effort and individual responsibility.

CHAPTER IV

SOCIAL INSURANCE

Social insurance is a part of social security. Its distinguishing feature is the financing of a substantial part of its cost by contributions from the beneficiaries or on their behalf from their employers, and the linking of benefits to contributions. Other parts of social security are financed by the state from the proceeds of taxation, and the benefits are not linked to special contributions.

In recent years it has become almost fashionable to argue that the term 'insurance' should not be used as a title for contributory systems of social security.[1] The expressions 'social insurance' and 'national insurance' mean something different from 'private insurance', and what is needed is to make the differences clear so that each expression can be used appropriately without being misleading. The term 'social insurance' is convenient, its use is widespread, it has come to stay and the arguments against its use can be challenged. So long as the objective 'social' or 'national' is included no confusion should arise.

The main arguments advanced against describing contributory systems of social security as a form of insurance are that the contributions are compulsory and are, therefore, taxes levied by the state, and that since the contributions by the beneficiaries are not enough to cover the risks, the state assumes responsibility for the difference which may be of uncertain amount and is borne by the general taxpayer. These issues will be considered not so much to counter the arguments against use of the term 'social insurance', which would be merely an exercise in terminology, but to emphasise similarities and differences between social and private insurance.

COMPARISON WITH PRIVATE INSURANCE

The basic element common to private and social insurance is the covering of risks, and the differences between them are essentially those of method. In private insurance, risks are pooled and the

[1] See, e.g. Alan T. Peacock, *The Economics of National Insurance* (London, 1952), p. 89, where the use of the term 'insurance' as in the British system of National Insurance is criticised as inaccurate and inappropriate.

contributions are paid voluntarily at roughly equal rates by people whose risks are approximately equal. People may insure for larger or smaller amounts and make correspondingly larger or smaller contributions according to their resources and circumstances and their estimate of the degree of risk they run.

In social insurance, also, the risks are pooled but, usually, large categories of persons are covered by a specified contribution without fine distinctions in degree of risk between individuals or groups. Thus, in British National Insurance, most risks for the whole population are covered at a rate of contribution that is uniform except for variations between men, women and young persons, and also between employed, self-employed and non-employed persons.[2] In other countries, however, allowances are often made for different degrees of risk, and benefits vary with earnings instead of being at flat rates as in Britain. Thus, industries that have had little unemployment may make smaller contributions to unemployment insurance than other industries with greater unemployment. In the United States, for example, it is the practice under the unemployment compensation schemes of particular states for the contributions to be reduced for business undertakings which maintain a good record of employment and of low claims on the fund. This practice is also often adopted in industrial injuries insurance, for example, in Ontario Workmen's Compensation, as an inducement to employers to maintain high standards of safety. Individual firms with good safety records pay reduced contributions, and payments also vary from industry to industry in accordance with the hazards of each.

In insurance, whether private or social, contributions are linked to benefits. The link is strong only when the beneficiaries contribute substantially to the cost, and is weakened in social insurance when the state takes over the major financial responsibility. It is, however, often appropriate for the state to bear a part of the cost although if it does, the difference is increased between social insurance and individual private insurance, for in the latter case, degree of risk, contributions, interest rates and benefits are the essential elements, rich and poor are treated alike if their risks are equal and benefits are actuarially related to contributions.[3] In social

[2] There is a separate insurance scheme for industrial injuries.
[3] Where schemes apply only to limited sections of the population, it is inappropriate for the state to bear a big part of the cost, as that would be unfair to the sections not covered. If, however, schemes are of general application or cover all people whose incomes are below a specified level, the contributions of the state may be substantial.

insurance there is a greater emphasis on needs, and no mathematical relation is maintained between contributions and benefits. Social insurance is closer to private group insurance than to private individual insurance.

In social insurance, contributions give title to benefits, and persons who do not contribute, or whose contributions are inadequate, receive no benefits. In some schemes, a participant must make a minimum number of contributions before he becomes entitled to benefit. This rule is frequent in pension systems, where contributions must be made for ten or some other specified number of years before the right to a pension is acquired. Again, unemployment or sickness insurance benefits may be drawn only for some specified period, often eight weeks, or three or six months, and title to benefit is not regained until a required number of new contributions has been paid.

In social insurance, social considerations override the principles of private insurance when bigger benefits are paid to a man with a family than to one with no dependants, though both have contributed at the same rate. In some systems in which contributions and benefits are fixed at different levels according to the wage category of the worker, the benefits may be more favourable to the workers with lower wages, who are, in effect, subsidised by the workers with higher wages. When an old age pension system is started on a contributory basis, the financing is usually determined actuarially on contributions throughout working life, but people who are late in middle life when the scheme starts are allowed full pensions when they retire, even though they may have contributed perhaps for as little as five years. They receive more than they should by actuarial standards, and are thus favoured compared with those who contribute during their whole working life. The deficit is made up by the state out of general taxes, or it is covered by payments made by long-term contributors.

CHANGES NECESSITATED BY INFLATION

It is sometimes argued that a government scheme cannot properly be termed an insurance scheme because the state may be called upon to bear the cost of increased monetary benefits necessitated by inflation. This conclusion is, however, erroneous, for it is based on a narrow mathematical accountancy relation and does not allow for the effects of changing conditions or real values. In periods of inflation, actuarial methods will need to be applied in real terms when relating values over a period of time. Already, accountants are increasingly measuring capital values in terms of replacement costs and recognise that the initial costs years ago have no significance when the value of money has substantially changed. Similarly, the nominal values of shares in companies are being brought into line with real assets. It is, indeed, a weakness of private insurance that it does not allow for changes in the value of money. The companies have been receiving premiums over a period of years during which the value of money was higher than it is when they pay the policyholders who, in effect, are much less insured than they intended or expected to be when they began to pay the premiums.[4] The companies pay in depreciated money.

If inflation persists and is substantial, contracts between insurance companies and policyholders, systems of social insurance and also more general contracts between lenders and borrowers will be increasingly arranged in real terms with allowance for changes in the value of money. Though more complex, they will resemble construction contracts in which increases in cost are made to allow for higher prices of materials or higher wages, or the sliding scale arrangements often made in collective bargaining between employers and trade unions that wage rates shall be adjusted to changes in the cost of living index.

CONTRIBUTIONS AND TAXATION

Contributions to social security schemes are usually compulsory, and some people claim that this feature makes the use of the term 'insurance' inappropriate. They say that individuals are not free to adjust their contributions to their estimate of the risk they run and to the amount of their resources. The contribution, because it is compulsory, is a tax.

As a compulsory payment to the state, the contribution has one of the characteristics of a tax, but it is also a payment or price giving title to specified benefits in defined contingencies. Social insurance thus resembles compulsory insurance by motorists to cover third-party risks, or insurance required of employers in some countries to cover their liability for industrial injuries. Its being compulsory does not make it any less an insurance against risks, and the payments made to cover the risks differ greatly from taxes

[4] When private insurance companies add bonuses to the sums insured, they make some allowance, partially and indirectly, for the fall in the value of money, as their opportunities for making profits in monetary units may be increased in periods of inflation.

which go into the general revenues of a country and are used for a multiplicity of purposes.

The term 'social insurance' would not be appropriately applied to a system where benefits are paid out of the ordinary revenues of the state, as, for example, family allowances in Britain or in Canada. Many schemes, however, include contributions by the beneficiaries, though the proportion of total cost borne by these contributions varies widely, as will be shown later in this chapter. In some systems, the proportion of total cost covered by the beneficiaries is high, and the proportion borne by employers and the state is low. In others, the benefits are financed largely by employers and the state, while in the United States Old Age, Survivors' and Disability Insurance scheme, the contributions are made entirely by the beneficiaries and their employers. Where the proportion borne by the state is great, and especially where the state undertakes to cover deficits so that the actuarial link between the beneficiaries' contributions and the amount of their benefit is broken, then the element of insurance in the system is slight. It is greater where the beneficiaries contribute big proportions of the total cost.

CONTRIBUTIONS BY WORKERS

Workers' contributions and also, largely, the contributions of employers on their behalf are deferred wages. Present consumption is reduced in order that future consumption in a time of greater need may be increased. If the social insurance system applies only to some parts of a country or to some industries, there may be a tendency for workers and also employers to move to other districts, with some reactions on wages; but this tendency, if it operates at all, will be slight, especially as social insurance schemes are frequently applied in districts and industries where conditions are attractive to labour. The tendency will disappear when social insurance is applied throughout the country.

A vital decision in planning social insurance is the amount which workpeople and other beneficiaries can afford to contribute. This will be determined largely by levels of wages, though another factor is the extent to which the benefits will relieve them of expenditure which they had previously met out of their wages, for example, the maintenance of aged parents. In countries where standards of living are low and where the wages of many workers are near subsistence level, workpeople can afford only small contributions, and that is one reason why comprehensive schemes of social insurance are rarely adopted in poor countries, one or two risks only being covered.

In countries with higher standards of living, contributions can be bigger and social insurance can cover more risks and provide better benefits. If a flat rate system of contributions and benefits is adopted, the deciding factor is what unskilled workers can afford to pay. Skilled workers are able to contribute larger amounts, and in many countries contributions vary with wages (often being a specified percentage), and benefits usually vary in proportion to contributions.[5] Where contributions are mainly at flat rates within the capacity of unskilled workers, the rates for women are less than those for men, in recognition of their lower average wages.

If the contributions by workpeople and employers are fairly equal and together cover about two-thirds to three-quarters of the cost of comprehensive social insurance, those of the workpeople are often about 4 to 5 per cent of average wages. When the employers' contributions are added, the total is equal to around 8 to 10 per cent of wages, not including a contribution by the state.[6] This would provide a basis for covering most risks including old age, but not family allowances or a health service. When contributions are at a flat rate for unskilled and skilled workers alike, the range is between $4\frac{1}{2}$ and $5\frac{1}{2}$ per cent of the wages of unskilled workers, and between 3 and 4 per cent of the wages of skilled workers. In countries where the difference in the wages of skilled and unskilled workers is small, for example in Australia, the percentage of wages paid for social security is only slightly less for skilled than for unskilled workers.[7] Where bigger contributions are paid by workers with higher wages, the percentage of the wage is generally fairly equal except where it is fixed somewhat higher for the better-paid workers, not for the purpose of providing them with bigger benefits, but as a means of subsidising the benefits of lower-paid workers. In all countries except those with very low standards of living, contributions at the

[5] In the New Zealand social security scheme, contributions are graded according to income, but benefits are at a flat rate; this method, however, is exceptional. In the United States Old-Age, Survivors, and Disability Insurance Program, which is the only joint, contributory, federal insurance scheme, the employee pays $2\frac{1}{4}$ per cent of wages, subject to a ceiling, the employer pays an equal amount, and self-employed persons contribute at a rate that is $1\frac{1}{2}$ times the rate for employees.

[6] In Britain from July 7, 1958, the total of the employer's and the worker's National Insurance contribution was 18s. 2d. for a man and 14s. 9d. for a woman, which included a contribution to the National Health Service.

[7] In many Australian industries, the difference between the basic wages of skilled and unskilled workers is only 10 per cent or less.

wage percentages indicated above are within the capacity to pay of the workers.

Workpeople recognise the reasonableness of making contributions from which they will derive benefits. By requiring beneficiaries to contribute, there is the implication that people should support themselves as far as their resources permit. It follows that the proportion of total cost borne by the beneficiaries should increase as their standards of living rise. Their contribution, being compulsory, is in some sense a tax which can be supported on the 'benefit' principle of taxation, and they can claim benefits as a right without a means test. If they make substantial contributions to the total cost, they are not likely to make irresponsible demands for increased benefits, as they know that these would result in higher contributions.

In effect, by providing benefits, social insurance reduces the need for private saving to a greater or lesser extent, and for many people, the contributions they are required to make represent an alternative form of saving for their own protection. It must be noted, however, that the introduction of social insurance may stimulate greater interest in making provision for old age and other contingencies, and may lead people to increase their savings in order to supplement the usually meagre social insurance benefits; they may now see a possibility of being able to provide realistically, whereas before it was hopeless to try to do so.

Contributions by workers are sometimes criticised as being regressive taxes, and the argument is advanced that benefits would be more equitably financed out of general revenues raised by progressive taxes based on capacity to pay. It is agreed that flat rate contributions have resemblances to a poll tax and, considered by themselves, are regressive. Also, even where the contributions vary with wages, the resemblances, though reduced, are not removed. However, social insurance contributions by beneficiaries have features which distinguish them from ordinary taxes. They are, in effect, prices paid for specified benefits, and the benefits are often heavily subsidised by the state. These subsidies modify if they do not entirely remove the regressive features of the contributions. Also, social insurance contributions must not be considered in isolation, but in relation to the whole system of taxes and distribution of income. Any one tax by itself may be regressive and inequitable, but other taxes may compensate for these defects and make the whole system equitable.

When, in 1911, social insurance was first introduced in Britain to provide sickness and unemployment benefits, the Lloyd George scheme was based on contributions of fourpence by workers, three-pence by employers, and twopence by the state, and to win support, the shrewd slogan 'ninepence for fourpence' was widely used. This was psychologically effective and politically expedient. The scheme was, undoubtedly, a good bargain for the workers, even though they may really have borne a higher proportion of the total cost than the nominal terms indicated by the slogan. In mid-century, wealth is more evenly distributed, there are new taxes on commodities and many workers are paying income tax, so the real share of the cost borne by the workers is greater than the nominal amount of their contributions. Under present conditions in Britain and in other countries where the incomes of a large part of the population do not vary over a wide range, the workers pay for most of the social insurance benefits they receive, and in effect, the schemes mainly result in a redistribution of resources among themselves.

CONTRIBUTIONS BY EMPLOYERS

Contributions by employers differ from those by the state in being a labour cost of production closely related to wages and employment. They are, in effect, a tax on employment and may, in some circumstances, reduce the demand for labour, but no more than would result from an increase in wages of a similar amount. The burden of the tax is greater on companies which employ many workers than on those which, though they may have an equal turn-over of goods or similar profits, employ few workers.

The burden of the contribution is shifted wholly or partly to consumers by a rise in price of the product, or to the workers when wages are adjusted. The extent and rapidity of the shifting will depend on the elasticity of demand by consumers, on the elasticity of demand for labour, and on the relative strengths of employers and workers in wage bargaining. In the long run, after time has elapsed for the processes of shifting to be completed, there will usually be little difference from the economic point of view whether the contributions are paid wholly by the employers, wholly by the workers, or are divided between them either equally or in some other proportion. The contributions are so closely related to wages that if they are paid wholly or largely by employers, wages will be correspondingly lower, and if they are paid wholly or largely by the workers, wage rates will be higher.

Joint contributions of fairly equal amounts by employers and workers frequently have psychological advantages and are usually preferable to systems which, apart from state contributions, are financed largely or entirely by employers alone or by workpeople alone. Employers' contributions can be supported because of their value in promoting better industrial relations and greater stability of labour. Without social insurance, the deterioration of labour would be greater because of loss of income from enforced idleness during periods of sickness or unemployment.

CONTRIBUTIONS BY PUBLIC AUTHORITIES

Governments, in addition to bearing the cost of public assistance, usually make contributions to social insurance. They do so in order that more liberal benefits can be paid than would be practicable under schemes financed only by the contributions of workpeople and employers. The fact that the government is contributing makes schemes more acceptable at the time of their introduction, as workpeople and other beneficiaries recognise that their contributions are small in relation to the benefits they will receive. Government contributions can be especially advantageous in countries where wages are low and there are wide differences in income between different sections of the community. Also, as the community as a whole gains substantial advantages from social insurance, it is reasonable that it should make a contribution towards the cost. Provision of social insurance benefits would reduce the number of people who would otherwise have to ask for public assistance, and any resultant savings could be used as a social insurance contribution. In special circumstances—when inflation reduces the real value of funds accumulated for pensions, for instance—the state should pay enough to make up the deficit; and in the early years of a pension scheme, it can reasonably make payments to enable people who are near retiring age when the scheme starts to draw adequate pensions on retirement, though their contributions will not have been nearly enough to cover the cost. In the United States, however, social insurance schemes are financed by contributions paid by the beneficiaries and their employers, without any government subsidies, this custom being the result of special economic and historical factors which have played a significant role in the adoption of methods different from those which have been applied in many other countries.

DISTRIBUTION OF COSTS

Different countries show great variety of method in distributing the costs of social insurance.[8] The tripartite system with contributions by workers and other beneficiaries, employers and the state is the most widely adopted, but within this system the proportions vary substantially. In some countries, only two of the three parties concerned contribute. In Soviet countries, the benefits are financed almost wholly by 'employers'; this method may have some psychological value and administrative convenience, but it is without economic significance, and the benefits might equally well be financed wholly by the workers or by the state, or be distributed in any proportions between them and the management side of industry.

In considering what would be an equitable balance in the sharing of costs between insured persons, employers and the state, the distribution of wealth and income and the standards of living of a country would be factors. Where the distribution of wealth and income between different sections of the population is wide, it would be equitable for the state to pay a high proportion of the total cost. Where the standards of living of the insured population are low, the state, within the limits of its capacity, should contribute substantially. Persons at or near subsistence level should have their contributions paid or subsidised by the state.

In countries where standards of living are high, and where the income of the majority of the population varies little from the average, the question of the proportion which the state should contribute is less important than elsewhere. It has been said of the Australian people that they 'form a middle class, without a proletariat or wealthy leisured class.'[9] From an economic point of view, in countries where this is true, there may be little to choose between financing by a tripartite social insurance system, by special taxes paid by the beneficiaries or by general taxes. By each of these methods, the same people would be likely to pay approximately similar amounts, and each method could be reasonably equitable.

In practice, the distribution of costs has been determined largely by political and social attitudes. Many early schemes were often

[8] An interesting table showing the variety in the distribution of costs in European countries is given in *Report III, The Financing of Social Security*, p. 21, prepared by the International Labour Office for the European Regional Conference, 1955.
[9] See A. D. Hope. 'The Literary Pattern in Australia', *University of Toronto Quarterly*, vol. XXVI, no. 2, January 1957, p. 125.

either tripartite or were financed jointly by employers and work-people, and whichever of these two methods of financing was adopted has tended to persist. Where employers and workers both contribute, they frequently do so on approximately a fifty-fifty basis.[10] In recent years, there has been a tendency for the state's proportion of the total cost to increase in a number of countries and for some schemes to be financed wholly by the state.

Where each risk is financed by separate contributions, the proportions borne respectively by beneficiaries, employers and the state differ from one risk to another. The cost of workmen's compensation for injuries from industrial accidents and diseases is borne entirely by employers in almost all countries, the idea being that they are liable and that compensation is a cost of production. The heaviest costs are in mining, transport and other industries with high accident rates. In the United Kingdom, however, after the Second World War when social insurance was being drastically reformed and co-ordinated, the policy was adopted that the costs of industrial injuries, including rehabilitation services, should be pooled, and that employers and employed should contribute at uniform rates in all industries and that the state should also contribute.[11]

The cost of family allowances is borne in most countries either entirely by the state, as in Britain, Canada and the Soviet Union, or entirely by the employers, as in France, Italy, the Netherlands, Czechoslovakia and Poland. In a few countries, the cost is financed jointly by employers and the state.[12] In France, the family allowance system was initiated by employers during and shortly after the

[10] In the United Kingdom in 1957, an adult workman paid about 44 per cent of the total contribution to National Insurance, excluding industrial injuries insurance, his employer's contribution was almost equal at 42 per cent, and the balance of about 14 per cent was paid by the state.

[11] In 1957, the weekly rate of contribution to the Industrial Injuries Insurance scheme by an employed worker was 5d., by his employer 6d., and by the state 2.2d.; a woman employee paid 3d., her employer 4d., and the state 1.4d. Greece is the only other country which has adopted the tripartite method of financing industrial injuries benefits. In Denmark, the cost is mainly borne by employers, but the state pays part of the accident premium due from small employers whose income does not exceed a prescribed amount.

[12] In Belgium the cost of family allowances is borne mainly by the employers, but there is a state subsidy of about 10 per cent; in Luxemburg the state pays the cost of administration; and in Switzerland, for agricultural families, about half the cost is borne equally by the federal and cantonal governments. In Iceland, family allowances are included in a comprehensive social insurance scheme which is financed by the tripartite method.

E

First World War, and they continued to finance it as it expanded to become nation-wide; the scheme evolved under their guidance and experience, and they have wished to retain control over its financing and administration.

Sickness and maternity insurance is financed jointly by employers' and workers' contributions in a considerable number of countries, including Austria, Finland, France, the Federal Republic of Germany, Portugal, Turkey, Burma and Venezuela. In others, the tripartite system of finance is used; in Denmark, Sweden and Switzerland, employers do not contribute.

The state bears substantial parts of the cost of financing public health services in many countries, the proportion very often being around 20 to 30 per cent. In some countries, it is much higher. In the British National Health Service, the state pays about 90 per cent of the cost, the balance being met by a contribution from the National Insurance Fund, which itself includes a state contribution.[13]

Old age pension schemes are financed by the tripartite method in most countries, though in Canada, Ireland and Denmark, for example, they are non-contributory, and in the United States they are financed from the joint contributions of employers and workpeople. In Norway and Sweden, as in Canada, the funds needed for old age pensions are obtained by special taxes together with subsidies from general revenues.[14]

Most countries apply the tripartite method of financing unemployment insurance. Thus, in Canada, the federal government contributes an amount equal to 20 per cent of the joint contributions of employers and employees, and it also bears the costs of administration. In some countries, however, for example the Federal Republic of Germany, the cost is borne jointly by employers and workpeople, and in the United States and Italy by employers only. In Finland and Sweden only workpeople and the public authorities contribute. The costs of administration of social insurance are often

[13] From July 7, 1958, the contribution towards the National Health Service was 2s. 4d. a week for an adult male worker, and 1s. 10d. for a woman, these amounts being paid partly by the workers and partly by their employers.

[14] In Soviet countries, the employees do not contribute, and in a few countries, including Finland, Portugal and Turkey, the cost is borne jointly by employers and workers in varying proportions. In the British system of National Insurance which covers sickness and unemployment benefits, old age and survivors' pensions and maternity and funeral payments, the cost is borne by the tripartite method. The cost of maternity and funeral payments is borne entirely by the insured persons, so the employers' contributions are somewhat smaller than the workers'.

borne in part by the state in proportions that vary from country to country.

The wide variety in the practises of different countries in distributing the costs of social insurance and family allowances between insured persons, employers and the state is indicated by Table I. The figures do not include revenues for public assistance, health services or veterans' benefits. The countries are in order as determined by the percentage of total revenue represented by the combined contribution of insured persons and employers.

TABLE I
Percentage Distribution of Receipts for Social Insurance and Family Allowances, 1953-4[1]

Country	From Insured Persons	From Employers	From the State and other Public Authorities	Other Receipts
Ceylon	—	100.0	—	—
Tunisia	—	99.5	—	0.5
Yugoslavia	—	97.6	—	2.4
Turkey	38.3	56.6	--	5.1
Israel	52.0	39.7	6.7	1.6
United States	31.5	59.8	0.4	8.3
France	19.7	69.2	2.7	8.4
Italy	6.2	82.2	7.4	4.2
Peru	23.9	59.4	9.7	7.0
Japan	36.8	43.4	11.6	8.2
Austria	29.2	48.4	16.5	5.9
German Federal Republic	36.5	38.6	15.6	9.3
Switzerland	47.0	26.7	16.8	9.5
Guatemala	27.4	44.6	26.9	1.1
Netherlands	19.8	52.1	22.5	5.6
New Zealand	64.6	4.8	20.9	9.7
Belgium	25.0	43.2	26.2	5.6
United Kingdom	35.9	30.7	26.5	6.9
Finland	11.7	51.6	26.0	10.7
Norway	39.5	17.1	40.8	2.6
Canada	10.3	18.9	41.3	29.5[2]
Denmark	20.5	5.3	74.2	—
Ireland	9.0	15.6	73.6	1.8
Union of South Africa	6.2	16.8	68.3	8.7
Sweden	15.5	5.2	75.7	3.6
Australia	0.2	11.6	87.1	1.1

[1] International Labour Office, *The Cost of Social Security*, 1949-54 (Geneva, 1958), pp. 180-3.
[2] Including special taxes, 26.3 per cent.

Of the twenty-six countries included in Table I, eighteen show the combined contributions of insured persons and employers to be more than two-thirds of total revenue, and two other countries—Finland (63.3 per cent) and Norway (56.6 per cent)—with somewhat less than two-thirds, may be grouped with them. The remaining six countries—Canada, Denmark, Ireland, the Union of South Africa, Sweden and Australia—form a quite distinct group; less than one-third of total revenue is provided jointly by insured persons and employers, and heavy reliance is placed on state contributions, which form 60 to 75 per cent of total revenue. Until 1951-2 the contributions of insured persons and employers constituted about 98 per cent of Australian Social Security receipts, but subsequently, as a result of a major change of policy, they became only about 12 per cent.

In the first group of countries there was wide variation in the proportions contributed respectively by insured persons and employers, the country in which the insured persons bore the biggest share being New Zealand, followed by Israel and Switzerland. The employers paid the total cost in Ceylon, Tunisia, Yugoslavia, Italy, France, the United States and Peru, in each case they paid around 60 per cent or more. As already noted, in the Soviet countries the employers pay almost the whole of the cost, and in France employers pay a high proportion because they alone pay for family allowances and their contributions to social insurance are substantially higher than those of the beneficiaries. In Italy, too, the employers pay the whole cost of family allowances and also of unemployment benefits. Employers in the United States pay for unemployment insurance.

In Canada a high proportion (70.8 per cent) including special taxes, is borne by the state largely because family allowances and old age pensions are financed from federal revenues. In Denmark and Sweden the percentages are high because a large part of the costs of old age pensions and unemployment insurance is borne by the governments. In Ireland family allowances are paid from the public revenues.

CHAPTER V

ACCUMULATION OF FUNDS *versus* 'PAY AS YOU GO' FINANCING

The cost of benefits may be met either from a reserve which has been built up by accumulating the revenues from contributions over a period of years, or they may be met mainly from current revenues on a year to year basis. These alternatives raise complex questions of public finance and aceountancy, the main features of which are discussed in this chapter.

It is only in certain social security contingencies that a choice between accumulating funds and financing from year to year need be made. Social security risks are of three main kinds: (1) those which recur fairly regularly year by year so that annual financing is mainly self-contained; (2) those which occur irregularly and uncertainly over a period of years; (3) those which seem fairly certain but remote for young people and those in middle life, the main risk of this kind being old age. The costs of a risk that occurs fairly regularly each year can be met annually. This is mainly true of sickness, although there is some irregularity because of epidemics the cost of which could be met by accumulating small reserves to compensate for year to year variations; large long-range funds are not needed. Health services, even including long-range capital expenditure for the construction or extension of hospitals, can readily be undertaken at a regular annual rate and cost. Year to year financing is suitable for maternity benefits, provision for orphans and for the victims of industrial accidents whose injuries are only temporary. Where the cost, even though it extends over many years, is relatively small and fairly regular each year (for example provision for widows, orphans and the blind), year to year financing would be practicable. For family allowances, too, the pay-as-you-go method is appropriate, for although the cost is large and payments for individual children continue during the fifteen or sixteen years of their dependency, the amounts are regular from year to year except for some variations in the birth rate and the size of the population. For all these benefits the problem of accumulating big funds to make provision for the future does not arise. They can mainly be financed year by year.

The contingencies where the problem of long-term financing claims special attention are unemployment, public assistance, permanent incapacity from industrial injuries and old age. There is no doubt that unemployment should be financed from funds accumulated in good years. This method of financing is essential for two reasons. First, unemployment may fluctuate greatly from period to period. Thus in Britain in the first decade after the Second World War, unemployment averaged less than 2 per cent of the working population, whereas in the 1920's it was 10 per cent or more, and in some periods in the early 1930's it exceeded 20 per cent. Years of heavy unemployment are also years of financial stringency for governments, and if funds had to be found from taxation or borrowing there would be a danger of economising at the expense of the unemployed. Governments would be much less likely to yield to this temptation if funds for unemployment benefits had been accumulated in years of prosperity, especially if the workers had made substantial contributions. In such circumstances, governments could scarcely break faith with the workers by reducing the rates of unemployment benefit. It would be politically inexpedient to do so.

A second reason in favour of this method of financing is that the accumulation of funds in years of prosperity acts as a brake on inflation and that the payment of large sums in unemployment benefits during depression tends to reduce the severity of the depression by sustaining purchasing power. The system thus acts as a built-in stabiliser in the economy. This use of unemployment funds and other social security resources as a means of reducing economic fluctuations has been more strongly emphasised in Canada and the United States than in Britain and other European countries.

Public assistance differs from unemployment insurance benefits in being financed from general revenues, and as these are voted annually, assistance is consequently financed by the pay-as-you-go method. Payments for public assistance, like those for unemployment, increase greatly in periods of depression, especially if unemployment insurance benefits are of limited duration and are insufficient for maintenance. In order to make adequate resources available for public assistance in periods of depression without involving increased taxation (which would be difficult to impose in stringent times and would tend to aggravate the depression), the appropriate method is deficit financing by borrowing, offset, in years of prosperity, by budgeting for a surplus. This method can be applied in other fields and bring greater economic advantages than those involved in the financing of public assistance alone.

The problem of financing old age pensions is different. The problem is to discover the extent to which people of working age can make provision for their retirement twenty, thirty or forty years ahead; it is not that the expenditure involved is necessarily irregular from year to year. With defined assumptions, including rates of benefit and pensionable age, the cost can be calculated actuarially by using information on the average expectation of life of men and of women. On this actuarial basis calculations are made of the amounts which must be contributed by individuals or on their behalf by their employers and the state to provide pensions of a given sum at the pensionable age, and these amounts are collected throughout the working life of the beneficiaries. People who are in middle life when the scheme is started will not be able to contribute fully and therefore will either receive proportionately smaller pensions or will need to have their contributions heavily subsidised either by the state or by the younger contributors and their employers, as in the United States.[1] The accumulation of big funds is often involved, and problems of their investment arise. However, before consideration is given to this question and to the extent to which present savings can provide for future needs, an outline may be given of ways, both private and governmental, of financing economic security.

PRIVATE SAVING

In choosing to save money to meet a future risk instead of spending it for immediate consumption, an individual makes the decision that he will obtain more satisfaction from having the money to spend in the future than from spending it now. If the risk against which he seeks to protect himself is realised, he may be poorer at that time than he is now and therefore the satisfaction to be obtained from spending a dollar then is likely to be greater than it would be now. By saving, he may be depriving himself of additional comforts or luxuries now, but at a later date the money may be used for necessaries. He may give thought to the probability of the risk and the severity of the conditions he will face if the risk becomes reality, and vary his savings accordingly. He will know

---

[1] In Britain, for example, people who at the start of the scheme were within ten years of the retirement age and who contribute during those years, are paid pensions at the same rate as people who contribute throughout their working lives.

that if he invests his savings they will earn interest, and his decisions will be influenced by the current rate. He will also need to think about the possibilities of his savings being lost either by theft if he hoards them, or by failure of the banks or other institutions in which he deposits them. These dangers are still very great in many underdeveloped countries, and the last was serious in the United States as recently as the depression years of the 1930's. More subtle but no less harmful are the insidious effects of inflation, whether creeping or rapid; and one of the injurious moral consequences of the failure of many governments to prevent or greatly to restrict inflation has been a weakening of habits of thrift.

An individual who saves in order to provide for future eventualities will either hoard his savings or invest them in any one of a variety of ways, the most usual being government bonds, industrial shares, private insurance, mortgage corporations or building societies; in the last two cases the purpose would be to secure ownership of a house. Similarly, private corporations, including industrial companies which have contributory schemes to provide retirement pensions for their employees, invest in such securities as industrial equities or debentures, real estate and government bonds. A few companies may be big enough to meet future obligations to their employees out of their general resources at the time when the pensions or other payments fall due. More companies, including those with employee shareholding schemes which encourage savings as a provision for the future, use the funds as part of their own finances, and their financial soundness determines the value of the savings. Most companies, however, set aside such savings in separate funds administered by trustees.

When an individual invests funds to provide for future needs, his investments, whether in the shares of private companies or in government securities, represent assets to him and liabilities of the companies or the government on which he has a claim. When, however, a government invests social insurance funds in its own bonds these securities are essentially claims on itself. As will be discussed later, this difference between private investment and government investment is significant, though the government is politically responsible and accountable to the community for meeting the social insurance obligations for which the funds were accumulated.

GOVERNMENTAL SOCIAL SECURITY FINANCING

Government schemes to provide social security benefits may be financed in one of several ways or by a combination of those ways. As already indicated, benefits may be paid out of the ordinary revenues from taxation each year, and some reserves may be built up to meet minor fluctuations in the annual cost of benefits so as to avoid the necessity for corresponding yearly changes in taxation. The beneficiaries make no special contribution, though they pay such part of the cost as falls on them as taxpayers. This method is used in the financing of·family allowances in Britain and in Canada, and for public assistance in all countries. As the benefits are dependent on annual votes by parliament there is no certainty of continuity: a change in economic conditions or in political attitudes might lead to alterations in the moneys voted.

This pay-as-you-go system is the simplest way of obtaining revenues for social security purposes. Each year estimates would be made of the total cost of the benefits. This total would be added to the estimates of all the other items of state expenditure, and the necessary funds would be obtained through the ordinary channels of taxation at rates fixed each year to meet the estimated total expenditure of that year. Except for relatively small reserves to provide for variations in expenditure from year to year, no funds would be accumulated for benefits such as old age pensions due to be paid in future years, and therefore no problem of investing huge funds would arise. The government would guarantee the payment of future benefits in the same way as it guarantees the interest and repayment of the capital of long-term loans. The taxes could be fixed at rates which would be as equitable as possible between different sections of the community according to their capacity to pay. No special machinery of collection would be necessary and no records required to relate the amounts paid in taxes by each person to the social security benefits he or she would receive.

There would be a danger of political pressure to increase benefits beyond reasonable levels. The risk would, however, be less serious in communities where wealth and income do not vary greatly in different sections of the population and where most of the people who receive the social security benefits are in the same income groups as those who bear the tax burden. In such circumstances, those who demand increased benefits would know that their demand would mean heavier taxes and that they themselves would have to carry a substantially greater load.

Another method is to collect money by special contributions and to keep records of each individual's contribution as a basis for the benefits which will be paid, but to merge the receipts in the general revenues of the government and to use the general revenues to meet both general expenditure and the social security benefits due each year. No social security fund is accumulated.

A third method is to collect special contributions for specified social security benefits. The revenues may be obtained either from taxes or from contributions made by employers, workers and self-employed persons, often supplemented from state funds.[2] The proceeds are accumulated in special reserves and invested by the government. Records are kept of the individual contributions which give title to benefits, and the benefits are paid as they fall due. It is essential to keep records if individual benefits vary in amount and duration according to the contributions paid by each person. Records must, for instance, be kept if contributions and benefits vary with the wages of the workers (as they do in the Canadian and United States unemployment insurance schemes) or if wage categories are used to determine the amount of the workers' and employers' contributions and of the cash benefits paid to the workers (as in the sickness and accident insurance system in Venezuela).

The method of special contributions for specific social security benefits is widely applied, especially in compulsory insurance schemes towards which employers and workers contribute.[3] It is used in the British system of National Insurance to cover a wide range of risks by comprehensive unified contributions from employers, workers, and the state. It is applied in Canada somewhat similarly to finance unemployment insurance benefits. The United States Old-Age, Survivors, and Disability Insurance Program is financed by the joint contributions of employers and workers, but unemployment insurance is financed by payroll taxes on employers only. In all these and other systems, funds are accumulated and the problem of their investment arises.[4] The interest derived from the investment of funds plays a big part in meeting the cost of future benefits, and that is a major reason for accumulating funds.

On the other hand, the Canadian old age pensions, which are

---

[2] If the contributions by the state from general revenues form a big proportion of the social security fund, the scheme approaches that of providing social security benefits from the yields of ordinary taxation.

[3] Differences between social insurance and private insurance were discussed in chapter IV.

[4] In workmen's compensation schemes where employers, or insurance companies acting on their behalf, are required to pay lump sums to provide pensions for permanently disabled persons, the accumulation of funds is necessary.

paid at a flat rate to all persons seventy years of age and over who satisfy specified conditions of residence, are financed by the pay-as-you-go method from the proceeds of special taxes at the rate of 2 per cent of personal taxable income (maximum tax $60.00 a year), a special 2 per cent. tax on corporate taxable income and a 2 per cent sales tax. In New Zealand, social security benefits are financed mainly on a pay-as-you-go basis, though appreciable balances have been accumulated.[5] The principal revenue is from a special social security tax at a flat rate of 1s 6d in the pound on salaries, wages, the income of companies and other income, together with a government grant from general revenues.[6]

An advantage of the actuarial method for old age pension schemes is that the people concerned know what is involved. The rates of contribution may be fixed from the beginning and remain at the same amount year after year, or they may be raised on dates that are announced at the beginning of the scheme.[7] These provisions may, however, have to be revised in course of time owing to changes in demographic forecasts, economic conditions and social attitudes, and experience gained in the operation of the scheme. The raising of contribution rates at intervals is a half-way house towards 'pay-as-you-go' financing.

INVESTMENT OF SOCIAL SECURITY FUNDS

The safeguarding and investment of big funds for future social security benefits raise major problems. There is a danger that in

[5] At the end of the financial year 1955-6 the balance in the social security fund was £16,805,826, which represented 23 per cent of the total social security payments during the year.

[6] In the financial year 1955-6 the revenue from the tax on salaries and wages yielded 47.6 per cent of social security revenues, on the income of companies and other income 33.2 per cent; almost all the remainder was the government grant (£14 million).

[7] For example, the United States Old-Age, Survivors, and Disability Insurance Program announced dates of increase, though subsequently the dates were changed. By the original legislation, the scheme was to be financed by contributions from employers and employees each at a rate of 1½ per cent of wages and salaries up to $3,000; but by amendments in 1939 the tax was fixed at 1 per cent till the end of 1942, then 2 per cent for the next four years, 2½ per cent for a further two years until the end of 1948 and then 3 per cent; but, by subsequent amendments, the rate remained at 1 per cent until the beginning of 1951 when it was raised to 1½ per cent. In 1957 the rate was 2¼ per cent, including contribution for total permanent disability after fifty years of age. The intention then was to raise the rate by ¼ per cent every five years until in 1975 it would be 4¼ per cent each. The ceiling had been raised to $3,600 in 1950 and to $4,200 in 1954.

times of financial difficulty a government may raid the funds and use them for other purposes. There is the risk of losses from corruption or maladministration. And the effective investment of large sums is complex. How can governments wisely invest such funds?

Many governments invest money in industrial undertakings. Thus, the British government has, at various times, held shares in such undertakings as Cables and Wireless and British Petroleum; and there was Disraeli's famous purchase of shares in the Suez Canal Company. Funds could be invested in nationalised industries, which have increased considerably in number in various countries during the middle years of the present century. Investments could be made in so-called joint ventures—undertakings in which the government of a country and private industry provide capital on a fifty-fifty or some other proportionate basis. This method has been adopted since the war in some Asian countries, for example Burma, where oil drilling and tin and lead mining are operated in this way. Then there are big projects such as the Volta River development in Ghana and the Kariba Hydro Electric undertaking in Rhodesia. Such opportunities, though increasing, are, however, usually unsuitable for the investment of social security funds, as some of them may involve too great risks and not satisfy the needs of the investment, which are to safeguard the capital against loss and to yield a fair rate of interest.

In practice, the annual social security surpluses are generally used by governments to meet regular current expenditure. In effect, the government borrows the funds and issues bonds bearing interest at current rates. The social security reserves, therefore, are loaned to the government and have a similar status to that of other government bonds. The reserve is a paper obligation or an accountancy device, and the capital and interest depend on the government's ability to meet its obligations in the future. The funds form part of the national debt, and the interest credited year by year comes from the taxpayers. Thus, the assets differ from those of private insurance companies which are the liabilities of industrial undertakings, governments and other bodies in which the funds are invested. Social security assets held by a government are a liability of the government to the beneficiaries, but are an obligation on itself. The integrity of a state insurance scheme depends, therefore, not on the building of a reserve fund, but on the government's willingness and ability in future years to find the necessary money for benefits by taxation. The obligation to beneficiaries who have paid contributions and who include the poorer sections of the population is, however, at least as strong as the obligation to holders of government securities, and deliberate default is unlikely.

Consideration must now be given to the main economic and financial effects of the government's use of the social security funds it borrows.[8] The government bonds held for social insurance purposes merely represent government obligations for stated amounts, they have no productive value and, as already noted, the interest is met by the taxpayers. The bonds are essentially an accountancy record of future obligations which can be met only by taxation out of real resources in the future.

PRESENT SAVING AND FUTURE RESOURCES

Because it seems fair and reasonable that the workers of today should contribute now towards their maintenance after they retire, it is easy to require them to do so, and the psychological attitude of the population is important in financing social security expenditure. The main problem, however, is the relation between saving now and consuming in the future. Joseph's problem was fairly easy once he had guidance about trends of production in Egypt and could convince the people that they should save resources during the seven fat years for the seven lean years. Already the people had experienced successions of plenty and of famine, so the plan seemed reasonable to them. What Joseph did was to save commodities— food which could be stored, would not deteriorate greatly and could be consumed years afterwards. Today, however, saving for the future is largely in terms of money. The people who are now saving for the years of their retirement (whether through private insurance, corporation superannuation plans or government pension schemes) will, when they are aged, have to depend on the people who are then of working age to produce the food, clothing, fuel and other goods they will be consuming. Only if the people then of working age prove willing to meet the obligations now being assumed by the government and other organisations will the goods needed by the aged be available. People pay taxes and other contributions today,

[8] An immediate effect of the use of social security surpluses by a government to meet current expenditure is that either current taxation or government borrowing from the public is less than it otherwise would be. If taxpayers or investors invest productively amounts equivalent to those they would have otherwise paid to the government in taxes or invested in government bonds, then future productivity will be increased and provide greater resources from which social security benefits in the future may be obtained.

but bread, eggs, meat, fish, milk and other perishable foods will have to be produced at the time they are consumed, perhaps thirty or forty years after contributions to retirement funds have been made.

Two major questions must be considered. First, what is the relation between the money now set aside and the future cost of the services which will be needed to provide for retired persons? Second, in what ways can money which is now being saved for the future be used to provide the basis for producing the goods needed twenty or thirty years hence by people who have ceased to be producers?

Effects of Inflation

The answer to the first of these questions must deal both with inflationary or other changes in the value of money and with changes in productivity. Clearly, those who now pay taxes or make contributions expect to receive adequate protection in the future. Money set aside today represents given quantities of goods and services at today's prices, and contributors can reasonably expect that in the future they will receive sufficient money to buy equivalent quantities of goods and services, together with an addition represented by a fair rate of interest on the money during the period of waiting.[9] Because of long-term inflations, the purchasing power of much past saving has fallen seriously, and those who saved have been subjected to an insidious and injurious form of taxation.[10] If benefits were originally fixed so as to meet needs wholly or in substantial part, their real value when they are received may fall far short of what was originally intended if an inflation has occurred in the meantime, and privation may result unless recourse is made to public assistance. When the contributions were made, maybe years

[9] Rates of interest may vary considerably. In Britain, for example, rates on long-term investments in 1958 were about double the rates nine or ten years earlier.

[10] Leaving aside the catastrophic collapse in the value of money in many European countries after the First World War for example, the real value of savings that were invested in government securities during and in the early years after the Second World War is now substantially less in terms of goods and services, even allowing for interest, than it was at the time of the investment. In other words, the savers have lost the difference between the original value in goods and services and the present value, and have received no real interest. So unfair did this become that prominent British leaders refused to take part in propaganda urging people to buy savings certificates and defence bonds, on the ground that it was immoral to do so when there was every likelihood that, although the securities were made to look attractive, those who bought them would lose thereby in real terms.

ago, the money unit had a higher purchasing power than that in which the benefits are paid. In other words, good money was paid for bad. Yet in the meantime the productivity of the community has probably increased and bigger resources are available to provide for those in need.

In these circumstances, the only fair course to take is to raise the benefits at least enough to allow for the increased cost of living and perhaps more, even though this action involves a departure from the original actuarial basis of the scheme.[11] But why not? Where the savings are made in a government scheme to provide retirement pensions, it is essential that when the pensions are paid, their purchasing power should be at a standard at least equal to that contemplated and expected at the time the contributions were made. The state both should and can make up the difference, as the inflation is a consequence of failure by the government to ensure monetary stability. It is true that the beneficiaries will receive more in money than would be forthcoming according to actuarial calculations, but the beneficiaries are not interested in money as such, but in what it will buy in goods and services.

To a greater or less extent, various countries have recognised their responsibility by increasing the rates of pension to offset the effects of inflation. The inference is that, in inflationary periods, there can be no close accountancy or actuarial relation in terms of money between accumulations of contributions and rates of pension, but there can be adjustments in real terms.

Growth in Productivity

Such adjustments are facilitated by increases in productivity, the rate of which in various countries over a period of years has been in the order of 2 or 3 per cent annually. These increases provide the basis for rising standards of living, because if productivity increases, the effort in terms of labour to produce a given quantity of goods and services will be less, and probably substantially less than it is today. Therefore money saved today is greater in terms of effort than the same amount of money in ten or fifteen years, even assuming there has been no inflation. The next generation of workers is thus in a favourable position to meet the material needs

---

[11] The need to make financial adjustments is not peculiar to social insurance; many private group pension plans introduced by companies for their employees require amendment about once every five years to take account of inflation and other changes in conditions, and the amendments are usually made on actuarial advice.

of people then living in retirement. Assuming increased productivity, there is a strong argument for raising pension rates so that allowance is made for the reduced effort required to provide them. They are likely to be raised, because conventional standards of subsistence or of human needs in any country are closely linked with changes in the country's productivity. A reasonable rate of pension in Canada or the United States today is much higher than at the beginning of the century, and very much higher than in India or Burma. The levels of acceptable social security standards in any country reflect the general standard of living of its people, and this in turn is linked with its productive efficiency.

Productive Investment of Funds

The second question raised above is concerned with the ways in which money saved now can provide the goods and services which will be consumed by aged people thirty or forty years hence. Clearly the relation is not close between money saved now and goods consumed many years ahead. Will people of working age at that time make the necessary provision? It is likely that they will do so on humanitarian grounds, for the aged at any time are the parents of the people of working age; but there are also powerful economic reasons. The savings of one generation become the working capital of the next. Each generation is born into a world that has a vast, complex organisation, and productive equipment which has been built up by the efforts of past generations. Present standards of living depend more than is usually recognised on our rich inheritance from the past. This includes roads, railways, canals, houses, farms, factory buildings and machinery and all the other instruments of production. Nor is there a break or division between generations; they succeed one another in continuous unbroken flow.

If the savings of today are used to build up capital for the future then present savers have a right to part of the future yield of that capital. Moreover, the augmented capital equipment which the next generation inherits from the past enables it to meet its own needs and honour its obligations to its parents. The obligation is reinforced by the fact that not only are the children of today provided with necessaries during the many years of their infancy, childhood and youth, but also that their productive capacity throughout their working lives is increased by the personal capital invested in them by their parents—both direct investment and indirect investment in the form of payments for a sound education. Thus, even though there is no direct connection between investment of social security funds in government bonds and the resources needed in the future to pay old age pensions, the next generation of workers is able to meet the taxation from which those resources will be provided.

The most satisfactory way of providing for the future, whether by direct government investment or investment in private under-takings, is in long-term productive capital developments which will maintain the real value of the capital and yield income. A few illustrations may be given. Present generations have benefited enormously from the labour and investments of earlier generations in constructing such great waterways as the Suez and Panama canals. The same is true of the labour and capital used long ago in building the transcontinental railways of Canada and the United States, including the immense efforts needed to tunnel the Rocky Mountains and bridge the torrents. Today similar gigantic engineer-ing schemes are being undertaken in various parts of the world; the St Lawrence Seaway and hydro-electric power development is an outstanding example. This will be of incalculable economic benefit to many future generations in Canada and the United States. Also the rapidity of its construction and the relative freedom from laborious physical effort by contrast with the sweat, toil and hard-ship involved in earlier big construction works are due to the vastly improved mechanical equipment which has been invented and perfected on the basis of past initiative invention, scientific work and technical engineering skills. Great irrigation schemes such as those in the Sudan, India and Pakistan which bring millions of acres into cultivation and greatly increase the output of food are based on the labour and saving of past and present generations. Invest-ments of labour and capital in docks, harbours and other transport systems and in public utilities progressively increase the national income and thereby raise future taxable capacity from which future social security benefits can be paid. Only if present resources are used unproductively, whether by governments or private investors, is there failure to make proper provision for the future.

There are other ways also in which the money saved today can provide goods which will be used in the future. Stock piling is one example which has important though limited application, usually as strategic reserves. Then, in addition to productive capital goods there are many durable consumer goods which can be produced now and used in a quite distant future. Housing is the best example: money used today by an individual in providing for himself a home or by a government in undertaking a housing scheme gives accom-modation not only in the present but for many years ahead. In

F

countries where the government promotes house building, present resources can be used to provide for future needs if economic rents are charged or if hire purchase schemes enable occupiers to buy their homes by regular payments over a period of twenty or twenty-five years. The work is done now but the value continues. The same is true of many durable articles of furniture, household furnishings, utensils and equipment. Period antique furniture of good design and workmanship appreciates in value. Some articles of clothing, such as heavy winter overcoats, have a long life. Women's winter coats may not have as long a life as men's because women's fashions change more rapidly and radically; even so, their fur coats are bought only occasionally and may continue in use for many years.

All these durable consumer goods constitute a substantial part of average current expenditure and avoid both future spending and production. Thus, the results of a survey of family expenditure made by the Canadian government in 1948 and used as basis of the present consumer price index show that in a sample, representative of a large section of the Canadian population, 31.7 per cent of total expenditure was for food, 14.8 per cent for housing, 11.5 per cent for clothing, 17.3 per cent for household operation and 24.7 per cent for other commodities and services. If it be assumed that 15 per cent is spent to buy houses and that this expense ceases once families have paid off mortgage charges, and that 3 per cent of the amount spent on clothing, 4 per cent of the amount spent on household furniture and furnishings and 4 per cent of the amount spent on other commodities represent an accumulation of durable articles, these total over 25 per cent of total expenditure. At a conservative estimate, therefore, it is fairly certain that many people at the time of their retirement from work will have accumulated, in the form of the house they live in and its furniture and other articles of personal use, a capital which will save them at least 20 per cent and often 30 or 40 per cent of the expenditure which families ordinarily incur during the course of their working lives. In other words the cost of living of retired persons for this reason alone will be so much less than the average cost of persons who are still at work. Most hire purchase payments for durable household goods and mortgage payments on the home will have ended before retirement, and the goods can be enjoyed without further expense, except for maintenance and repairs. Also the cost of maintaining children will usually have ceased. These factors have an important bearing on the rates of pension that should be planned for, and consequently on the contributions to be paid throughout working life.

The extent to which the present generation of workers can provide resources in the form of durable goods which it will still use after retirement, or of capital goods which it will hand over to the next generation of workers for productive uses, will depend on the way present resources are used. Some individuals may make little or no direct provision for their future needs, but spend most or all of their income on immediate consumption. Governments may do the same: they may obtain funds from the community by taxation or social insurance contributions, but spend the money on current consumption, for example on military defence. Such expenditure is indeed necessary for one form of security, and in these critical years one of the most difficult questions with which governments are faced is how to distribute the resources of the community. They have to decide in what proportions they are to be used for immediate consumption, military security, and investments in material capital investments to meet the economic and social needs of the future, or in human capital by making better provision for health, education and welfare.

Wherever resources are consumed in the present, whether necessarily or wastefully, less capital is accumulated for the future. Moreover, a considerable part of capital expenditure on such works as the St Lawrence Seaway and hydro-electric power development is financed by borrowing, and therefore, although the work is done and the capital equipment provided in the present, the monetary cost is spread into the future, because the interest charges have still to be met and capital (including capital sinking fund charges) has still to be repaid.

The burden on future generations of workers varies with changes in the relative proportions of persons who are working and those who are not working. If the proportion of people over working age increases (as it will in Britain during the next twenty-five or thirty years), a given number of people at work have to support a larger number of retired people. The burden is similarly increased by raising the age of leaving school and the age of entry into industry.

Reference must be made here to the position of underdeveloped countries with low standards of living. In many such countries the standards of living of large numbers of the people are so meagre and immediate consumption so inadequate that the possibilities of saving are severely limited: any saving would reduce still further an already very low level of productive efficiency. There is therefore great difficulty in building up capital for the future to increase productive equipment whether for raising standards of living or providing a minimum of social security. So there is a vicious circle of poverty, low productive efficiency and difficulty in finding capital to increase productivity. The problem is aggravated by a recent growth of population at rates so rapid as to absorb in immediate consumption most if not all of the gains which may be made in productivity, and in consequence the standards of living remain low or rise only very slowly. In some less developed countries, for example India, contributions by people with low incomes to social insurance or provident funds, especially for retirement benefits, offer one way of obtaining appreciable financial resources for productive capital investment which will tend to raise future standards of living.

On balance, the pay-as-you-go method has advantages over the accumulation of huge funds for the financing of increasing future obligations (particularly old age pensions) in advanced countries where social insurance is highly developed, its financial aspects well understood and the whole or a large part of the population covered by the schemes. Future generations will be able to meet growing demands if each generation hands on to its successors improved productive capital equipment. It is desirable, however, that the combined rates of contribution in the early stages of old age insurance should be greater than the rates needed to meet the relatively light payments of current benefits, so that some funds can be accumulated; otherwise, the increases in contributions in the later stages may be unduly large.

For schemes restricted to particular industries or other relatively small sections of the population the creation of an earmarked fund is preferable. This method also has psychological advantages in the early stages of social insurance, especially in the less developed countries, as people will more readily understand the relation between contributions and benefits if there is an earmarked fund.

Any reserves that are built up in the pay-as-you-go system are relatively small and the interest they earn is not a vital element in the finances of the system. Where big funds are accumulated the interest is important and enables contributions to remain constant or to increase relatively little as the cost of benefits grows. The interest on the earlier accumulations is used to cover deficits of expenditure over contributions in the later years.

CHAPTER VI

PROPORTION OF SOCIAL SECURITY PAYMENTS TO NATIONAL INCOME

At any given time calculations can be made to show the proportion which social security payments form of the national income of a country. The proportion will differ from country to country and from period to period according to circumstances. If benefits are increased substantially or if the scope of social security is widened, the proportion will increase. For example, the introduction of cash benefits for sickness, a lowering of the age at which old age pensions can be claimed or an increase in the amount of pensions will raise the proportion. Variations from year to year in the volume of un-employment will result in changes in the proportion. In a period of inflation, if benefits are not adjusted upwards in relation to the fall in the purchasing power of money or the rise in the cost of living, there will be a fall in the real value of the benefits and in the pro-portion they form of the national dividend.

It would be useful to have an estimate of the proportion of national income that would have to be spent in order to provide an adequate standard of social security. In attempting to establish such a proportion, it would be necessary to define the scope of social security and to make assumptions about suitable scales of benefit. Estimates would be necessary of the cost of each element in social security—provision for the aged, the unemployed, the sick, invalids, children in need, widows, the blind and others. These estimated costs would then be added together and the total expressed as a percentage of the national dividend. It would also be advantageous to establish a minimum proportion which would be appropriate for good years, a 'maximum' proportion for bad years and an average proportion for a sufficiently long period of years to smooth out variations caused by short-term conditions. If such proportions could be established even very approximately they could be used as a kind of standard with which the actual proportions in any country could be compared.

The purpose of this chapter is to consider the establishment of such a tentative standard. One method is to construct a hypothe-tical standard of social security and on specified assumptions to relate its cost to national income. This can only be done for each country separately, taking account of the actual standards of living and the distribution of incomes in relation to national productivity and the extent to which voluntary methods of providing security are effective, particularly among the poorer sections of the population. A second method is to tabulate the proportions of national dividend actually spent on social security in various countries, and then, in countries where the social security system leaves gaps (an absence of cash benefits for sickness, as in Canada, or of children's allowances, as in the United States), to estimate the cost of meeting such deficiencies. Much investigation over a long period and more extensive experience of social security schemes in various parts of the world will be necessary to change early crude estimates into more refined standards for measuring the appropriateness of different systems at different times and in different countries.

INTERNATIONAL COMPARISONS

Several calculations have already been made of the proportion of the national income of various countries spent on social security in recent years, and this information will now be reviewed. The most comprehensive in range of countries covered are estimates by the International Labour Office showing the total receipts, total expenses and benefit expenditure for social security as percentages of national income in the years 1949 to 1954.[1] The social security expenditures in 1953-4 expressed as percentages of the national income of various countries are given in Table II. These total expenditures as a proportion of national income are generally somewhat higher than benefit expenditures because of administrative costs.

It must be noted that considerable changes have been made since these figures were compiled. Thus, the United States Old-Age and

[1] *The Cost of Social Security,* 1949-1954 (Geneva, 1958), pp. 161-4. The national income figures are of national income at factor cost, defined as being equal to private and public expenditure on consumption plus net domestic capital formation plus net exports, plus net factor income from the rest of the world less indirect taxes after deduction of subsidies. Included in the social security statistics are systems established by legislation and administered by public, semi-public or autonomous bodies, particularly compulsory social insurance, public assistance, family allowances, public health services (curative and preventive), benefits for war victims, compensation for industrial accidents and special schemes for public employees. For the full definition of social security used by the International Labour Office in its compilations, see *ibid.,* pp. 2, 3.

Survivors Insurance has been extended to more categories of people and Disability Insura͏ ͏e has been added, though the bigger expenditure may have been offset as a proportion of the national income by the continued growth of that income. Emphasis must also be placed on the fact that the figures are solely of social security expenditures, and there is wide variation from country to country in the extent to which security is provided by private sector expenditures.

TABLE II

Social Security Expenditures as Percentages of National Income, 1953-4

Country*	Percentage	Country	Percentage
German Federal		Finland	9.9
Republic	19.2	Netherlands	9.6
France	18.5	Canada	9.1
Austria	17.0	Norway	8.8
Belgium	16.2	Australia	8.1
Italy	14.7	Switzerland	7.6
New Zealand	12.6	Japan	6.7
Luxemburg	12.4	Israel	6.2
Czechoslovakia	11.6	United States	5.4
Sweden	11.5	Union of South Africa	4.5
Yugoslavia	11.4	Ceylon	3.2
Denmark	11.1	Peru	2.4
United Kingdom	10.7	Guatemala	2.2
Iceland	10.0	Turkey	1.4
Ireland	10.0		

* Arranged according to size of percentage.

The wide range from under 2 per cent to over 19 per cent is due to the fact that the countries with the lowest percentages covered only a small part of the social security field while the countries with the highest percentages went beyond it. Thus in Turkey the expenditure was mainly for public officials and military personnel, and for limited schemes of social insurance and public health services; there were no family allowances and little public assistance. Most of the countries with fairly comprehensive schemes had expenditures within a range of from 6 to 13 per cent of the national income, but in varying degrees the systems either had gaps or extended in some of their features beyond the limits of social security. The arithmetical average of the seventeen countries within this range was 9.3 per cent of national income.

For purposes of comparison, figures compiled by the Social

Security Section of the Research Division of the Canadian Department of National Health and Welfare are given in Table III. They show for Great Britain, the United States, Canada, Australia and New Zealand the percentage of national income spent on income maintenance and health and welfare services in 1949-50.[2] The figures are all appreciably higher than those compiled by the International Labour Office, partly because of some differences in the scope of the statistics and changes in systems and benefits, but mainly because the Canadian Department's data are for 1949-50 whereas those of the International Labour Office are for 1953-54. During this interval all the five countries experienced inflation and also growth in productivity resulting in a substantial rise in national income, but social security benefits were not increased proportionately and lagged considerably behind the growth in national income.[3]

TABLE   III

*Social Security Expenditures as Percentages of
National Income, 1949-50*

Country	Income Maintenance	Health and Welfare Services	Total
Great Britain	6.07	5.80	11.87
United States	3.90	1.62	5.52
Canada	5.53	2.46	7.99
Australia	5.09	2.21	7.30
New Zealand	9.23	3.95	13.18

More recent figures have been calculated by the Canadian Department of National Health and Welfare. They show social security expenditures expressed as percentages of national income as follows:

	1953-4	1954-5
Great Britain	10.3	—
United States	5.5	6.5
Canada	8.5	10.0

[2] Dr. Ronald Mendelsohn in his book *Social Security in the British Commonwealth* (London, 1954), made comparisons for the United Kingdom, Canada, Australia and New Zealand showing the relation between national income and social security payments for income maintenance in 1938 and 1948-9 (p. 299). His figures do not include expenditure on health services, and allowing for this and for differences in date and changes in benefits, productivity and prices, they correspond fairly closely with those compiled by the International Labour Office and the Canadian Department of National Health and Welfare.
[3] This is shown by the International Labour Office figures which are given separately for the years 1949, 1950 and 1951 in *The Cost of Social Security 1949-51* (Geneva, 1955), p. 93. The average fall in the proportions in the five countries during these years was 12 per cent, ranging from 6 per cent in Canada to 20 per cent in New Zealand.

The figure for Great Britain is less than that shown above for 1949-50, because the social security expenditure is compared with the gross national product at factor cost instead of with the lower net national income figure and, also, the gross national product used includes Northern Ireland, whereas the social security expenditure is for Great Britain only.

In countries with economic development and standards of living approximately similar to those of Britain, the United States, Canada, Australia, New Zealand and countries of Western Europe, a basic or minimum system of income maintenance would require an expenditure of around 6.5 to 8.0 per cent of the national income. To this should be added about 2 per cent of the national income to provide health services.[4] The services would be free for people in receipt of public assistance; other people would pay amounts up to, for example, 3 per cent of an average wage, say £20 annually, towards the cost of medical services and standard hospitalisation which they and their families needed in any year; but beyond that amount the health services would be free.[5] These estimates are based on a study of the data given above; additions have been made to allow for gaps and inadequacies of benefits, and reductions have been made to allow for systems which provide benefits outside the scope of basic social security. Thus, about 8.5 to 10 per cent of the national income of such countries is required to provide a minimum income and health services, including benefits for war disabilities. In countries with little or no expenditure for war veterans the percentages would be 1.0 to 1.5 per cent less.

The estimates are for countries where less than 4 per cent of the workers are unemployed. If unemployment rose to 12 per cent the social security percentages of national income would have to be raised by 2 or 3 per cent to provide unemployment insurance benefits and public assistance for the additional unemployed persons and their dependants.

On the basis of a study of medical costs in thirteen countries, Miss Laura Bodmer of the Social Security Division of the International Labour Office estimated that a general public health service that covered medical expenses including hospitalisation would cost about 2 per cent of national income. The results of this study are given in a paper, "Quelques observations sur le coût des soins médicaux", *Revue Belge de Securité Sociale, May-June* 1956.
[5] Consideration is given in chapter ix to payments by individual beneficiaries of some part of the cost of health services which they themselves receive.

HYPOTHETICAL EXPENDITURES

The above estimates are crude approximations, based on actual systems of social security in various countries and modified to make allowance for gaps and for benefits beyond basic standards. An alternative method of estimating what proportion of the national income is required to provide a comprehensive basic system of social security is to build up a hypothetical scheme for the provision of specified benefits, evaluate the total costs on the basis of the number of beneficiaries in a country and relate the aggregate to the national income. For purposes of illustration the method will be applied to Great Britain and Canada; no attempt will be made to provide refined or detailed calculations but only to give a general indication of the method and of the main order of magnitudes and proportions.

The essential features of these hypothetical calculations are provision of old age pensions from seventy years of age, and allowances for children under sixteen years of age for the third and succeeding dependent children in a family. These benefits are at flat rates for all, and therefore are paid to some people who are not in need.[6] The system also includes unemployment benefits, sickness benefits, compensation for industrial accidents and diseases, maternity grants, pensions and allowances for invalids and for widows and orphans, pensions for war victims and public assistance. The cost of a public health service and administrative expenditures are also included.

The standards used for various income benefits are those defined in the Draft Convention concerning Minimum Standards of Social Security adopted by the International Labour Conference in 1952. They are established as percentages of the wages, including any family allowances, of an ordinary unskilled labourer in the engineering industry, as follows:

Contingency	Standard Beneficiary	Percentage of Wage
Employment injury	Man with wife and two children	50
Sickness or unemployment	Man with wife and two children	45
Invalidity	Man with wife and two children	40
Old age	Man with wife of pensionable age	40
Survivors	Widow with two children	40

[6] Hypothetical estimates could be made along similar lines by using benefits which vary with wages.

The percentages are higher or lower according to the number of dependants. For maternity the percentage in the Convention is 45. No percentage is given in the Convention for family allowances; for the purpose of the present calculation 5 per cent of the wage is used as the rate of benefit for each dependent child after the second.[7] This percentage is much below the proportion necessary to maintain the children, and for large families with low incomes the allowances would need to be supplemented by public assistance, though a preferable alternative would be to increase the rate of allowance as the number of children in a family increased.

In making estimates for Britain, an ordinary labourer's wage in engineering is taken to be £10 a week. The unemployment percentage used is 1.5 per cent of the working population, which is representative for the early 1950's, but 12 per cent is also taken to indicate the magnitude of additional costs of social security in a substantial depression. For sickness the calculation is based on an average of twelve days' sickness a year for the working population, but only nine days' benefit, the first three days being unpaid.[8]

On these assumptions the figures of annual expenditure would be:

[7] In some countries the rates are much higher, the allowances being intended to cover a large part if not the whole of the cost of maintenance of each child. In France the allowance for the second dependent child is 20 per cent of a 'basic wage', and for each subsequent child it is 30 per cent. The problems of family allowances are discussed in some detail in chapter viii.

[8] The expenditure for old age pensions is calculated by taking an average pension as £2 a week for each of 3,700,000 persons aged seventy years and over. Children's allowances are at 10s. a week for 4 million dependent children from the third in a family. The unemployment benefit rate is £4 10s. a week for one-half of 1.5 per cent unemployed of a working population of 20 million, for a man with a wife and two dependent children, and the remainder at half the rate. For sickness the rate is £4 10s. a week for 1.5 weeks for one-half of the working population of 20 million, for a man with a wife and two dependent children, and the remainder at half the rate. Other contingencies and services consist of the following rounded estimates based on current expenditures, the rates of benefit corresponding closely with the international standards of benefits adopted: industrial injuries, £25 million; widows, orphans and child care, £50 million; nutritional services (school milk and meals), £80 million; maternity, £10 million; war pensions and disability services, £100 million; public assistance, £125 million. Administration is at a rate of 5 per cent of direct expenditure on benefits and services.

	£
Old age pensions	384,800,000
Family allowances	104,000,000
Unemployment	52,650,000
Sickness	101,250,000
Other contingencies and services	390,000,000
Administration	51,635,000
Total	£1,084,335,000

The total for income maintenance and nutritional services is about 6 per cent of the gross national income (at factor cost) of £18,750 million in 1957.[9] If 2 per cent, that is, about £375 million, were added for health services and hospitalisation, the percentage of the national income would be 8. The actual expenditure is a higher percentage partly because the standards of benefit are generally above the minima specified in the Convention of the International Labour Organisation. Other main differences from the system in operation in Britain are that in the above hypothetical scheme, pensions are paid only at seventy years of age instead of at sixty-five for men and sixty for women. Also, family allowances are paid only from the third child, but at higher rates. If unemployment rose to 12 per cent of all employees, the social security expenditure would increase to more than 10 per cent of the national income. It must be emphasised that these percentages of the national income are based on minimum standards and they would be greater if the rates of benefit were higher.

For Canada, an ordinary labourer's wage in engineering is taken to be $50.00 a week. The unemployment figure used is 4 per cent of a total force of 4,700,000 wage earners, but 12 per cent is also taken to show the additional costs of social security in a substantial depression. For sickness the estimated cost of income maintenance is based on an average of twelve days' sickness a year for the labour force, but with only nine days' benefit, the first three days being unpaid.[10]

---

[9] Central Statistical Office, London, *Monthly Digest of Statistics.*

[10] The expenditure for old age pensions is calculated by taking an average pension of $10.00 a week for each of 700,000 persons aged seventy years and over. Children's allowances are at a rate of $2.50 a week for 1,700,000 dependent children from the third in a family. The unemployment benefit rate is $22.50 a week for one-half of 4 per cent unemployed of a total of 4,700,000 wage earners, for a man with a wife and two children, and the

On these assumptions the annual expenditure would be:

Old age pensions	$364,000,000
Family allowances	221,000,000
Unemployment	164,970,000
Sickness	118,969,000
Other contingencies and services	515,000,000
Administration	69,200,000
Total	$1,453,139,000

This total for income maintenance is about 7.6 per cent of a national income of $19,000 million.[11] If 2 per cent were added to this for health services and hospitalisation, the percentage of the national income would be 9.6. The actual percentage, as estimated by the Canadian Department of National Health and Welfare, was 8.5 per cent in 1953-4 and 10 per cent a year later. The main differences in coverage are that the 9.6 per cent includes cash benefits for sickness and a more comprehensive health service, but family allowances at $10.00 a month for dependent children only after the second in a family. The percentage would be considerably greater if the country experienced a substantial depression, as increased provision would have to be made for the unemployed; if 12 per cent of insured workpeople were unemployed the social security expenditure would rise to about 11.5 per cent of the national income.

DISTRIBUTION OF SOCIAL SECURITY EXPENDITURES

The distribution of social security expenditures is significant in indicating the political and social attitudes, policies and conditions in the various countries. This distribution is illustrated in Table IV.

remainder at half the rate. For sickness the rate is $22.50 a week for 1.5 weeks for one-half of 4,700,000 wage earners, for a man with a wife and two children, and the remainder at half the rate. Other contingencies and services consist of the following rounded estimates based on current expenditures: industrial injuries, $100 million; widows, orphans and child care, $50 million; maternity, $15 million; war pensions and disability services, $200 million; public assistance, $150 million. Administrations at a rate of 5 per cent of direct expenditure on benefits and services.

[11] The estimated national income of Canada in 1954-5 was $18,808 million.

TABLE IV

Percentage Distribution of Social Security
Expenditure for Specified Purposes, 1953-4[1]

Country	Social Insurance and Assimilated Schemes	Family Allowances	Public Health Services	Public Assistance	Public Employees Military and Civilian	War Victims
Austria	61.1	13.0	—	6.2	11.3	8.4
Belgium	48.1	15.3	1.2	8.4	18.7	8.3
Denmark	50.5	6.2	18.1	13.3	9.6	0.6
Finland	17.2	29.7	17.3	18.0	9.3	8.2
France	40.1	27.8	—	6.7	18.4	7.0
Germany (Fed. Rep.)	55.5	—	0.5	11.6	18.1	13.4
Ireland	49.8	11.6	12.3	12.9	11.1	—
Italy	38.2	22.0	1.5	7.9	19.8	10.6
Norway	50.1	6.7	14.5	12.6	14.4	1.5
Netherlands	56.0	18.6	—	7.8	16.4	1.2
Luxemburg	54.0	13.8	—	4.8	23.9	3.5
Sweden	45.5	12.2	21.4	13.5	6.0	0.3
Switzerland	51.7	0.7	14.8	17.2	15.6	—
United Kingdom	37.8	6.6	31.7	13.5	5.1	5.3
Canada	39.3	20.9	17.6	8.5	2.8	10.9
United States	42.1	—	10.0	17.2	9.0	21.7
Peru	42.1	—	9.8	24.3	23.8	—
Israel	53.1	—	32.3	9.7	—	4.9
Japan	53.5	—	11.2	19.5	15.8	—
Australia	48.2	16.6	14.0	2.0	5.1	14.1
New Zealand	50.8	19.1	16.6	0.5	5.4	7.6

Generally the proportion spent for public assistance is low when
the proportion spent on social insurance benefits and family allowances is high. The converse is also true. The highest proportions for
public assistance were spent in Peru, Japan, Finland, Switzerland
and the United States. The percentage (21.7) for war veterans in the
United States in 1953-4 was much the highest in the world. If expenditure on war victims were excluded from the comparisons, the
expenditure on public assistance in the United States would be about
22 per cent of all social security expenditure, this being higher than
in any other country except Peru (24.3 per cent).

The high proportionate expenditures on family allowances in
Finland, France, Italy, Canada, New Zealand and the Netherlands
are noteworthy, the proportions in these countries ranging from
nearly 20 to nearly 30 per cent of the total. In some of these

[1] In a few countries there were small percentages for administrative expenses
not allocated among the schemes.

SOURCE : Statistics compiled by the International Labour Office. See
The Cost of Social Security, 1949-1954 (Geneva, 1958), pp. 172-5.

countries the system goes beyond the limits of social security and makes provision for many families who are not in real need. The same is true of public health services. For these the highest proportionate cost is in the United Kingdom, closely followed by Israel, and in these countries services are provided for people who could afford to meet most of the cost themselves.

In the United States the absence of family allowances is a noteworthy gap in providing basic security. Also, as already indicated, the percentage for war veterans in the United States is exceptionally high, and the amount spent on these services will not reach its maximum until near the end of the present century. In the United States and also in Canada the proportions spent on social insurance would be somewhat increased if a system of cash benefits during periods of sickness were adopted. In Canada the high percentage spent on family allowances could reasonably be reduced on the assumption that Canadian wages are generally sufficient for a man, wife and two children and that social security allowances for children should be concentrated where the need is greatest, that is, among the larger families. The Canadian proportion for old age was increased when (partly because of the higher cost of living) the rate of pension was raised to $55.00 a month in 1957.

Statistics compiled by the Canadian Department of National Health and Welfare show in greater detail the distribution of income maintenance payments in five countries in the fiscal year 1949-50 for the main categories of beneficiaries. The proportions are shown in Table V.

TABLE V

Percentage Distribution of Income Maintenance Payments

Country	Old Age	Family Allowances	Disability	Veterans	Mothers, Widows and Survivors	Unemployed	Other
Great Britain	50.1	10.3	15.1	13.2	3.7	4.0	3.6
United States	27.5	—	6.6	26.5	9.3	26.1	3.9
Canada	17.2	41.0	5.7	16.1	2.2	12.4	5.4
Australia	31.5	26.2	12.3	19.3	3.8	2.2	4.7
New Zealand	39.5	33.9	8.9	12.2	4.8	0.02	0.6

Great Britain spends a much higher proportion of its income maintenance payments for old age pensions than other countries do. The proportion could with advantage be reduced by raising the age at which National Insurance pensions become payable from the present age of sixty-five years for men to sixty-eight years, and from sixty years for women to sixty-three years. This would be appropriate in view of the greater fitness of older people now than a generation ago and the need in periods of full employment to encourage people to continue longer at work. The proportion spent on family allowances is lowest in Britain (leaving out of account the United States, which has no general system of allowances for children), mainly because in Britain no allowance is paid for the first dependent child in a family where the father is working. This practice is sound enough on the assumption that the wage is adequate to maintain a family with at least one child and that resources should be concentrated where the need is greatest, that is, on large families. The proportion spent in the United States on unemployment benefits is very high for a period in which business was booming.

In a comprehensive system of social security, excluding special schemes for public employees and war veterans, a proportion of 40 to 50 per cent of the social security budget could appropriately be spent on social insurance, the most costly item being old age pensions. For family allowances the proportion might be around 15 to 20 per cent, for public assistance a similar proportion and for public health services approximately 20 to 25 per cent. The public health services would provide for all the medical needs of the poorer sections of the population, and, whether by insurance or otherwise, for the heavy medical expenses (particularly hospitalisation and surgical treatment beyond a specified amount) of the other sections of the population. Where the proportions of national income spent on particular social security contingencies vary widely from the proportions suggested above it can be concluded that there are considerable gaps for which the social security system does not provide, or that unnecessarily high proportions are being spent on some items to the neglect of others or that the system has been extended beyond the boundary of basic social security and, for various reasons, makes provision for people who could cover their needs at least in part from their own resources.

The standards and proportions reviewed above are minimum standards. For example, the rate of benefit for family allowances is much below the standard necessary for the maintenance of the children, and bigger allowances, especially for larger families, would increase the costs. On the other hand the flat rates of benefit for old age, sickness, unemployment and family allowances involve payments to some people who are not in need, and the cost of social security could be reduced either by requiring people to meet a greater part of their needs from their own resources, or by limiting social security benefits to people whose incomes generally do not exceed a specified amount. The proportion of the national income spent on social security and its distribution over the different risks will vary from country to country according to economic conditions and sense of social responsibility. The data reviewed in this chapter may, however, serve as a measuring rod or guide for determining minimum standards.

G

CHAPTER VII

AGE AND RETIREMENT

Old age pensions rank with children's allowances and comprehensive medical care as the most costly items of social security. In Great Britain, expenditure on National Insurance and non-contributory old age pensions is about 24 per cent of the total cost of social security.[1] In Canada in the month of September, 1956, the number of people aged seventy years and over who were receiving pensions was 788,966 and the total net payment to them was $31,586,932, or an annual rate of about $380 million.[2] For 1958 the estimated total was about 4 per cent more because of higher pension rates and more pensioners. This annual amount together with old age assistance grants totalled more than $400 million, which, as in Great Britain, represents about one-quarter of all social security expenditure, not including the cost of veterans' pensions, allowances and services. The cost of old age pensions may amount to $2\frac{1}{2}$ per cent or more of the national income.

Because of the high cost of old age pensions, care is needed when adopting systems to resist political pressures that would tend to make them too generous. 'It is dangerous to be in any way lavish to old age until adequate provision has been assured for all other vital needs, such as the prevention of disease and the adequate nutrition of the young.'[3] Lavishness can be exhibited not only in granting too large a pension but, even more, in fixing too young a pensionable age. There is growing awareness of the cost of old age pensions because the proportion of older people in many countries is increasing. The true cost, is, however, determined not only by the

---

[1] The 24 per cent does not include national assistance payments to aged persons to supplement their pensions, or pensions for war and other service disabilities. It was officially estimated that National Insurance retirement pensions in 1958-9 would amount to £622 million out of a total National Insurance expenditure of £897 million.

[2] For the fiscal year ended March 31, 1956, the total net amount paid in old age pensions to people seventy years of age and over was $366,037,582, according to statistics compiled by the Department of National Health and Welfare.

[3] Sir William Beveridge, *Social Insurance and Allied Services* (London, 1942), p. 92.

rates of pension and the age at which they are paid, but also by the loss of the productivity of large numbers of people who are required or influenced to cease working while they are still fit. Retirement by people who are fit and wish to work, contrasted with retirement due to invalidity or incapacity for work caused by age, is partly in effect a form of unemployment. Many of the people who are faced with compulsory retirement at sixty-five or even sixty years of age are at the height of their powers, and their retirement is often a substantial loss both to themselves and to the community. 'The greatest hurt which comes with advancing years is the sense of uselessness which society so often imposes on the elderly. . . . It is, therefore, cruel as well as stupidly wasteful that our social system commonly enforces the rule that an individual must retire and cease carrying responsibility just because he has reached a certain chronological age.'[4] To many people whose work has been their vital interest, whose habits of work are deeply engrained, and who are unable to engage in satisfying leisure activities, compulsory retirement is almost a sentence of death.

In periods of labour shortage, when expansion of output is prevented not by lack of machinery and plant but of workpeople, the economy would benefit by making greater use of the inadequately tapped resources of manpower among older people. Also, there is often a considerable time lag in adapting social thinking to new conditions. Present attitudes and policies on old age pensions and retirement are unduly influenced by periods of depression, particularly those of the inter-war years when it was considered to be in the interests of the economy to remove older people from the labour market by early compulsory retirement in order, so it was thought, to make way for younger people. The policy of early retirement during depressions is based on an untenable work fund theory which claims that the amount of work is limited and that employment of older men implies unemployment of younger workers. The depriving of older people of the right to work is no remedy for depressions.

CHRONOLOGICAL AND BIOLOGICAL AGE

The practice of some business undertakings of fixing a chronological age for retirement is bad on both economic and social grounds. There is often a big difference between chronological and biological

[4] Edward J. Stieglitz, M.D., *The Second Forty Years* (Philadelphia, 1946), p. 250.

age. Some people are young at seventy and others are old at fifty. Economic capacity and not age should be the essential test of employability. In other words, the vital test is whether the value of the work done is worth what must be paid for it. Capacity at different ages varies with the nature of the job. Where very great physical energy is required, the output of many men may decline in their forties, and there would be advantages in replacing them by younger men. This does not mean that the older men should retire from work. They should be released from heavy work before the strain has broken their health and should be trained for and transferred to lighter work which they may be able to continue for many years. It would often be better for many miners, seamen and others whose work is strenuous to be transferred to lighter work than to stipulate an earlier age of retirement for them than for workers in other industries.

There is no one answer to the question, 'What should be the age of retirement?' It varies between individuals and occupations. It also varies between countries, especially where there are wide differences in health standards, nutrition and expectation of life.

The age at which pensions are paid has a considerable influence on the age of retirement, and often the two are closely linked together. Some people tend to think they must be old as they near retiring age, and the psychological effect may be that they age prematurely. Yet in many countries and in many undertakings the pensionable age has been fixed arbitrarily without sufficient investigation into the fitness of people to continue working longer, or sufficient flexibility to encourage them to do so.

Governments and universities and some industrial undertakings often fix compulsory retirement rigidly at sixty or sixty-five years of age. However, people rarely reach their highest responsibilities in the key positions of intellectual, professional and administrative work until they are well on in their fifties, and many are at their best between sixty and seventy. In almost every field of human endeavour the leaders are the older people who have gained the knowledge and experience which time alone can provide, and their trained judgment and greater stability and maturity of outlook should be fully used. Manual work also can effectively be continued longer than it is at present.

Early retirement is often supported on the mistaken assumption that, like the shorter working day and week and longer annual holidays with pay, it represents an improvement in labour standards. To reduce the age of retirement from seventy to sixty-five or from sixty-five to sixty is thought to be of great benefit by giving people the right, after many years of toil, to have leisure in their old age while they are still fit to enjoy it. Thus early retirement is regarded as a reward towards the end of a long working life. Also, as a country's productivity increases, support is given to the idea of a progressive reduction in the age of retirement. There is, however, no true relation between earlier retirement and a shorter working week and paid annual holidays. One purpose of these last is to make people fitter for continuing their work, whereas early retirement has no such objective.

This line of argument fails to distinguish between aged people whose health is so poor that continuing at work involves severe and even dangerous strain, and those who, though chronologically aged, are fit for work and desire to continue. For the former, retirement is a gain; for the latter it means not only that their standard of living is likely to be greatly reduced but that they will suffer from the feeling of being unwanted.

Special consideration is needed for many older workers who, though not 100 per cent fit, are capable of doing much productive work. Some of them may be fully fit for lighter jobs, and in many large undertakings, with a little ingenuity by management, such jobs can be found, and perhaps reserved mainly for older people. Similarly, opportunities should be made available for people whose productivity is below standard but who, while remaining in their original occupations, can still attain, for example, 75 or 80 per cent of standard. Such productive resources should not be wasted, and arbitrary barriers which at present prevent their use should be broken down.

The results of medico-scientific research together with evidence from industry show that chronological age is not a sound standard for compulsory retirement, and public opinion is increasingly recognising these findings. The difficulty, however, is that up to the present no adequate objective standard or measuring rod has been devised for determining biological age and for measuring the loss of physical and mental powers due to age. It is more likely that such tests will be discovered for manual work than for other types of work, but until reasonably reliable measures are available, the less refined methods of trial and error have to be used.

PRODUCTIVITY AND WAGES

Employers will decide whether any worker who wishes to remain at work is worth the wage that must be paid to him in his present job, or whether less exacting work can be found for him at a lower wage. Sometimes it is better to transfer older men from piecework, where the pace is fast and intensive and the machines are of high capital value requiring big output, to time rate work, where, even though the wages are less, the men can work at their own pace without strain. Older men can also be employed at piece rates on jobs where they will not need to maintain high speed to keep up with other workers and where the capital overheads of the machinery are low; their earnings will be in proportion with their output, so their labour costs per unit of output will be similar to those of other workers whether faster or slower than themselves.

The question is often raised whether the rates of pay of older workers on any job should be less than those for younger workers. The answer should depend on relative efficiency and not on chrono-logical age. But how is relative efficiency (and therefore relative wages) to be measured? Some employers might pay unduly low wages to older people and thus get cheap labour. The ideal would be to equalise the labour costs of old and young according to their relative productivity, but this is often difficult to measure, and the trade unions generally favour payment at the same rate for a job whether it is done by old or young. Some collective agreements, however, provide that, by mutual arrangement between the employer and the union, rates may be reduced where an employee is below average efficiency because of age, physical handicap or infirmity. To fix special rates for older people is not easy, and co-operation between management and trade union representatives would be necessary to avoid abuses. Given a sympathetic and co-operative approach, the problems could be solved.

THE EFFECTS OF LABOUR-SAVING MACHINERY

A second cause of prejudice against the employment of older people is failure to recognise the major change which has been effected in industrially developed countries since the beginning of the century by the use of machines to do much of the heavy work formerly done by men's muscles in almost back-breaking toil. A large part of the work of the St Lawrence Seaway was done by men sitting in the driving seat of bulldozers, whereas the Panama Canal was dug by the sweat and toil of men wielding picks and shovels. Heavy weights are raised and lowered mechanically, and ships at modern ports are loaded and unloaded by lifts, cranes and, where the cargo is suitable, by suction systems and conveyor belts. Automation is on the march. Many men may be too old at forty or fifty to handle loads weighing 200 or 250 pounds, as workers still must do at ports in some parts of the world, but many men seventy years of age or more are fully competent to move such loads mechanically by pulling a few levers, and can do so without strain to themselves. Studies have shown that no significant differences are observable in the performance of moderate work between the ages of seventeen and seventy-one.[5] Today, in Western countries, most industrial work can be classified as moderate.

The grim phrase 'too old at forty', which has been more widely heard in the United States than in Western Europe, is mainly used with reference to jobs requiring great physical strength. Older applicants for such work tend to be rejected and the younger ones given the jobs. But all that this usually means is that such work is too heavy for older people. For example, the writer, in the years preceding the First World War, visited a salt works in England where brine was being evaporated in great pans; the crust that kept forming on the brine prevented the steam from escaping, so the workers, dressed only in shorts, had to keep running along narrow gangways over the steaming liquid to break up the salt crust with heavy wooden rammers. Their hours of work were only four a day, which were all they could maintain, and many of them were unable to continue on the job beyond the age of forty or fifty. That process is now mechanised, but strenuous physical toil is still necessary in mining and other industries and is proportionately greater in countries where methods are relatively primitive than in industrialised countries where labour-saving equipment has been widely installed.[6]

Labour saving machinery makes work less physically arduous, and improved efficiency of production permits shorter hours and longer holidays with pay, higher standards of living and nutrition and better medical services. All these extend the years during which

[5] This conclusion was reached on the basis of experience in the United States by Dr Nathan W. Shock, Chief of the Cardiovascular Diseases and Gerontology Section of the United States Public Health Services.
[6] In Western industrialised countries the proportion of men under forty is high in building and contracting, and also, by contrast, in the manufacture of precision instruments where good eyesight and the ability to handle and assemble small, delicate parts are essential. It is high also in forestry and fishing, and in new industries such as aircraft manufacture. In most of these industries, however, some men well on in their sixties are remarkably efficient.

people can work efficiently. Also, the time spent at school has been extended and provides a better preparation for work, thus raising the personal 'capital' value of all people, including those who are elderly. Skill and employment qualities are enhanced and it is desirable that they should be used as long as possible.

DECISIONS ON RETIREMENT

Retirement is determined partly by the decisions of employers and partly by the choice of workpeople. Clearly, employers will not usually retain people if the value of the work done is less than the money paid in wages; if they do, it will be for sentimental or charitable, not economic reasons. To continue in employment, workers must be worth their keep. Yet many people still fit for work are compulsorily retired because of company rules or pension fund regulations. When, however, an elderly worker has been dismissed, he may experience considerable difficulty in finding a new employer. His best chance of working as long as he is fit is to be retained in his job.

Where the decision rests with workers, they may choose to retire for a variety of reasons. They may find the work an increasing burden, and may risk a breakdown of their health if they try to maintain the standard of efficiency expected of them. If easier work is found for them, they may continue to work regularly without strain; but often the change may involve lower status and wages, and they may prefer to retire, especially if, with their pension and savings, they have enough for comfortable living.

Some retire at the earliest pensionable age not for reasons of health but because they wish to have more time and freedom than their regular employment allows them for things in which they are interested. They have hobbies and other activities and interests, their time is well occupied and they can adjust their efforts to their strength, so they do not experience the frustrations of idleness. This is the happiest form of retirement, but it usually depends on having developed stimulating interests long before reaching pensionable age. Some people, with little imagination, retire early because they wish to enjoy what they think are the delights of unlimited leisure. Often their work has been monotonous and uninteresting and they look forward to freedom from it as a prolonged holiday. If, however, they have no hobbies or other interests to occupy their time with satisfaction to themselves, they find after a few weeks that their life is one of boredom, they miss the regularity of work and are deprived of the daily companionship of their workmates and the busy activities of their former place of work.

Recent investigations in the United States have shown that as many as 56 per cent of those who retire at sixty-five or over do so because of their employer's retirement policy. They thus have little or no chance of working longer unless they can find a new employer, and that is a difficult accomplishment for people of that age. Poor health or accidents accounted for the retirement of 26 per cent, and no doubt some of these could have continued to work if they had been transferred to lighter jobs. Only 9 per cent retired because of a desire for more leisure, and the remaining 9 per cent retired for various reasons—their jobs were discontinued, they had to undertake the care of a sick wife or other dependant or they moved to another district.[7]

THE PROBLEM OF PROMOTION

One argument frequently used in support of early retirement and of making it compulsory is that it provides opportunities for the promotion of younger people. Unless opportunities for promotion are adequate, young people may feel frustrated by being kept waiting too long in junior posts with insufficient responsibility. When they finally reach the senior positions, their outlook has become so stereotyped by years of subordinate routine or limited work that they are unable to show the freshness of outlook, the initiative and qualities of leadership which the top posts require. It has even been argued that those in key positions should be required to retire early, while they are at the height of their powers, in order to open channels of promotion for younger, untried and less efficient people.

These arguments apply only to a relatively small part of the whole working population and have little significance in fixing a pensionable age for purposes of social security. To the extent to which they are valid they are concerned largely with administrative posts in government service and private industry, with academic appointments, with the armed forces and similar organisations with hierarchies of authority and control. They have little application to the main body of unskilled and semi-skilled workers and even to the ranks of skilled manual workers; many skilled workers do not seek promotion to foremanship, and those who have the qualities needed for progressive advancement to executive jobs are often

[7] See *Hanover Pension Bulletin*, Nov. 1956 (monthly publication of the Hanover Bank, New York).

sought out and given opportunities while they are still in their late twenties or early thirties, when pensionable age is an irrelevant consideration.

The arguments in favour of early, compulsory retirement frequently have less force for administrative and similar appointment than is sometimes urged. In any large organisation, whether governmental or private, efficiency demands a balanced age structure with, as far as possible, a sufficient number at each age level. If younger people are promoted too rapidly, so much disharmony may be created in the organisation that any gain from the possibly greater competence of those who are promoted is more than offset. To state this drawback is not to imply that promotion by seniority should be adopted, but that a careful blend of seniority and efficiency in promotion policy should be maintained. If responsibility is delegated to younger personnel, their keenness and efficiency can be maintained until they move up to key positions. Unfortunately some top administrators seem unable to delegate responsibility, often to the consequent disadvantage both of themselves and of the organisation, and when they retire they leave a vacuum not because of the age at which they retire but because they have concentrated even the details of control too much in their own hands. The policy of having understudies who are given full insight into the work both at the top and at each level in the hierarchy has much to commend it, and is a valuable feature of promotion systems. It reduces the risk of conflicts between youth thrusting for advancement and age hanging on to power. It is sometimes practicable and advantageous not to retire people who have held the top jobs when they reach an age at which they can appropriately be replaced by younger people, but to retain them for special work in which their wide experience, judgment and advice can be available for the organisation. The vital test throughout should not be age but fitness and efficiency.

THE EFFICIENCY OF THE AGED

Vast amounts are spent to maintain the aged, but relatively little attention is given to ensure that their productive capacities are well used. Convincing evidence is accumulating to prove the magnitude of their potential output. Wartime experience in industry, for example, demonstrated the contribution they can make to productivity.

In posts of responsibility and also in skilled manual craftsmanship, the maturity of outlook which older people have acquired from experience is an asset. As already indicated, it is particularly valuable in executive posts and in academic and professional work. Judgment improves as experience accumulates. Nor is there evidence to prove that older people show less drive, initiative and willingness to adopt new methods and to try experiments than their younger colleagues. In administration and in reaching decisions about policies and courses of action their qualities usually increase during their fifties and sixties if their work in earlier years has been sufficiently stimulating to prevent them from becoming limited by dull routine and insufficient responsibility.

Some business firms by a kind of 'self-denying ordinance' adopt a universal rule that all employees from unskilled labourers to the president shall retire at sixty or sixty-five. There is an advantage in cutting out dead wood and in avoiding the difficulty that is presented when some people who are well past their best try to cling to their jobs too long. This gain is, however, often minor, and heavily counterbalanced, especially in the top ranks of management, by the forced retirement of executives at the peak of their powers. Those who devise such rules would not scrap machinery that was running at a high rate of efficiency, yet that is what they are doing with human capital, which is the most valuable of all. The argument here is made only partly in support of raising the retirement age; it is mainly a plea for abandoning unnatural and wasteful rigidities in favour of intelligent flexibility.

Investigations show that elderly men are generally as efficient as younger workers, except at heavy work and work done at a rapid pace, and a majority are worth retaining until they are about seventy years of age. Their output may be slightly lower than that of younger men, but the quality of their work is high, they are steadier and more reliable, they require less supervision and are a good influence in the workshop. Their record of punctuality is good and absenteeism among them is little if any greater than among younger people. They are better on time work than where incentive bonuses are used to stimulate high speeds, and they should not be included in teams of people doing such work or on rapidly moving assembly lines. Though they may not so readily adapt themselves to new machines and processes, many of them show no great difficulty in learning new ways of working. Evidence does not support the widely accepted assumption that learning new ways is specially difficult for the elderly. Their experience enables them to conserve their energy, and they are particularly good where reliability and craftsmanship rather than speed are needed. If they work somewhat more slowly than younger workers, they are often able to do as much because of their greater steadiness and application. The toughness and resilience of many aged people is surprisingly great.

Statistics show that much higher proportions of people continue to work at ages from sixty-five to seventy-five in districts where light industries such as textiles and light engineering are established than in districts where mining and other heavy industries are predominant.[8] For older people in the latter districts the problem may arise of moving to districts with light industries, though people well settled in their own homes and with friends and associations in the neighbourhood may be reluctant to change their locality. An alternative would be for the light industries to move into the heavy industry areas so as to use the work of older men and also of women of all ages for whom employment opportunities would otherwise be scarce. This would be sound industrial policy in periods of labour shortage. All the evidence shows that it is only in the heavy industries that age is much of a handicap to the employment of men up to about seventy years of age.

It is widely believed that accident rates are considerably higher among older workers. This belief is not, however, supported by the results of investigations, which show that older workers, because of their greater experience, have fewer accidents, whereas younger men are often more careless.[9]

Shortages of labour since the war, contrasted with the surplus in the years of depression before the war, and the productive efficiency

[8] Recent data for Great Britain show that in light industries, about 25 per cent of men between the ages of sixty-five and seventy and 22 per cent of those between seventy and seventy-five remained at work, there being little falling off until after seventy-five years of age. On the other hand, in mining only 15 per cent of those between sixty-five and sixty-nine continued to work, and as low as 4 per cent of those over seventy. In the case of women, all in light industries, the percentages were much smaller: only 5 per cent of those over sixty remained at work. The percentages were much higher during the war, being double or treble in light industries.

[9] For Britain, the *First Report of the National Advisory Committee on the Employment of Older Men and Women* (Cmd. 8963, London, 1953) states: 'The existing evidence does not support the common assumption that older workers sustain more accidents proportionately than the young. The rate of award is nearly twice as high among men under 30 as among men over 60, and, even with greater length of absence per injury, the average number of days lost by those over 60 as a result of accidents compares well with the 40-49 age group and is only slightly higher than the average for all ages.' Experience in the United States and other countries is similar to that in Britain.

shown by older workers during the war have resulted in the employment of larger numbers of elderly men in recent years. This is shown by data for Great Britain, where in recent years many firms have employed four times the number of men of pensionable age employed before the war.[10] In the main these men have not been earning less than younger workers. About 60 per cent of those who reached pensionable age and remained at work continued at their former jobs, and about 40 per cent changed their jobs. Among skilled workers the percentage who remained in their former occupations was higher than among the unskilled; a higher proportion of the latter were transferred to lighter work, and semi-skilled workers were often employed in light assembly work or as gatekeepers and cleaners. Some firms have separate workshops for elderly workers who are efficient but who are not suited to working under normal workshop conditions, this arrangement being similar to those which firms sometimes make for workers who are handicapped by the results of accidents.[11] Certain firms make slight adjustments of hours of work so as to enable older workers to avoid travelling to and from work at peak times when they might have to stand during the journey.

Part-time work—three days a week or morning or afternoon shifts of four hours a day—if it can be conveniently organised, may provide some men with an alternative to full employment. Part-time work is particularly attractive to women, including older women. Many are available for part-time employment in later life, for although they still have domestic responsibilities, the care of children is often less exacting. There are opportunities for such work in domestic service, in retail distribution at its busy periods and in nursing, teaching and clerical work. More opportunities could usefully be organised by industrial undertakings.

Big increases in productivity would result from encouraging people reasonably fit for work to continue in employment until they are at least seventy years old. Medical and rehabilitation services could also increase the productivity of older workers. If inducements and obligations to retire were removed, and if prejudices and obstacles against continuing to work were broken down, valuable additions to output could be gained. In Britain, for example, where retirement pensions are paid to men at sixty-five and to

[10] *Ibid.*
[11] Some blind workers are excellent at certain kinds of assembly work and have shown themselves able to work by touch at least as rapidly and efficiently as those with unimpaired sight.

women at sixty, there are some 900,000 men aged sixty-five to sixty-nine and about 1,400,000 women aged sixty to sixty-four. Approximately 375,000 of these men remain in fairly regular employment but over 500,000 are mainly idle. If half the latter continued to work and earned only two-thirds of an average wage of, say £9 a week, their earnings would aggregate £78 million a year. Also, if, of the large number of women between sixty and sixty-four who remain at home, as few as 150,000 more were to go out to work, their annual earnings at two-thirds of a weekly wage of £6 would total more than £30 million. The combined total for men and women would be a gain of about £110 million for the economy.[12]

The British government gave a lead in the employment of older people when, in 1955, it made special provisions for recruiting people (men and women) between the ages of forty and sixty for the clerical officer and clerical assistant grades of the civil service The posts are pensionable. The arrangements are made in accordance with government policy on the employment of older men and women. They also take account of the changing age distribution of the population and the need to make the fullest use of the country's manpower in conditions of full employment.

The whole problem calls for much further investigation by governments, employers and trade unions. Too little is yet known about the causes and consequences of the processes of ageing in terms of productive efficiency, and only a tentative beginning has been made in the systematic study of them. Detailed information is needed about the capacities of people of sixty years of age and over for different kinds of work, about their heart defects and other ailments not severe enough to exclude them from work. The studies should be directed at productivity, capacity to learn, reliability, fatigue, accident and sickness rates and other factors bearing on fitness for work at successive ages beyond sixty, especially between sixty-five and seventy. The respective psychological effects of compulsory retirement and of opportunities to continue at work as long as possible also need to be studied. Some investigations may be done under laboratory conditions by testing energy, the onset of fatigue and the suitability of different kinds of work for older people, including those who are suffering from ailments of the aged. Such aptitude tests are needed for adequate samples of people succes-

[12] This is in the order of one-sixth of the total cost of National Insurance retirement pensions, but represents output instead of merely a transfer payment.

sively from sixty to seventy or seventy-five years of age. Other data can be obtained under workshop conditions by co-operation between industrial doctors and personnel officers. More medical studies are needed into the kinds of work which older people can do without causing deterioration of their health, and into diseases that can be held in check so that work can be continued longer. Such researches will pay big dividends in productivity and in reducing the cost of pensions.

PROVISION FOR OLD AGE

Old age is the greatest cause of poverty. Because of their own incapacity due to the infirmities of age or because of the rigidities of the employment market, large numbers of people do not work for the last eight or ten years of their lives. They have to be maintained somehow during this long period, but since their earnings stop on their retirement they are generally a low income group. In the United States in 1950 the median income of families whose head was over sixty-five years of age was $1,903 whereas for families whose head was between fifty-five and sixty-four it was $3,258.

One way to provide the necessary resources is to spread the earnings from work over the working years and also over the years of retirement. A man who began work when he was twenty years of age and continued to work at the same rate of pay until he was seventy could spend five-sixths of his earnings during his fifty working years and enjoy the same standard of living for ten years of retirement on the one-sixth he had saved, not counting the addition of interest. Allowing for interest, he would be able to maintain his standard of living by saving one-tenth or less of his earnings during his working years, the proportion depending on the rate of interest.

The problem is, however, much more complex and difficult. It is impossible for a man to forecast whether he will live long enough to retire, how long he will live in retirement or whether his wife will be dependent on him during his retirement or will have died before then. Some people are spendthrifts; they take little thought for the future and make little provision for it. Others, with no higher wages, accumulate enough to live comfortably after they retire from work. Saving should be started early in life, but to people who are only twenty or thirty years old, retirement from work seems remote, whereas current expenditure for necessaries or enjoyment makes insistent claims. Usually at these ages the cost of setting up a home and maintaining children must be met, and it requires an iron will, which few possess, to set aside enough for old age. Earnings in the early working years may be low and saving for old age may be deferred until later years when it is hoped that income will be higher and savings will involve less sacrifice. The earnings of many people may be so low all through their working life that they are unable to save for their old age. Then again, misfortune in the form of unemployment or sickness may drain away many or all of the resources intended for the years of retirement.

Finally, many may put their savings into so-called gilt edged government securities only to find that the gilt has worn off and that in old age their income is in depreciated paper which has perhaps only half or less of the real value set aside. Their savings have been eaten into by inflation, and the bonds in which they innocently invested, often as a result of government propaganda, would better be described as 'guilt' edged if the depreciation is due not to inevitable wartime expenditure but to the ineptness of the government's financial policy or its failure to show political courage in controlling and stabilising the economy. Inflation is in effect a form of taxation without representation against which our forbears fought so strenuously, being a consequence of executive action not effectively controlled by parliament. Much as we despise sixteenth- and seventeenth-century monarchs who debased the currency, their manipulations were modest compared with those of governments in our own time. Inflation is the cause of much poverty, and the aged are the chief sufferers. They cannot protect themselves by higher monetary earnings, and they have a big interest in having inflation stopped.

When there are such hazards, with which even economists find it difficult to cope, it is not surprising that large numbers of people reach old age without having been able to make adequate provision. Investigations show that in many countries two-thirds or more of the people who cease to earn because of old age are unable to maintain themselves and are dependent on their families, private charity, public assistance or social security pensions.[13] Where such large proportions are in need, the arguments are strong in favour of a general system of old age pensions without a means test. A minority will

[13] These high proportions were shown by the writer's investigations in British Guiana and Barbados in 1954. In the United States in 1937, before the Old-Age and Survivors Insurance system was introduced, about two-thirds of the people over sixty-five were without sufficient means for their maintenance.

receive pensions who could do without them, but against the cost must be set the advantages of avoiding the discouragement of thrift which a means test involves. Also it is reasonable that the thrifty, who have their own savings to augment their pension, should enjoy a higher standard of living than the improvident, who have no other income than the state pension.

AGE FOR SOCIAL SECURITY PENSIONS

Although the age of unfitness for work varies with the individual and ranges widely from under sixty years to seventy or more, it is possible in any country to estimate the age at which a majority of the people become unable to work regularly enough to keep a job and maintain themselves by their earnings, and then to use that estimate to determine a normal pensionable age. It is necessary to have a normal pensionable age in order to organise and finance a system of pensions. Moreover, individuals who are undertaking voluntary savings and insurance need to know what they may expect from the state scheme, and companies that are making supplementary superannuation arrangements for their employees can only plan effectively if they know the age at which state insurance pensions are payable and for what amount. As has already been emphasised, those who are able to continue working should be given the fullest encouragement to do so. On the other hand, it is convenient to have a system of means test pensions, say for five years preceding the normal pensionable age, so as to provide for the minority of people who become unfit for work because of age and have not sufficient resources for their maintenance. The incapacity of still younger people who became permanently unfit could be regarded as the result of sickness or accident rather than of age, though the line of demarcation is arbitrary and varies with individuals.

Rarely are detailed researches made to determine an age of retirement appropriate for each country, and the standards have often been fixed by hit or miss methods resulting from the balance of political forces.[14] A few illustrations may be given, mainly from countries with high standards of living and expectation of life. A standard which has fairly wide application is a pensionable age of

[14] It must be noted that the fixing of a normal pensionable age does not necessarily involve retirement on reaching that age.

H

sixty-five for men and sixty for women.[15] This is applied in the United Kingdom and in Australia. In New Zealand the age is sixty-five and in Canada seventy; no distinction is made between men and women in either country. In the United States the pensionable age for men is sixty-five; the age for women was lowered to sixty-two in 1956.[16] The average age at which men actually retire in the United States is about sixty-eight and a half or sixty-nine. In some Latin-American and other countries, impracticable demands are not infrequently made by trade unions for pensions equal to full wages or high proportions of wages at sixty years of age or even earlier. These would throw unduly heavy burdens on the community, and one effect would be to reduce substantially the real wages of people of working age.

In many Western countries with high standards of living, the expectation of life at birth is from sixty-five to sixty-nine years for boys and from sixty-nine to seventy-two and a half for girls; the life expectancy of people who reach sixty-five years of age is around eleven or twelve years for men and thirteen or fourteen for women.[17] By contrast, in some heavily populated countries with low standards of health and nutrition the expectation of life is very much less. In India, for example, the 1951 census returns showed life expectancy at birth to be 32.45 for boys and 31.66 for girls, or less than half that in the West, while the proportion of people in India who would be regarded as chronologically old in Western countries is very small. Also, the appropriate age for most people to retire from work because of age is much lower in India.

For countries where the expectation of life of people at sixty-five years of age is ten years or more, it is likely that a considerable

[15] Among twenty-five European countries with pension systems, 'the (pensionable) age for men in the European laws is fixed above 65 in four countries, 65 in thirteen countries, 60 in seven countries, and 55 in one country. The age for women is above 65 in four countries, 65 in seven countries, 60 in eight countries, 55 in five countries, and 50 in one country.' Wilbur J. Cohen, *Retirement Policies under Social Security* (Berkeley, 1957).
[16] Widows and surviving mothers are entitled to the same benefit they would formerly have received at sixty-five, but female workers who retire and wives of retired workers receive an actuarially reduced benefit.
[17] These countries include England, Sweden, Denmark, Norway, the Netherlands, Canada, the United States, Australia and New Zealand. In these countries life expectancy greatly increased between 1900 and 1950. Thus in the United States in 1900 the life expectancy at birth was under fifty years, whereas by mid-century it had risen to nearly seventy. The increase in these countries since 1900 is about as great as in the whole of the preceding nineteen centuries of the Christian era.

majority would be able to do suitable work efficiently to maintain themselves for at least half those years and that seventy could be regarded as the normal age of retirement. Much evidence is available in support of this claim, particularly the wartime experience of the efficiency of workers between sixty-five and seventy years of age. Yet some of these countries, including Britain, the United States, Australia and New Zealand, fix the normal pensionable age for men at sixty-five. This age is a rough approximation based on conditions a generation or more ago and does not allow for subsequent changes such as improved standards of health and mechanical progress which enable people to work longer.

Whatever age is chosen on the basis of adequate information about the fitness of people to continue working should be regarded as a guide and not a guillotine, remembering that some people are unfit for work at that age or should retire earlier and that others should work beyond it. 'To attempt to force people to retire before their powers and desire for work fail, and to compel them by a rise in the minimum age of pensions to struggle on after their powers have failed, are two errors and injustices which should be avoided in any system of social insurance designed to increase human happiness.'[18] In many Western countries it seems probable that for men seventy would be a suitable age for standard pensions, but not earlier than sixty-seven or sixty-eight.[19] The system should, however, be flexible both ways, so that higher pensions would be paid to people who continued to work beyond the standard age and lower pensions to those who, because of infirmity, ceased work earlier.

There are two main alternatives. One is to pay the pension from the standard age and to take no account of any subsequent earnings. People who reached that age would be free to decide for themselves whether to continue working or to retire, according to the available opportunities for employment. It could be objected that some workers, because they were receiving a pension, might be willing to work for lower than usual wages and thus endanger wage standards. It would be appropriate for them to work for lower wages if their efficiency were below average and if they were paid according to their ability or productivity, but if they were fully efficient they should be paid at standard rates.

[18] Sir William Beveridge, *Social Insurance and Allied Services*, p. 96.
[19] A lower age would be appropriate for countries where health standards are low and life expectancy short, but it should be progressively raised as the effects of improved health standards are realised.

The second alternative is not to pay the pension to those who continue to work, but to guarantee them a higher pension—increased progressively according to the length of time they do not draw it, and calculated on the basis of their shorter expectation of life—when they do retire. In Britain pensions are payable to men at sixty-five and to women at sixty, but during the first five years the pensions are reduced by deducting part or all of earnings beyond sixty shillings a week, and if earnings are substantial no pension is payable. However, workers who continue in employment become entitled when they retire to a pension increased by one shilling for every twenty-five weekly contributions made after the minimum retiring age. This inducement to continue working is only slight. From seventy years of age for men and sixty-five for women, the pension is paid without any deduction of earnings.[20]

It might be advantageous to pay a bonus in addition to an actuarially calculated supplementary benefit in order to induce people to stay off pension as long as they are fit and can earn a living. The question would also have to be decided whether people should cease making contributions to the pension system when they reach standard pensionable age, or whether they should continue to make contributions so as to earn an increased pension when they retire. There seems no reason why individuals should not be given this option. It would also be useful to consider the practical possibilities of paying a part pension to those who do part-time work and of augmenting the full pension when they cease work.[21]

It would also be useful to include a provision that when a man who had continued working beyond standard pensionable age finally retired, an appropriate lump sum would be paid to him or into his estate to be available for the dependants. The latter arrangement would be equitable for people who 'die in harness' or draw pensions for only a short time after their deferred retirement, and would prevent the system from being a sort of gamble with death.

[20] In Britain the deduction for earnings of men between 65 and 70 years of age and of women between 60 and 65 years of age is only half the additional earnings for earnings between 60s. and 80s. a week. In the United States, for men between sixty-five and seventy-two years of age, deductions are made only if earnings exceed $1,200 a year. For each $80.00 earned by employment above that amount, one month's benefit is deducted. No deductions are made in the United States after seventy-two years of age.

[21] This scheme would, however, be somewhat similar to the system now frequently adopted of deducting earnings of more than a specified minimum from the amount of pensions drawn. Ways could be devised of avoiding the deterrent to continuing in employment which tends to result from this system.

Considerable numbers of people are compelled by infirmities to retire from work before they reach the standard pensionable age. For reasons of health, it is desirable to encourage them to retire early, lest they struggle on with increasing strain and risk a complete breakdown which may make them helpless invalids and shorten their lives. For, say, the five years before standard pensionable age, retirement at reduced rates of pension should be available for people who wish to cease work or for people who lose their jobs during this period because their efficiency has declined. These lower pensions could be paid either without a means test, or, as is already the practice in some countries, subject to such a test.

There are advantages in fixing a rather high age at which full or standard pensions will be paid without a means test and in having an earlier period, as a kind of 'buffer state', during which lower pensions are paid. These might be below subsistence level, but for most people they would, together with personal savings, provide reasonable standards of maintenance. For people without other resources, these lower pensions would be supplemented by public assistance with a means test, and if experience showed that large numbers of people required such assistance, the age for payment of full pensions should be lowered. In countries where standards of living are high and expectation of life is long, the age for full pension might be seventy and for lower pensions sixty or sixty-five. The lower pensions would be suitable not only for people with disabilities, but for others who, though fit to continue working, prefer to retire early so as to engage in leisure activities. There would be a case for raising the rate for people, say, five years older than the age at which full pensions begin, especially if the pension during these five years were somewhat less than sufficient for maintenance. For example, many people seventy-five years old who had been on pension for five years would no longer be able to earn much and might have used up a large part of their savings, and a higher pension would then enable them to continue without needing to apply for public assistance.

The value of having a kind of 'buffer state' before standard pensions are paid is recognised in a number of countries. A usual method is to fix a minimum age at which pensions without a means test are paid. This age is seventy in Canada, but old age assistance is paid to people between sixty-five and sixty-nine. In New Zealand a distinction is drawn between 'superannuation' and 'age benefit'; the superannuation pension is paid without a means test to people at sixty-five years of age, and the age benefits, which are subject to a means test, are payable to people from the age of sixty. Such methods are based on the recognition that age, in the sense of fitness or unfitness for work, varies between individuals. However, they also draw an arbitrary distinction between age and invalidity as causes of inability to earn a living.

Consideration must be given to the age distribution of the population. In various countries the proportion of older people is increasing and will continue to do so for several decades. Early retirement, since it involves failure to make the fullest use of the productivity of the elderly, will throw a heavy burden on people of working age. Thus, in England and Wales in 1944 the number of people of pensionable age (sixty-five for men and sixty for women) was 12.6 per cent of the total population; ten years later it was 14.1 per cent and by the end of the century it may be nearly 20 per cent. Here it may be noted that as this percentage grows, older people will be able to exert increasing political pressure to secure remedies for unsatisfactory treatment, including the removal of obstacles to their continuing to work if they are able and willing to do so. The growing numbers of older people should be given more opportunities to continue at work not only in their own interests, but also in order to reduce the cost of social security borne by the younger generation.

The International Labour Organisation at its Philadelphia Conference in 1944 adopted a recommendation that benefits should be paid on the attainment of a prescribed age, which should be the age at which persons commonly become incapable of efficient work because of serious sickness and invalidity and, in consequence, likely to experience heavy or permanent unemployment. An age of not more than sixty-five for men and sixty for women was recommended as the minimum, but provision was made for fixing a lower age for persons who had worked for many years in arduous or unhealthy occupations.[22] Also, if the basic benefit was considered to be sufficient for subsistence, payment was to be conditional on retirement from regular work, but small casual earnings would not constitute a disqualification.

An interesting method of determining a suitable age of retirement was considered by the International Labour Conference in Geneva in 1952 during the drafting of the Convention concerning Minimum Standards of Social Security. The proposal was that the

[22] The International Labour Organisation's Convention on Seamen's Pensions, 1946, provided that pensions would be paid at fifty-five or sixty years of age at rates based on length of service at sea and on remuneration.

prescribed age for payment of old age pensions should be 'not more than 65 years or such higher age that the number of residents having attained that age is not less than 10 per cent of the number of residents under that age but over 15.'[23] An argument in support of this method is that it relates the burden of providing for the aged to the number of people of working age available in any country to support them. It would allow for a higher retiring age than sixty-five in countries where the expectation of life among the aged is high, and where, presumably, many older people are able to maintain themselves by working beyond sixty-five. It would not, however, allow for variations between one country and another; for instance, it would not take account of large additions to the population of working age, caused by high birth rates in the recent past and a large immigration of young people, in countries where there is also a high expectation of life. These factors would be significant in Canada and Australia in the 1950's. The application of the 10 per cent standard on the basis of the figures on Canadian population for the year 1956 would have resulted in a pensionable age of somewhat under sixty-eight.[24] Taking account of the factors mentioned, the age of seventy fixed for federal government pensions is more appropriate.

Because of population differences from country to country, the International Labour Conference of 1952 rejected the 10 per cent formula at the last moment and adopted the more flexible one that 'the prescribed age shall be not more than 65 years or such higher age as may be fixed by the competent authority with due regard to the working ability of elderly persons in the country concerned.'[25] As the Draft Convention adopted by the Conference sets a minimum standard, any country which ratifies the Convention could fix a pensionable age below sixty-five, and this change might be desirable in countries where, because of health conditions, only a small proportion of the population reaches the age of sixty-five and few are then fit enough to maintain themselves by working.

[23] For example, a country in which there were 20 million people between the ages of fifteen and seventy could fix its pensionable age at seventy years provided there were at least 2 million people who were seventy years of age or over.
[24] In the United Kingdom in 1953 the age would have been about sixty-nine. The formula would give a lower age for men than for women.
[25] Convention concerning Minimum Standards of Social Security, article 26(2).

RATES OF BENEFIT

The pensions must be sufficient for the maintenance of people without resources. Means test pensions are flexible and in fixing their amount the cost and standards of living in each locality can be taken into account. Thus lower payments may be made in rural areas than in big towns and cities where rents and other costs are considerably higher. The payments can also be adjusted in big countries such as the United States and Canada where there are substantial differences in standards of income in different regions: a higher pension is needed in New York State and New Jersey than in Mississippi and some other Southern states, and in Ontario and British Columbia than in Prince Edward Island and Newfoundland.

In deciding the amount of a means test pension the problem arises, what allowance should be made for help which members of the family can provide and what account should be taken of savings and property? Under poor law systems, assistance was provided, and still is in some countries, only to destitute persons virtually without resources of their own. In recent years, however, more liberal policies have been applied along lines indicated in chapter III and usually savings of limited amounts are not taken into account in fixing the amount of assistance. These policies have the advantage of not unduly discouraging thrift, though the use of a means test inevitably does penalise thrift to a greater or less extent. To avoid discouraging thrift is a strong argument in favour of restricting means test pensions and other social security benefits to relatively small numbers of people. As far as is practicable, thrifty people who by effort and sacrifice have made substantial provision for their old age should not be brought down to the level of those who have been wasteful and improvident.

Pensions paid as a right without a means test may be set at flat or uniform rates, usually related to the standards of unskilled workers, or they may vary with wages. Flat rate pensions have three main merits. They are easily administered, people with higher wages are free to make additional provision by voluntary savings (including private insurance) and supplementary occupational pension schemes can be readily adjusted to them.[26] Also, since they are paid

[26] In the Canadian *Report of the Joint Committee of the Senate and House of Commons on Old Age Security* (Ottawa, June 28, 1950), the view was expressed (p. 106) that in devising a system of pensions care should be taken 'not to diminish the area of incentive for private savings or for supplementary provision of old age security through employee pension schemes or individual purchase of annuities'.

without a means test, they, like pensions which vary with wages, do not discourage thrift. On the other hand, both these kinds of pension involve payment to some people who are not in need, but this disadvantage is largely compensated by administrative convenience, by the fact that the great majority of beneficiaries will have low incomes on retirement and that thrift is promoted instead of being discouraged.

Pensions are usually set at a rate considerably less than the wages people earn from their work, often at less than 50 per cent of average wages, partly because the need is generally less, partly because of cost and partly also to avoid giving pensioners an unfair advantage over employed persons in districts where wages are very low.[27] Flat rates of pension form a bigger proportion of the average wages of unskilled than of skilled workers. Thus in the basic British system of uniform National Insurance benefits, the pensions for a man and wife were 50 per cent or more of the wages of low-paid workers but less than 30 per cent of the wages of highly paid skilled workers. Where, however, the rates of pension vary with wages, the proportions do not vary so much, though in the United States and other countries the systems are so devised that the lower paid get a higher proportion than those in the upper wage brackets, and also there is often a ceiling or maximum pension.[28]

In the International Labour Organisation's Convention on Seamen's Pensions, 1946, the rate of pension at fifty-five years of age is to be not less than 1.5 per cent, and at sixty years 2 per cent, of the remuneration on which contributions paid by or for a seaman for each year of sea service were based. For thirty years' service the rate of pension would be 60 per cent of the remuneration.[29]

[27] The Canadian Joint Committee considered that 'the rate of benefit paid should be set at such a level as to avoid as far as possible the social inequalities of a situation in which the retired beneficiary group might find themselves in more favourable economic circumstances than those not yet retired who are still actually engaged in productive employment' (ibid., p. 106). To a limited extent in one or two of the eastern provinces a man and wife who together receive $110 a month in pensions may have an income bigger than the wages of some low-paid workers.
[28] In a scheme considered in 1957 by the British Labour Party, the lowest-paid wage earners would receive a pension up to 75 per cent of their earnings, and people earning more than £12 a week would get a pension of 50 per cent of their earnings up to a maximum pension of £750 a year.
[29] The Convention gave an alternative method of determining the amount of pension which would be an amount based on contributions from all sources of not less than 10 per cent of the total remuneration of the seamen.

In Britain in 1957, in a project prepared for the Labour Party, it was recommended that everyone should be in a supplementary pension scheme.[30] The proposed method for accomplishing this aim was to control supplementary pension schemes at the workplace and to make them compulsory for persons who were not in an approved pension scheme or who did not have adequate provision for old age. Supplementary pension schemes that were already in existence would be continued, but would be required to enable workers who moved to jobs with other employers to benefit from the full value of their own and their employers' accumulated contributions, and the interest.[31] This is a reasonable proposal, as it would avoid tying workers too closely to employers and would facilitate mobility of labour. The proposal that contributions and pension rates should vary with earnings is in conformity with the practice already adopted in many schemes. Recognition of the need to adjust pensions to changes in the cost of living and in national productivity is desirable, and the method proposed is similar to that devised for pensions in Western Germany, as outlined on page 125.[32]

The plan is to build up the necessary revenues by contributions of 3 per cent of wages by workers, 5 per cent by employers and 2 per cent by the state.[33] Here it may be argued that if the state contributes substantially to National Insurance and bears the whole or a large part of the cost of public assistance, family allowances, public health and other services which provide comprehensive basic provision it should not be expected to incur much additional expense for supplementary pensions. If it is able to contribute more towards social security, it could do so with greater advantage by improving basic security benefits than by subsidising supplementary

[30] *National Superannuation,* a policy statement prepared for the British Labour Party for the provision for aged persons of benefits additional to the basic pensions under National Insurance.

[31] A sound method of doing this is to 'vest' or hold the accumulations until the worker reaches sixty-five or whatever age is specified for entitlement to the appropriate pension. The main difficulty would arise with casual workers who frequently change their employers.

[32] The suggestion is that if, for example, a worker's earnings throughout his working life averaged four-fifths of average wages, then he would be granted a pension of four-fifths of the average pension at the time of the award, and that it would subsequently be adjusted to changes in the cost of living.

[33] It was expected that these contributions would enable workers to receive pensions at sixty-five years of age equal to half pay, that there would be a minimum pension of £3 a week after forty years' work, or less for earlier retirement, and that the maximum would be two-thirds of the wage.

pensions. Also, flexibility seems preferable to the rigidity of requiring all workers to belong to supplementary schemes, as is proposed.

In October 1958, the Conservative government, recognising a growing desire that pensions should be related to earnings, announced its intention of developing the system of old age pensions by introducing a scheme of wage-related pensions.[34] The former policy of flat rate contributions and pensions is to be retained for people earning up to £9 a week, but their rates of contribution will temporarily be somewhat reduced. On this is to be grafted a graduated system providing supplementary pensions which will vary with earnings between £9 and £15 a week. Employed adults earning £9 a week or more, and their employers, will contribute amounts graduated according to the worker's earnings between the £9 and £15 limits. In effect the joint contributions to the graduated part of the scheme can be regarded as deferred earnings. On earnings between £9 and £15 the initial contributions will be $8\frac{1}{2}$ per cent of earnings, half paid by the employer and half by the employee, in addition to the flat rate or minimum contribution which is paid by all whether their earnings are below or above £9 a week. Thus workers earning more than £9 a week would pay the same flat rate contribution as workers earning less than that amount, and would also contribute $4\frac{1}{4}$ per cent of their earnings between £9 and £15.[35]

Workpeople earning more than £15 a week will pay the flat rate contribution and also the variable rate on their earnings up to £15 but not on their earnings beyond that amount. The government's view is that the state should use compulsory powers only to ensure basic provision and that people in the higher wage and salary brackets should, beyond the level of £15 a week, be completely free to make such additional provision for their old age as they consider desirable, taking account of their own individual circumstances.

The pensions will range from a minimum of £2 10s a week based on the flat rate part of the scheme up to just over £6 a week for people earning £15 or more a week. They will be payable on retirement at the age of sixty-five for men and sixty for women, but for people who continue to work, they will be reduced or withheld on

[34] The government's proposals are given in a White Paper, Cmd. 538, entitled *Provision for Old Age: The Future Development of the National Insurance Scheme* (Oct. 14, 1958).

[35] It has been estimated that in 1961, when the scheme is expected to start, there will be 7,750,000 workers, mainly women, earning £9 a week or less, a similar number earning between £9 and £15, and 5,250,000 workers, predominantly men, earning over £15.

the basis of earnings up to the age of seventy for men and sixty-five for women.

The government plans to make the scheme financially sound and to avoid the growth of deficits and increasing burdens of uncertain amount on the taxpayer. Thus the Exchequer's support is to be limited to a fixed annual charge of £170 million, to be concentrated mainly in the flat rate part of the scheme for the benefit of the lower-paid workers. This policy is sound: the state should not contribute proportionate amounts towards pensions which vary with earnings. The method adopted is 'pay-as-you-go', instead of that of accumulating large capital funds, and, in order to keep the revenues level with the growing cost of pensions, the contributions both to the flat rate and the variable rate parts of the scheme will be raised at four intervals of five years each for the first twenty years. These increments will raise the graduated part of the contribution from the initial 8½ per cent to 9½ per cent. The policy of increasing the contributions at intervals resembles the method adopted in the United States for financing its old age pensions.

Employers in private industry, organisations in the public services and authorities administering the nationalised industries which have their own voluntary occupational pension schemes will be allowed to contract out of the graduated part of the state scheme, provided the voluntary arrangements are approved as equivalent alternatives, are financially sound and ensure continuity of rights for persons changing their employment. The government's scheme is also designed to provide supplementary pensions related to the wages and salaries of those who are not covered by approved occupational schemes.[36] It served as the basis for legislation in 1959.

Continued inflation and consequent fall in the purchasing power of money make necessary successive increases in the monetary rates of pension in order to maintain their real value for the beneficiaries, and this requirement also applies to other social security cash benefits. Such adjustments have usually been made at irregular intervals when opinion in Parliament was favourable, and when financial resources and parliamentary time could be found. There are advantages in maintaining a high degree of stability in the

---

[36] The Government Actuary estimated that in April 1958, about 8,750,000 employees were covered by voluntary pension schemes (about 5 million in private industry and 3,750,000 in public employment). These comprise less than one-half of all employed persons. Probably schemes which would satisfy the conditions for contracting out would cover under one-third of the 8,750,000 employees.

monetary amounts of pensions, and frequent changes should be avoided as far as practicable. If, however, the monetary amount lags seriously behind the rise in the cost of living, the amount must be raised.

Various methods may be used. If the trend of the cost of living is uncertain and irregular, the timing of changes may be left to the government and to Parliament, and account may be taken of all relevant factors. If, however, the trend is persistently upward, some more systematic method of adjustment will be increasingly demanded. One method would be automatic adjustment by a sliding scale—the pension would be increased in proportion to the rise in the cost of living whenever the cost of living had risen by a specified percentage.

An interesting alternative is a scheme adopted in West Germany in 1957. This bases both old age and invalidity pensions on current rates of wages and salaries. It provides protection against inflation, because in the fixing of monetary wages account is taken of changes in the cost of living. Wages also increase in relation to rises in the productivity and prosperity of industry, and the scheme adopted would therefore enable old age pensioners to share in industrial progress. The method thus has advantages over adjustments only to changes in the cost of living. Each year a standard pension will be fixed on the basis of average earnings during the previous three years. Pensioners who had earned an average wage during their working life and who retired after forty years' work would receive a pension of 60 per cent of the standard, and if wages continued to rise subsequently, the pension would be increased in proportion to the increase in the general level of wages. Workers who had earned more or less than the average wage would receive proportionately higher or lower pensions, subject to a maximum. The amount of pension also varies according to the number of years of contributory employment.[37]

---

[37] It is useful to note that British civil service pensions are based on the salary of the individual during his last three years. They, therefore, make allowance for his promotion and also to some extent for inflation up to the time of retirement. In an inflationary period they have advantages over the Federated Superannuation Scheme for Universities, a method applied to university staffs and certain other categories, by which, throughout his service, the employee contributes 5 per cent of salary and the employer 10 per cent, so that no allowance is made for a fall in the value of money between the earlier and the later years of service. Unlike the German method, neither of these systems makes adjustments for inflation after retirement, although some supplements have been provided.

METHODS OF FINANCING

The four main methods of providing revenues for old age pensions are: (1) provident fund contributions; (2) pooled contributions; (3) special or earmarked taxes; (4) general taxes. These methods are not necessarily sharply separate and may be combined in varying proportions. Also, when the second and third methods are used there are the alternatives—accumulating and investing a fund, or using the 'pay-as-you-go' system—which have been discussed in chapter v.

Provident Funds

The main feature of provident funds is that they are individual. A separate account is kept for each person in which all contributions made by or for him are accumulated and interest is added. When he retires, he can have the accumulated amount converted into a life annuity by actuarial calculations based on expectation of life, or choose some other option according to his circumstances. Thus he may choose a joint annuity to be paid to himself and his wife, or make provision for annuities to be paid him for at least a specified number of years and, in the event of his dying earlier, for the remaining value to be paid into his estate.

Contributions may be at a flat rate, or may vary with wages, either as a percentage of each contributor's wage or according to wage categories; for example, the required contribution from workers with wages below $200 a month might be $8.00, from those with wages from $200 to $300 it might be $10.00, and from those with wages over $300 it might be $12.00. The workers' payments are supplemented by contributions from their employers, either of equal amounts or at a substantial rate. The government undertakes payment of interest and cost of administration and may also contribute.[38]

In the provident fund system there is no pooling of the finances.[39]

[38] In the early stages of a scheme there would be advantages in having the government pay more than its standard contribution into the accounts of people who were then in middle life or within a few years of retirement so that their benefits on retirement would be bigger than would be possible from the accumulation of funds at standard rates during the relatively short time they would contribute.

[39] This is subject to the qualification that, in the calculation of annuities based on the average expectation of life of the whole group of beneficiaries, individual variations, ranging from death soon after retirement to the drawing of pensions for many years are pooled.

In some other schemes, if a contributor dies before reaching retiring age, the money that has accumulated on his behalf is pooled and enables bigger pensions to be paid to those who draw pensions after retirement. Again, by pooling, higher benefits can be paid to people who are within, say, ten or fifteen years of retirement when the scheme starts, or, in schemes where contributions vary with wages, relatively higher pensions may be paid to lower-paid workers, who are in effect subsidised by the better-paid workers.

The provident fund system has the advantage of being readily understood. It is akin to individual saving, and in countries where such saving is well developed, as it has been in West Indian communities by the Friendly Societies, that experience can be used to explain the system and to gain public support. Benefits are in proportion to contributions, except in so far as the government may subsidise the scheme to increase the funds for the older people in the initial years. The scheme is flexible, as people who are near retirement age when it starts can contribute for a few years and, on their retirement, can draw a small annuity, perhaps supplemented by the government; if their accumulation is too small for an annuity, they can be paid a lump sum, perhaps spread in quarterly amounts over the first two or three years of their retirement. If contributors die before pensionable age, the amount standing to their credit is available for their dependants and can be integrated with schemes for the benefit of widows and orphans. People whose contributions are interrupted for any reason, for example by unemployment, build up smaller accumulations, and their annuities will be smaller than those of regular contributors. Contributors who continue working long into their old age accumulate larger amounts; on the other hand, those who are compelled by infirmity to cease work early, for example at sixty years of age, still have significant, though smaller, amounts available to them.

The scheme is particularly suitable in countries which have had no previous system of old age pensions other than those based on a means test, and also where the provision of old age pensions is limited to specified industries or other groups and does not extend widely throughout the country. It gives experience in the payment of contributions and in administration and can be replaced by other methods if a wide extension of old age pensions is planned; equitable arrangements, based on accumulations, can be made for those who have contributed to the provident fund.

One difficulty in the provident fund method, as in all funding systems, is that the purchasing power of money falls during periods of inflation and in consequence the annuities have a lower real value than was originally intended and are unfair to the contributors. The appropriate remedy is for the government to make up the difference in real value lost by inflation. This remedy is preferable to, though more costly than having to supplement the annuities by public assistance payments with a means test—a method which would otherwise be necessary to ensure subsistence to long-term contributors.

Pooled Contributions

In most contributory pension systems the funds are pooled in the sense that some people receive more than in proportion to their contributions and others less, mainly because of individual variations in expectation of life. As Professor D. C. MacGregor has indicated, 'of 1,000 men living at the age of 40, only some 600 will reach the age of 70.'[40] A man in his twenties may have an even chance of living to seventy and drawing the appropriate pension at that age, whereas a man in his fifties who is ill may live ten years or less and receive nothing from the pool, his contributions being pooled for the benefit of people who live for many years beyond pensionable age.[41] In varying degree this problem is somewhat mitigated by the contributions of employers and especially by those of the state, since the chances are that the great majority of people will draw from the pool more than the value of their own direct contributions.

An argument in favour of pooling is that those who die before they draw pensions do not need them and that the risk they were protected against was the risk that they might live for a long time and require pensions for many years. Another argument is that the rates of contribution may be somewhat less or the pensions somewhat bigger than they would be if each contributor (or his estate) were entitled (as he would be in provident fund schemes) to receive the full value of the contributions made by him or on his behalf. Another aspect of pooling found in many systems where contributions and pensions vary with wages is that the pensions paid to people in the lower wage grades may be bigger in relation to

[40] Canadian Tax Papers, no. 4, *The Proposed Old Age Pensions* (Toronto : Canadian Tax Foundation, 1951), p. 18
[41] This difficulty is overcome to a greater or less extent in those pension schemes which also pay benefits for the dependants of persons who die before reaching pensionable age or draw their pensions for only a short time afterwards.

their contributions than those in the upper wage grades. Such systems, therefore, involve a transfer of resources from the higher paid to the lower paid with the object of promoting greater social equality.

Special or Earmarked Taxes

Special or earmarked taxes, such as those used in Canada to finance federal old age pensions and in New Zealand to finance superannuation pensions and other social security benefits, can be used effectively where the whole or a large part of the population is covered and where wealth is distributed fairly evenly among the main body of beneficiaries. Such taxes are preferable to general taxes as a means of financing pensions because they are less subject to political influence and because pressure to increase benefits is held in check by the knowledge that the special taxes would also be increased.

General Taxes

Where old age pensions and other social security benefits are paid out of the revenues from general taxes, there is no close link between taxes and benefits. Financing by general taxes is supported by some on the ground that the tax burden can be distributed equitably, whereas financing by special contributions or earmarked taxes may place an unduly heavy part of the cost on the poorer sections of the population. The cost of benefits paid from general revenues is lumped together with expenditure on defence, education, transport, communication and all the other activities undertaken by the government, and then income taxes, import duties, purchase and other taxes are imposed at rates sufficient to meet the required total.

The state may cover the whole cost of pensions and other social security benefits from general revenues, or (as in many countries) it may make a contribution from general revenues towards the cost, and this may be a large or a small part of the total. Before a decision is made on whether to rely wholly, in part or not at all on revenues from general taxation to finance old age pensions, consideration should be given to the differences in wealth and income between the main sections of the population and to differences in the standards of living of the beneficiaries. Where the disparities are wide and taxation is progressive, there is a strong case for substantial participation by the state from general revenues in the interests of better distribution. Means test pensions for the benefit

I

of people with low incomes are generally financed from general revenues.

THE CANADIAN SYSTEM

The Canadian system of old age pensions came into operation at the beginning of 1952 in accordance with the federal Old Age Security Act. It is a good illustration of the use of earmarked taxes to finance pensions without a means test, and of general taxation to provide pensions with a means test. It also has other interesting features and is well adapted to Canadian conditions. Its main provision is the payment of universal, monthly, flat rate pensions, originally of $40.00 but raised in 1957 to $55.00, to every Canadian who is seventy years of age or over and who has resided in the country generally for the ten years immediately before the approval of his application.[42] In the adoption of the age of seventy, there is recognition of the fact that large numbers of people below that age are able to maintain themselves by continuing to work, or have saved enough to live on until they are at least that age. Because the pension is paid without a means test, and because it is much below most people's average earnings, it does not discourage thrift among people of working age. Moreover, people over seventy who are able and willing to work are not discouraged from doing so, because the amount of their pension is not affected by their earnings. Naturally, many ageing people who find regular work a heavy strain will, on reaching seventy, be induced by the pension to retire even though they could have continued to work for a year or two more. Consideration could, however, be given to the advisability of having a minimum rate of pension at seventy and higher rates for those who defer drawing pension for one or more years up to the age of seventy-five, at which a maximum pension would be paid.

The Canadian federal pensions are financed on a pay-as-you-go basis, not by the usual contributory system, but from the proceeds of earmarked taxes. These are a 2 per cent sales tax, a 2 per cent corporation profits tax, and a 2 per cent personal income tax which, however, is subject to a ceiling of $60.00.[43] In effect, these taxes are

[42] It is significant that the system is based on recommendations unanimously adopted by a committee of forty members of the Canadian Senate and House of Commons from the four main political parties. A constitutional amendment was required to give the federal government authority to operate a federal system.

[43] The pensions have cost more than the yield of the three taxes, but the pensions themselves are taxed.

not basically so different as they might at first seem to be from the more usual tripartite contributions by workers and other beneficiaries, employers and the state. The 2 per cent income tax is a contribution by beneficiaries and those who will become beneficiaries, except for those whose income is below taxable level; the sales tax is similarly borne and the corporation tax is a contribution by employers, though not in proportion to the number of their employees.[44]

In Canadian conditions, there were strong reasons for the earmarked tax method of financing. The machinery for collection of each of the three taxes was already in operation and could easily undertake the additional work, so its use avoided the setting up of a new system and the collection of special contributions from employers, workers and others scattered over a very large territory, some of them in sparsely populated agricultural, forestry and mining regions. The earmarked tax method also avoided the difficulty, which has been encountered in the United States, of excluding certain occupational groups from the scheme because of the trouble of obtaining contributions from them, and of making ineligible for full pensions people whose contributions have been insufficient in number or amount. It has the advantage of simplicity of administration, because the revenues are easily obtained, no means test investigations are required and no individual contribution records need to be maintained. In more compact countries, however, especially where an effective administration has been built up over the years for the collection of contributions, there are advantages in the direct contributory method. This is favoured by the trade unions in Britain because it seems to give a stronger title to benefit without a means test than would a system financed by special or general taxes.

Another merit of the Canadian federal system is that this payment of pensions to people over seventy years of age is immediate; there is no waiting (as there is in Britain and the United States) for contributions to be made for specified periods before entitlement to pension. The reason is that there is no direct link between contributions and benefits: the cost of aged people at the time of the

---

[44] It would be an interesting research into the incidence of taxation to try to determine to what extent the distribution of the burden under the Canadian taxes for old age pensions is similar to the distribution under the more direct contributory systems where (as in Britain) the state, employers, workpeople, self-employed persons and non-employed persons provide the revenues.

inauguration of the scheme in 1952 was met by a form of social budgeting mainly from income drawn from the population of working age, whose burden was made easier by the substantial long-term growth of Canada's population.

The cost of administration is low, totalling in 1955-6 only 0.86 per cent of the amount paid in federal pensions and in family allowances, with which the administration of pensions is combined. Because the scheme of federal pensions is uniform and simple, it is easy to devise occupational schemes for providing supplementary pensions.

In Canada, in addition to the federal non-means test pensions at seventy, there are means test pensions for people between the ages of sixty-five and seventy whose resources are meagre.[45] They provide for people who, because of infirmity due to age, are unable to maintain themselves by continuing to work and who have not saved enough to live on. The cost is shared equally between the federal and provincial governments.[46]

OCCUPATIONAL PENSIONS

In recent years pension schemes for the employees of individual undertakings have been widely adopted. Many such schemes were established in the inter-war years and their number has rapidly increased since the Second World War. Some of them are introduced by the employers as part of their industrial relations policy. They believe that such schemes contribute towards better relations between workpeople and management, that they tend to attract and retain good workpeople, that they give recognition for long service and that they make termination of employment easier when the time of retirement comes. Where trade unions are strong, pensions are often provided as a part of 'fringe' benefits and the conditions are defined in collective agreements.

The schemes in private industry are usually voluntary, but some are required by legislation, for example, the scheme for railroad employees in the United States under the Railroad Retirement Acts. That schemes supplementing social security pensions have been extensively applied is shown by the fact that in Canada in 1956

[45] The scheme is a liberalisation of a previous scheme for the assistance of the aged that was based on federal grants-in-aid and had operated since 1927.
[46] Some provincial governments have schemes for the supplementation of the basic federal old age security allowances and federal-provincial old age assistance.

nearly a million employees worked in undertakings with occupational pension plans; they include employees of the federal and provincial governments and municipal authorities, hospitals, banks, insurance companies and industrial undertakings.[47]

In the United States, the number of employees covered by private pension plans at the end of 1954 was estimated to be 12,500,000, and this total does not include employees of federal, state, municipal and other public authorities.[48] The private pension plans may be illustrated by the position in New York State at the beginning of 1957, when it was estimated that 2,400,000 employees were covered in that way.[49] Among 290 plans in undertakings with 1,500 or more employees, 181 were in accordance with collective agreements and the remainder were not. In about three-quarters of the plans the employees did not contribute. More than two-thirds of the plans put their funds into trusts, and one-sixth used insurance companies. Most of the plans had a normal retirement age of sixty-five, some sixty-eight and a few seventy; in many of the plans retirement was compulsory at the specified age. Usually, size of pension was related to length of service, and a minimum service, often fifteen to twenty years, was required to secure the normal pension which, in many undertakings, was at a flat rate. Some two-thirds of the plans paid pensions to persons who became totally and permanently disabled before reaching normal retirement age. In the United States, as in other countries, the requirement in many private plans that pensions can be paid only to workers who have remained with the same employer for many years has the important consequence that the proportion of covered workers who will actually receive pensions may often be relatively small.

In Britain, according to a survey made by the Government Actuary, about 5 million people in private industry will benefit from occupational pension schemes which supplement their National Insurance pensions, and in addition, 3¾ million in public service, the armed forces and the nationalised industries, including

[47] For a review of the provisions of pension plans, see *Industrial Pension Plans in Canada* (Ottawa, 1955), prepared by the Economics and Research Branch, Department of Labour; also William M. Mercer, *Canadian Handbook of Pension and Welfare Plans* (Toronto, Montreal, 1956).
[48] *Welfare and Pension Plans Investigation,* United States Senate Report 1734, 84th Congress, 2nd session, 1956.
[49] State of New York Department of Labor, *Pensions: Larger Plans in New York State,* 1957, Special Bulletin no. 232 (New York, July 1957).

coal-mining, will receive supplementary pensions.[50] Salaried personnel are much more fully covered than wage earners, and men than women. In private schemes, the provisions apply to 71 per cent of salaried men and only 38 per cent of wage paid men; for salaried women and wage paid women the percentages are 34 and 23. In private schemes, the employers' contributions amount to more than double the employees', partly because, when these schemes were started, many employees with long years of previous service had to be taken into the plans and pension rights provided for them at the expense of the employers. Employees make no contributions in about 30 per cent of private insured schemes and 44 per cent of non-insured schemes. More than half the private schemes are arranged through insurance companies. Some schemes carry no protection against insolvency of the employer. In many schemes, an employee loses the value of the employer's contributions if he transfers to some other job, and this stipulation restricts mobility. Many employers regard pension schemes as a means of retaining employees. In most private non-insured schemes, the transfer of pension rights is not permitted, and where it is permitted it is subject to restrictions.

These occupational pensions are supplementary to the social security pensions provided by governments, and the question of what their relation should be therefore arises. The social security pensions could be regarded as minima and the occupational pensions as additions, so that people would draw both. Or occupational schemes approved by the government could be regarded as alternatives to social security provision. The government would have to be satisfied that benefits provided were at least as good as those under social security, and the employers and workers covered would then be exempted from paying contributions to social security. Some difficulty would arise if workers changed jobs part way through their careers and took employment in an undertaking which had no approved scheme, though this could be met by requiring the original employer to transfer to a contributory state scheme funds equal to those which would have been accumulated if he and the workers concerned had been paying into the state fund.

Some occupational schemes are integrated or dovetailed with the social security pensions. For example, in Canada the government pays pensions of $55.00 a month from seventy years of age.

[50] *Occupational Pension Schemes* (London: H.M.S.O., 1958). The data are based on a sample survey in 1956 with adjustments to allow for subsequent increases.

An occupational scheme may pay pensions of, say, $100.00 a month from sixty-five or some other age below seventy, and reduce them by $55.00 when its pensioners reach the age of seventy. This plan enables contributions to the occupational scheme to be less during working life than if no account were taken of the social security pension.[51] The more clear-cut the government scheme, the easier it is for occupational pensions to be appropriately adjusted.

Occupational pensions often began as *ex gratia* payments to employees for long and faithful service, but these were uncertain and open to other objections. Now most schemes are financed by joint contributions by employer and employees, either at equal rates, or, if unequal, usually higher for the employer than for the employee.[52] In British universities, for example, the employer's contribution is 10 per cent of salary and the employee's 5 per cent. Often government superannuation schemes are financed entirely by the government, this being the practice for the British civil service and for teachers. Usually the pensions in occupational schemes, unlike the flat rate uniform pensions of some social security systems, vary in amount according to the salary or wages of the employee. They are related both to length of service and earnings, either throughout the employee's career or during the last few (e.g., five) years before he retires. Some schemes require retirement at a rigidly fixed age, and others show considerable variety and flexibility. Pensions are sometimes paid at a given age regardless of whether the recipients keep on working and earning wages; usually, however, pensions are deferred until the actual time of retirement and are then paid at a higher rate. Often schemes take the form of group life insurance by arrangement between the business undertaking and an insurance company.

Many schemes are so devised that if an employee leaves to work for another employer, he receives only the amount of his own contributions with interest, but not those paid by his employer. This and other features reduce mobility. A more equitable method if an employee leaves after, say, fifteen or twenty years' service, is for his

[51] Some private occupational schemes were able, without changing the contributions, to pay pensions between the ages of sixty-five and seventy at rates from $20.00 to $25.00 a month higher than before, and then at seventy years of age to deduct the amount of the federal pension. Others made no increases of pension in these earlier years but reduced the contributions to allow for reduction in the occupational pension at the age of seventy when the federal pensions are drawn.

[52] In a project by the British Labour Party in 1957 the contributions proposed were 3 per cent of earnings by employees and 5 per cent by their employers.

pension rights for that period to be vested; when he reaches sixty-five or whatever is the minimum pensionable age, he becomes entitled to the appropriate pension, or, if he dies earlier, the benefits may be paid to his dependants. Alternatively, the sums accumulated during his old job could be transferred to the superannuation fund operated by his new employer, or to a government annuity fund to mature until he reached a specified pensionable age.

As already noted, schemes in private industry are usually voluntary. They could, however, be made compulsory by legislation which would also define the minimum conditions they were to observe. It seems preferable, however, that they should be voluntary and be regarded as supplementary to social security pensions. The vesting or transfer of superannuation rights should, however, be made compulsory so as to prevent workers from being too much tied to an employer. If occupational pension schemes conform with conditions laid down by the government, valuable concessions are granted in the form of exemption from income tax of contributions to and interest earned by superannuation funds.[53]

WELFARE SERVICES FOR THE AGED

As has been indicated, the best contribution to the welfare of most elderly people is to enable them to continue at work as long as practicable. However, there comes a time when they reach Shakespeare's sixth age of man that 'shifts into the lean and slipper'd pantaloon', and can no longer undertake regular employment even on light half-time work. The transition may be abrupt or gradual, but when this stage is reached social security involves more than a cash pension. A whole series of welfare services is needed, including suitable accommodation, opportunities for recreation, domestic aid for the infirm and nursing and medical care during sickness. Here is where kindliness and friendly personal care are essential and can do far more than any cash payments to bring brightness and comfort in the declining years.

The great majority of people after retirement from work continue to live in their own home, sometimes sharing the house with their grown-up children or other relatives, or else go to live in the home of a son or daughter. This is the most natural and satisfactory way of living for most elderly people, and probably more than 90 per

---

[53] The schemes must be genuine pension schemes and not savings, the money accumulated must be funded, and the employer's contributions must be irrevocable.

cent of them live in this way, though some prefer not to live with their children and some children want to have their homes to themselves. The aged people may help by doing some of the housework and by sharing in the care of their grandchildren. An elderly couple, so long as they are reasonably active, can manage comfortably together, dividing the chores, preserving privacy and independence and living a pleasant Darby and Joan life. If they become more feeble and have no relatives living with or near them, a system of home help arranged by the local authority is valuable in doing some of the cleaning and perhaps preparing a meal. When the aged become almost helpless and seriously ill, the question arises whether they should be moved to a hospital or home where regular nursing services can be provided, for the attention and care they require becomes a heavy burden on relatives, though it is often cheerfully borne.

For aged people not living in their own homes or with relatives, accommodation has long been provided in almshouses and in institutions. Almshouses are usually built as groups of small dwellings each for an aged person or for a man and wife. Accommodation in large institutions has been generally less satisfactory than in private dwellings or in medium-sized homes provided by the public authorities or voluntary associations, because people living in them often suffered from strict discipline and lack of privacy, and were isolated from their friends. In consequence many aged people would only go to a poor law institution as a last resort.[54]

Some aged people are accommodated in foster homes, and this method of boarding out with suitable people could usefully be extended. There is, however, need for more accommodation for aged people who are unable to live in private homes. Some institutions can be made more comfortable and be administered with greater sympathy and understanding. New accommodation should, however, be provided mainly in the form of small dwellings in groups, or homes with accommodation for about thirty to fifty people. Both types should be located among houses occupied by younger people: there should be no segregation or isolation in large remote colonies. They should be in pleasant surroundings near shops, libraries, parks and places of worship, and the people living in them

---

[54] In Britain after the Second World War, just before the National Insurance scheme came into operation, more than 60,000 people of pensionable age were living in poor law institutions. Although conditions in these institutions had been much improved, many still lacked the amenities needed by aged people.

should be mainly from the neighbourhood so that they can stay within easy reach of their friends and of the associations with which they are familiar. When dwellings for the aged are in groups near to one another, it is easier for helpers to go in to assist them, for activities to be organised for them and for nurses and doctors to visit them. Among the homes with accommodation for several dozen people, some would be for those who had only their pension to live on, but others could be run like small private hotels for those with modest private means who could afford to pay towards the extra cost of additional comforts.

For many people the main burden of old age is the monotony of having nothing to do and nowhere to go. Many clubs for the aged have been organised but they have often been dull, drab and badly run. Segregation is undesirable, and activities for the aged should if possible be arranged at community centres, perhaps a room set aside for their use. More thought should also be given to arranging for useful productive work to be done. Women, of course, often do knitting, and for men many activities requiring only simple tools or machines would be practicable. If necessary 'sheltered' markets could be found for the products, and payment made for the work done. The output of what might be called 'armchair producers' could be considerable, but its main value would be the satisfaction and therapeutic benefits which would result.

Then there is the problem of the accommodation of the aged when they are sick. Some need hospital care until they are convalescent. The chronic sick, who may be almost helpless through rheumatism, arthritis or partial paralysis, may live for months or years. Doctors may be able to do little for them except in times of crisis, but they need nursing care and attention. Often they are kept in hospitals but usually a sick bay with nursing facilities in a home for aged people would be preferable. For people suffering from dementia resulting from senility, care in institutions is essential.

In view of the increasing number of aged people in many communities and of their special and varied welfare needs, more trained personnel will be required. There is a place also for counselling services and for trustees to safeguard the interests of those aged people who are no longer able to handle their legal and financial affairs.

CHAPTER VIII

FAMILY ALLOWANCES

Most social security cash payments for income maintenance are for people whose wages have stopped because of such causes as unemployment, sickness, disability, old age or the death of a breadwinner. Usually the payments vary with the number of dependants, as the purpose is to meet essential needs and these vary according to the number of people in the family. No difficulty arises in obtaining the necessary information about the number of dependent children, so the detailed inquiries and objectionable features of a means test are not involved. Family allowances are therefore often a regular part of social security benefits paid to those whose wages have ceased.

The family allowances considered in this chapter are, however, payments made for children in families where the breadwinner is at work and is receiving his wage or salary. They therefore seem to differ fundamentally from allowances paid to families whose income from work has temporarily or permanently ceased. If the primary object of social security is to meet the basic needs of people who are unable adequately to supply those needs themselves, then to pay family allowances for this purpose to wage and salary earners implies that the wages and salaries are insufficient for family needs. How far is this implication true?

Powerful arguments for family allowances were put forward in the 1920's by Miss Eleanor Rathbone in her book *The Disinherited Family,* and during her forthright and successful campaign in Britain for children's allowances. It must be emphasised that her disinherited families were mainly the large families of the lower-paid workers whose wages were insufficient for their needs. Investigations in many countries have shown that after old age the next greatest cause of poverty is large families of low-paid workers. This arises largely from the dilemma that in the wage system, workers in the main are paid either by time rates or according to output, and not according to their needs. The wage principle is 'equal pay for equal work' or in other words there is a 'rate for the job'. In the operation of this system, therefore, people working side by side and doing the same kind and amount of work rightly earn equal amounts, though some of them are bachelors without dependants, others have a wife and one or two children, and still others a wife and a family of six, eight or more children. If the wage is only sufficient for the needs of a family of average size, it follows that bachelors and those with smaller than average families will have a surplus or will live at higher standards of comfort, whereas those with larger families will experience shortages or suffer privation and poverty.

Thus there is no close relation between wages and size of family, and, though it is often assumed that the wages even of workers in the lower-paid occupations can with careful management provide for the minimum needs of families of average size, it is widely recognised that the wages of such workers are insufficient for large families. It is true that workers with large families may deny themselves of all but the necessaries and that they may do additional work by overtime and odd jobs in order to increase their earnings. A wife may also do some paid work, though it is usually undesirable and impracticable for her to do so if she has many young children. The opportunities for extra earnings are limited and precarious, and although there is some flexibility both in earnings and in expenditure it is not sufficient to meet the problem of the large families of low-paid workers.

Wages are mainly related to the grade, skill and productivity of workers and are not closely adjusted to the varying needs of the different families, and it is this which has led to the introduction of family allowances. The problem is illuminated by the following quotation from a paper by Dr George F. Davidson, Deputy Minister of Health and Welfare in Canada: 'The fact is that our wage structure is geared inevitably, and rightly so, to industrial skills and productivity. It is an industrial, not a social wage. In compensating our men and women for the contributions which they make to the society in which we live, we recognize that their skills should be paid for to the extent that they add to the technological, industrial, commercial, intellectual, and cultural wealth of modern times. At the same time, we largely fail to compensate the parents of our nation for the extra financial and economic burdens which they voluntarily assume in rearing a generation of future citizens.'[1]

How this dilemma between wages and needs has arisen, why it did not exist or was less acute in earlier times and what solutions have been adopted, will now be reviewed.

[1] Paper on "The Role of Children's Allowances," read at the 76th annual meeting of the National Conference of Social Work, Cleveland, Ohio, 1949.

THE EVOLUTION OF FAMILY ALLOWANCES

The payment of cash allowances to families whose breadwinner is working is a recent development and is limited mainly to countries with relatively high standards of living. Conditions were very different in earlier times and they still are very different in countries which are mainly agricultural and whose people for the most part live in rural communities and sometimes, as in Africa, under tribal organisation. In such conditions, children are not the economic burden which they have become in other parts of the world, and indeed large families are often an economic asset. Food is produced locally and shared among the numbers to be fed, shelter is primitive and easily provided as families grow in size, and children often begin to do useful jobs in the fields and around home at the age of eight or nine.

By sharp contrast, the advanced countries have passed laws that require children to remain at school until they are fourteen, fifteen or sixteen years of age, and laws that fix the minimum age at which children are allowed to enter industry or other paid employment. Housing is expensive because it must conform to legal requirements as well as customary standards. These and other factors have imposed heavy economic burdens on parents for the maintenance of children, especially on parents of large families, and the problem was not one that could be solved by any practicable changes in the wage system.

One of the first measures that recognised the need to ease the financial burden of providing for a family allowed income tax deductions for a wife and dependent children—a man on a specified income who had a large family paid a smaller tax than a man who had few or no dependants. Such allowances are often substantial, but they have the disadvantage that they are of no help to the poorest families whose incomes are below taxable level, and of relatively little value to others with low incomes and large families.

The main development in paying cash allowances for the maintenance of workers' dependants occurred during and shortly after the First World War. Wartime and post-war inflation with rapidly rising prices and shortages of commodities caused severe hardship especially among large families with low incomes. Increases in money wages were inevitable but usually lagged well behind rising prices so that real wages fell. Customary wages had been relatively stable for decades, and employers were often reluctant to increase basic wages during the war as they hoped that when it was over wages would return to their previous level. They, therefore, preferred to pay cost-of-living bonuses rather than increase basic wages, as they thought that it would be easier to remove the bonuses than to cut back basic wages. In considering different kinds of bonuses to compensate for the rise in the cost of living it was easy to demonstrate that the rise bore most severely on those with large families and it was a simple step to devise bonuses that varied according to the number of each worker's dependants. In this way the family allowance system came into being.

There were many other motives for its introduction. There was the humanitarian or paternalistic motive of helping those with large families in a period of great need. Some employers recognised that if allowances were paid for dependent children instead of adequate flat rate wage increases for all workers to cover the rise in the cost of living, a saving in the wage bill could be made at the expense of the unmarried workers and of married workers with few or no children. Less purchasing power would be distributed, and a family allowance system could therefore be less inflationary than general increases in wages. This was the main reason why John Maynard Keynes at the beginning of the Second World War included family allowances, along with compulsory savings, among his major proposals on wartime finance.[2] In the 1920's family allowances had been supported in France and some other countries with the object of arresting and perhaps reversing the decline in birth rates, and in Germany under Hitler they were designed to increase manpower.[3]

For a combination of these reasons, family allowance systems developed in many Western European countries, especially in France and Belgium, towards the end of and shortly after the First World War. Almost every conceivable variety was tried. In some schemes allowances were paid for the wife and for each child. Others were for children only. Some paid no allowances for the first child or for the first two children, on the assumption that the wage was adequate for a man with a wife and one or two children and that allowances should be reserved for the larger families. In some schemes no allowances were paid in respect of children after the fifth or sixth in a family, and in others they were paid in respect of all dependent children however great the number. In some schemes

[2] *How to Pay for the War* (London, 1940).
[3] Countries such as Canada, Australia and New Zealand with their vast opportunities for increased population need not fear but could welcome any possible effect which family allowances might have on raising the birth rate.

the allowances were paid at the same rate for each child; in others, specially favourable to large families, they increased with each successive child; in still others they diminished with each successive child.

Often in the early stages the allowances were paid by individual employers either direct to their workers or to the workers' wives, though sometimes the system was established by agreement among employers in the same industry and locality. Thus at first the allowances were closely linked with wages, they were a direct labour cost and, as already indicated, were often regarded as a special form of cost-of-living bonus added to wages. Therefore, an employer paid more to a man with a large family than to one with few or no dependants, though the output of the latter and his value as a worker to the employer might be equal to or even greater than that of the former.

THE WAGE DILEMMA

This system presented no difficulty during the manpower shortages of the First World War or in the early post-war boom. Trouble began, however, when the slump started towards the end of 1920 and unemployment became severe. Employers were forced to consider means of reducing their costs, and they soon realised that, because of family allowances, they were paying much more to workers with large families than to those with few dependants. They could, therefore, economise by dismissing the workers with the largest families, but by doing so they would injure the very people whom the family allowances were designed to help.

Much thought was given especially in France to ways of removing this danger, and French employers by the exercise of characteristic French logic soon devised an effective method. The employers in different industries and localities agreed to form common funds out of which the allowances would be paid. The contributions by each employer to the fund were based on a criterion independent of the number of children in the families of the workers. The most usual criterion was the number of workers employed, so that an employer with 100 workers would pay twice as much into the fund as an employer with only 50 workers, and in respect of any one worker he would pay the same amount whether the worker had six or eight children or none at all. The employer would therefore have no financial inducement to dismiss workers with large families. Other criteria used in some funds were the total wage bill of each firm, in the textile industry the number of spindles and looms and in coal-mining the tonnage of coal produced, these various criteria being considered more suitable in some industries than the number of workers employed. Each criterion was, however, independent of the number of children of the workers employed by any firm. The funds were appropriately called 'equalisation funds' (*caisses de compensation*), as they equalised or provided compensation among employers for the cost of the family allowances paid.

This equalisation fund system was adopted also in Belgium and to a lesser extent in some other European countries. In France it spread rapidly, funds being extended to cover more employers and bigger localities, and as early as 1921 more than sixty equalisation funds had been established. So widespread did the system become that in 1932 an act was passed requiring all employers in industry, commerce, agriculture and the liberal professions to belong to an approved equalisation fund, unless a large undertaking employed so many workers that it was able to maintain a system of paying allowances without recourse to a fund, in which case it was authorised to establish its own system of allowances. The act provided for the payment of allowances in respect of all children up to the age of sixteen years of workers in the employments covered, and it stipulated principles and methods for the operation of district and occupational funds. Although the equalisation fund system broke the close connection between allowances and wages, the schemes were still financed by the employers, and the allowances were a labour cost.

During the 1920's and 1930's the development of family allowance systems in Continental European countries attracted much attention in other parts of the world. In this period the introduction of family allowances was widely discussed in Great Britain but little progress was made, largely because the trade union movement was not convinced that the workers as a whole would benefit, and in the Trades Union Congress a majority was not in favour. The French model was not acceptable mainly because the financing and administration were undertaken by the employers, who had full control, subject to conditions regulated by legislation. Even with the safeguards of the equalisation funds, there was unwillingness to accept modifications of the wage system, which would imply that the remuneration of labour was based on any other principle than that wages were paid for work done and were based on the grade, skill and efficiency of workers without regard to their family obligations and other responsibilities outside working hours. Any other principle would be likely to result in distortion, confusion and even chaos.

Fear was also expressed that if family allowances were paid, the total amount of money paid to the workers in wages and allowances combined would be less than if a wage system without family allowances were retained. In collective bargaining the solidarity of the workers would be weakened because their interests would be divided: those with few dependants would be mainly concerned with the amount of wages, and those with many dependants might benefit more by concentrating on better scales of allowances than on wages. This fear was very real during the depression years of heavy unemployment in the 1930's when employers were seeking ways of reducing labour costs and when workers' resistance to reductions in wages was weakened by shortages of work. Trade unions would be likely to find that those of their members who had families of more than average size and who were benefiting most from the family allowances would not be so firm in their resistance to wage reductions or in their demands for wage increases as they would be if they were dependent only on wages. This situation may arise in any system of family allowances, but it is more likely to do so when the allowances are financed by employers than when they are paid from state revenues and therefore not directly linked with industry and employment.

If family allowances were to make much headway in the British Commonwealth and other countries a new approach had to be found. In many countries laws were in operation for the fixing of minimum rates of wages by wage boards or councils so as to provide reasonable wages for workers in sweated and low-paid industries. These laws and also the legislation establishing courts of arbitration in Australia and New Zealand (which not only made awards to settle industrial disputes but also fixed basic rates of wages) often stipulated that the minimum or basic wage for adult male workers must be a living wage, and must be adequate for the needs of a family of average size. This wage was usually defined by law or practice as an amount necessary for a man with a wife and two or three dependent children. In collective bargaining also, trade unions usually emphasised the cost of living, and in negotiating wages for the lowest-paid grades they had specially in mind the needs of workers with families of average size. For such workers this was often the critical point in negotiations. But larger families were still left without adequate provision for their needs. Wages

K

were standardised by grade, and were based on the amount and quality of work done, the value of the work and the demand for and supply of labour. The wage system could not provide for the wide variations in the size of the families of the different workers. Minimum wages based on the needs of families of average size were no solution.

The first tentative steps in a new approach were taken in Australia (New South Wales) and in New Zealand in the 1920's and 1930's where arbitration courts and other wage-fixing bodies faced the impossibility of reconciling the wage system with the needs of large families. Realisation gradually came that the right solution was not to attempt any distortion of the wage system but to meet the needs of large families by paying them state allowances entirely separate from wages. Cash allowances for dependants were paid in social insurance and assistance systems in many countries during periods when wages had ceased, but these allowances did not meet the needs of large families whose breadwinners were working but earning too little to provide a decent living. The best solution seemed to be for the state to pay cash allowances to supplement the family income from wages, and leave the wage system operating on established and well-tried lines.

STATE ALLOWANCES

Decisions in a number of countries to pay family allowances from state revenues still left important issues to be settled. Should the scheme be applied generally, or only to the families of employed persons? Should allowances be paid only to families whose incomes were below a specified level, and should they be paid in respect of all dependent children or only after the first or second child on the assumption that the wage was sufficient for families consisting of a man, his wife and one or two children? Should the allowances be at a flat rate for each child or should they be on an increasing or decreasing scale according to the number of children? Should the allowances be smaller for young children and increase progressively as they grew older? How should the state obtain the necessary funds? Should they be obtained by a tax on bachelors, by a tax on employers, by joint contributions of employers and workers as in social insurance or from the ordinary revenues of the state?

These questions, which indicate the main issues involved, will be considered in relation to the systems adopted in Britain, Canada, Australia and New Zealand. The United States has no general system of family allowances; it may be argued that wages are so high that a majority of parents can provide adequately even for large families, but there must still be many large families in the lower income brackets who are much below what is regarded as adequate according to living standards in the United States.

In financing allowances paid by the state, a tax on employers may be suitable in a system restricted to the dependants of employed persons, but it is inappropriate in a system that is applied more widely. A tax on employers also maintains a link with employment and labour costs which is open to objections. This method has been retained in France, and is firmly established on the basis of experience from the 1920's onwards. In New South Wales the first family allowance scheme in 1927 was financed from a tax on employers, mainly because the allowances were linked to the application of the living wage principle. In 1934 the special tax was abandoned and the allowances were paid out of the general revenues; and this method was adopted when in 1941 the Australian government applied a system of child endowment to the whole country. Family allowances have been financed in this way in New Zealand since 1926, and the same method of finance was adopted in Britain and Canada when the present comprehensive family allowance schemes were introduced in 1945.

In all four countries, not only are the allowances financed from general revenues but they are paid without a means test. It is desirable to avoid means tests, for they require highly trained staff and have objectionable features even when they are conducted liberally and sympathetically. The avoidance of means tests is more costly but it has the substantial advantage of removing considerable numbers from the scope of means tests and therefore conforms with one of the principles proposed in chapter III. In the initial schemes in New South Wales and in New Zealand a means test was applied but was later abandoned.

The question is how extensive the system should be. The main problems that arise are whether allowances should be paid in respect of virtually all dependent children or only in respect of children in families with incomes below a specified amount, for example $4,000 a year. Evidently people with substantial incomes can support large families without any cash allowances from the state, and where (as in Britain, Canada, Australia and New Zealand) allowances are paid to such people the system goes beyond the scope of basic social security. Perhaps the strongest reason for such a system is that it avoids dividing the community into classes on the basis of income; as citizens, all are treated alike. Though it over-rides the principle of using limited state resources where they are most needed for social security purposes, it may be accepted as a desirable element of social policy. The arguments against limiting allowances to the families of persons working under contracts of employment are also strong, as there are other sections of the community whose needs are just as great.

Clearly outside the scope of basic social security is the payment of allowances for families with only one or two children in countries with high wage and income standards. This is done in Canada, Australia and New Zealand. In these countries wages are high enough for the needs of a family of average size. In Britain, allowances are not paid for the first child in a family but only for the second and each subsequent child, the assumption being that ordinarily the wage even of unskilled workers is sufficient for the needs of a family consisting of a man with a wife and one child. Wages and incomes are lower in Britain than in Canada, Australia and New Zealand but even in Britain the allowance could with advantage be concentrated on families with three or more dependent children. Here is where the need is greatest. The state should not provide for those who can meet their own needs, and people with families of average size or less should be fully responsible for them. Substantial amounts now being paid for the first and second child could be used instead to increase the rates of allowance for larger families, to provide or improve other kinds of social security now inadequately covered, or even, where other social security needs are sufficiently met, to reduce taxation.

· The issue may be illustrated from the position in Canada where the cost of family allowances as a proportion of social security expenditure is one of the highest in the world. Until the recent increases in old age security payments it was the biggest single item in Canada's social security budget. In September, 1956, family allowance expenditure was at a rate of $397 million a year, the average allowance per child was $6.04 and the average allowance per family was $14.41. This family average of $14.41 represented an addition of roughly $4\frac{1}{2}$ per cent to the average wage of a Canadian worker. For workers in the upper wage brackets it was under 4 per cent and for those in the lower wage brackets it was about 7 per cent. These percentages are broadly representative for workers with families of average size. For a worker in the lower wage bracket with six dependent children the family allowances formed a much higher proportion of the wage, being in the order of 20 per cent.

The total number of Canadian families receiving allowances in September 1956 was 2,296,709 and the total number of children in respect of whom allowances were paid was 5,479,973, so that the average number of children per family in respect of whom allowances were paid was 2.386. Of the total number of children, 2,171,030 or about 40 per cent were in families with one or two dependent children, and 3,308,943 in families with three or more dependent children. If allowances had been paid only after the second dependent child in a family the number would have been 1,680,963 and the cost would have been approximately $123 million a year. Thus about $275 million a year would have been saved if no allowances had been paid for the first and second dependent child in a family, and part of the saving could have been used to increase the rate of allowances for those with large families. The value of the allowances is now considerably less than it was when they were originally fixed, owing to a rise in the cost of living between 1945 and 1959. If the allowances had been increased so as to equal their purchasing power when the rates were established, the cost in September 1956 would have been at an annual rate of about $212 million if paid only for children after the second, or not much more than half the cost of paying for all dependent children. If higher allowances were paid to the larger families the money would be concentrated where it is most needed, and that is the essential purpose of social security. Here it may be noted that by the Family Allowance Act of 1944, the allowances for each child after the fourth were progressively reduced, but the act was very properly amended in 1949 in favour of uniform rates.

The relation between cash family allowances and the income tax allowances for children is considered later. At this point, political factors must be considered. Canadians have become accustomed to receive family allowances since they were introduced in 1944, and any government that proposed to cease paying them for the first two children would be likely to encounter strong opposition. An alternative that might provoke less protest and bring the Canadian and other schemes closer to basic social security principles would be to keep the allowances for the first two children at their present rates, recognising that their real value had fallen heavily because of the rise in the cost of living but, when the time was appropriate, to increase the allowances for the third and subsequent children. This plan would involve the political and financial problem that the provinces with the largest families would benefit most. They already do so under the present system, although not so much now as formerly, when provincial differences in average size of families were greater. As Dr Joseph W. Willard has pointed out, the highest family allowance payments per head of the population are in Newfoundland, New Brunswick and Prince Edward Island, followed by Quebec and Nova Scotia; the lowest are in British Columbia and Ontario, with Alberta, Manitoba and Saskatchewan in between.[4] In September 1956, the average allowance per family was highest in Newfoundland ($18.22), and lowest in British Columbia ($12.34), the average for Canada in that month being $14.41.[5] The provinces that gain the most are, however, the ones where the need is greatest: in the Atlantic provinces and Quebec not only are families larger, but wages and incomes are smaller than in other parts of Canada, and the allowances therefore form a higher percentage addition to average family incomes.[6]

In Canada the rate of allowance increases with the age of the child. Originally the rates were $5.00 a month for each child under six years of age, $6.00 between the ages of six and nine, $7.00 between nine and twelve and $8.00 between thirteen and fifteen. By contrast, Britain, Australia and New Zealand all have uniform rates that do not vary according to age. The Canadian system is rational, as the cost of maintaining a child increases as it becomes older. This has been shown by many studies, and scales have been established showing the cost at different ages.[7] The original Canadian rates listed above corresponded approximately with the results of these scientific studies. In view of Canada's high standards of living it is doubtful, however, whether there is any advantage in varying the rate according to age, and the system would be adequate if a uniform rate were adopted for each child irrespective of age, or, at most, if two rates were adopted—one rate for younger children and a higher one for older children. Acting along these lines, the Canadian government in 1957 reduced the number of age categories

[4] "Some Aspects of Family Allowances and Income Redistribution in Canada," *Public Policy*, vol. V, 1954.
[5] Statistics compiled by the Department of National Health and Welfare.
[6] In some of the Atlantic provinces the economy operates in certain occupations in such a way that cash plays a relatively small part in family living, and the introduction of old age pensions and family allowances has brought substantial cash incomes to various families, with the consequence that there may have been a weakening among some people of the spirit of independence and self-reliance. This, however, is in part a transitional situation and not of great significance when viewed in relation to the whole of the Canadian scene.
[7] One of the earliest was by Quetelet, and there are many more recent scales.

from four to two, with allowances of $6.00 a month for children up to ten years of age ar. ! of $8.00 a month for children from ten to sixteen years of age. These allowances were never intended to cover the cost of maintaining children, and since they were fixed they have lost more than one-third of their value because of the rise in the cost of living: at 1957 prices the average allowance of $6.04 per child a month did not, in many families, cover more than one-quarter of the cost, and in some families not more than one-fifth or one-sixth.[8] Consequently, the refinement of varying the allowances according to age would seem to have little value.

In New Zealand, as in Canada, allowances are paid for each child in a family, including the first, the rate being ten shillings a week for each child up to the age of sixteen, or up to eighteen if he continues his education. At March 31, 1956, the total number of children for whom allowances were being paid was about 721,500. If, however, allowances had been paid only for the third and subsequent children, the number of children receiving them would have been about 203,740, and about 72 per cent of the cost of the allowances would have been saved. In the financial year 1955-6, the saving would have been about £13,450,000 out of a total actually spent on children's allowances of £18,860,866. The saving in subsequent years would have been in approximately similar proportion.

In Australia the child endowment system is a kind of half-way house between the system in Britain and those in Canada and New Zealand. When the scheme was first introduced in 1941, as an extension to the whole of the Commonwealth of Australia of a system already operating in New South Wales, no allowance was paid for the first child, but subsequently an allowance was introduced at half the rate paid for each of the other children. The allowance for the first child is five shillings a week, and for the second and each subsequent child it is ten shillings a week. The number of children for whom allowances were being paid at the end of June 1955 was 2,764,167, and the allowances were at an annual rate of £52,529,902 (Australian). If allowances had been paid only after the second child, the number of children eligible would have been 632,384. At ten shillings a week, the cost would have been at an annual rate of £16,441,984, or less than 32 per cent of the cost of paying allowances for all dependent children.

[8] In many families during 1944-5 when the scheme began to operate, the allowances would cover not far short of one-half of the cost of maintaining children, because the dollar had higher purchasing power and standards of living were lower.

If national productivity continues to rise at about the same rate as it has in recent decades, and if this rise results in corresponding increases in standards of living well distributed among the large masses of the population, then by about 1975 or 1980 most incomes will be 40 or 50 per cent higher in real value than those in 1958. In such circumstances, most incomes will be high enough to enable families to maintain three children in health and decency, and allowances may then properly be reserved for families with more than three dependent children. It is true that as standards of living rise, the minimum considered essential for health and decency also rises. Allowing for this, however, the increased resources would enable adequate provision to be made from wages by families of medium size, and the moral and psychological advantages of parents shouldering as much responsibility as they can reasonably carry are substantial. The administration of family allowances is not made more complex by omitting one or more children from the system or by paying allowances at lower rates per child in small than in large families.

INCOME TAX ALLOWANCES FOR CHILDREN

For many years in various countries, deductions from gross income have been allowed to people with dependent children. The amount of tax they have to pay is thereby reduced, and their spendable income is increased in just the same way as are incomes supplemented by family allowances paid in cash. As already noted, income tax allowances for dependants are restricted in their benefits to those with incomes sufficient to render them liable to pay such taxes, but considerable numbers of people whose need is greatest derive no help from this system because their incomes are too low. The introduction of family allowances in the form of direct cash payments removes this disadvantage.

The question must be raised whether it is necessary to operate both systems in Britain, Canada and other countries which now have family allowance payments in cash. There would seem to be advantages in using only one method. It would seem preferable to discard the income tax allowances for children, and after removing anomalies, to fix the rates of family allowances in such a way as to achieve a rational social purpose.[9] At present, although some adjust-

---

[9] The abandonment of income tax allowances for children would not preclude special allowances to parents who send their children to private schools at considerable cost, and who by so doing reduce the amount spent by governments to provide places in schools administered by the public authorities.

ments in income tax allowances for children have been made in consequence of the introduction of family allowances, various discrepancies remain. The essential common objectives of the two schemes should be merged in a unified family allowance system.[10] There are disadvantages in using two stones to hit one bird.

For many people above the lower income groups the government takes away with one hand (income tax) a part or the whole of what it gives with the other. This point is illustrated in Table VI, which shows for various levels of income from $2,500 to $6,500 a year and for families of different sizes, the amounts paid annually in tax in Canada and the amounts received in family allowances. No income tax is paid on earned incomes up to $2,150 in families with a wife and one dependent child.

TABLE VI
Annual Income Tax and Family Allowances in Canada*
(in dollars)

Gross Income	Number of Children in Family							
	1	2	3	4	5	6	7	8
	Annual Income Tax							
2,500	57	33	9	—	—	—	—	—
2,600	73	49	23	—	—	—	—	—
3,000	137	113	89	65	41	17	—	—
3,500	224	197	188	145	121	97	73	54
4,000	314	287	260	233	206	179	153	129
4,500	411	381	351	323	296	269	242	215
5,000	511	481	451	421	391	361	332	305
5,500	603	576	549	521	491	461	431	401
6,000	693	666	639	612	585	558	531	501
6,500	793	762	730	702	675	648	621	594
	Annual Family Allowance							
	72	144	216	288	360	432	504	576

Table VI shows that all families with incomes of $2,600 a year and only one child entitled to family allowance pay more in tax than the amount of the allowance. For larger families the relation is progressively more favourable, but even with eight children people whose gross income is over $6,400 pay out more in income tax than they receive in family allowances. For families with more

[10] The process of merging would involve the complication of separate assessments of the incomes of husband and wife. Another issue is whether family allowances should be counted as income for tax purposes or not.

* The incomes are assumed to be wholly earned, and allowances are made for the wife and for each child entitled to family allowances. The family allowances are calculated conventionally at the rate of $6.00 a month; the average monthly rate for the whole of Canada in September 1956 was $6.04.

than eight children, family allowances exceed tax at higher incomes.[11]

ECONOMIC AND SOCIAL VALUE

The payment of family allowances is one of the constructive elements in many social security programmes. By ensuring better standards of nutrition, clothing and other needs of children in large families who otherwise would suffer privation because of unduly low wages, the system provides a firmer basis for the efficiency of the next generation of workers. It can make a substantial contribution to economic productivity and to a progressive raising of the national income. A beneficial by-product of family allowances which has been experienced in Canada is improved school attendance, as the allowances are withdrawn if attendance at school is not satisfactory. In Britain, allowances are not paid for children who leave school between thirteen and sixteen years of age.

Family allowances should, therefore, form a high proportion of the total expenditure on social security in all countries where conditions are favourable.[12] In Canada, Australia and New Zealand the proportions which family allowances form of total social security cash benefits are among the highest in the world, other countries with high percentages being France, Belgium, Italy and the Netherlands. The figures for Canada, Australia and New Zealand are given in Table VII

TABLE VII

Family Allowances as a Proportion of Social Security Cash Benefits: Canada, Australia and New Zealand*

Country	Family Allowances	Total Social Security Cash Benefits	Family Allowances as Percentage of Total
Canada (1953-4)	$355,700,000	$1,137,100,000	31.3
Australia (1952-3)	£A53,244,000	£A141,505,000	37.6
New Zealand (1953-4)	£17,618,581	£48,992,762	35.9

[11] The number of families in Canada with more than eight children was only 14,877 in September 1956.

[12] In overpopulated countries where growth of population is proceeding rapidly because of high birth rates and declining death rates resulting from improved health conditions and medical care, and where productivity per head and standards of living are low, family allowances may be inappropriate and other measures claim priority.

* The figures do not include expenditure for health and hospital care, or for veterans.

Family allowances have an economic as well as a social value. Not only do they tend to strengthen the future economy by building up the human capital of a country, but the regular payment of substantial sums of money, a very large part of which will be used for immediate consumption, helps to stabilise the economy by sustaining the demand for goods and services. They are therefore a factor of considerable value, along with old age pensions, unemployment benefits and other social security expenditure, in reducing the severity of depressions. It might be argued that the maximum effect would be obtained if family allowances were paid for all dependent children, not just for children after the first or second. The effect, however, depends on the rate of allowance. A low rate spread over all the dependent children in a family might involve a total expenditure on allowances no greater than if bigger allowances were paid for fewer of the children. From the standpoint of social security the advantage would lie with the payment of allowances where the need is greatest, while as a stabilising factor in the economy the effects of a given total expenditure could be about the same with either alternative.

One further point must be emphasised. The payment of allowances to a family while the breadwinner is earning a wage, salary or other income from gainful occupation removes or reduces a danger often confronted in fixing rates of benefit when income ceases from such causes as sickness and unemployment: the danger that the social insurance or assistance payments for workers with low wages and large families may be almost as big or even bigger than the wages they receive while working.[13] Take the hypothetical example of a worker who has a wife and eight dependent children and whose wage while working is $40.00 a week; when his wages are interrupted by sickness or unemployment he receives benefits at $12.00 a week for himself, $6.00 for his wife, and $2.00 a week for each child; his income from benefits when not working is therefore $34.00, and he would get only 17 per cent more for doing a week's work. For some people this would not be a big incentive to return to work as soon as possible. If family allowances were paid for each child after the second, the family income of such a man when working would be $52.00, or about 53 per cent more than when he is unemployed.

[13] The difficulty under discussion does not arise where, as in Canadian Unemployment Insurance, the benefit for unemployed workers is paid in respect of the unemployed worker and only one dependant, but then provision is not made for larger families, who may therefore have to apply for public assistance.

CHAPTER IX

HEALTH

Health—physical, mental, moral and spiritual—is the most valuable of all human possessions. It is a main factor in security. Nowadays, medical science and practice are rapidly advancing in the conquest of disease and are making a vital contribution to welfare and pro- ductive efficiency. One after another, diseases which formerly killed large numbers of people prematurely or caused serious debility, suffering and misery have been brought under control. The effects are shown in detail by medical statistics, but more generally by the big increase in expectation of life, which has almost doubled in many countries since the latter part of the nineteenth century, especially as a consequence of reduced mortality among infants. Particularly remarkable are the results of campaigns against such diseases as malaria, smallpox, and yellow and typhoid fever by the use of drugs, inoculations, the killing of insects by spraying and better water supply and sanitation. Indeed so successful have these measures been in preserving life that they have created social and economic problems in over-populated countries where birth rates have not yet been adapted to the greater life expectancy which medical knowledge has brought.

Yet in all countries sickness is still a heavy burden, involving loss of production, loss of income and costly medical expenses. Even in Canada, where health standards are among the highest in the world, 60 per cent of the population ordinarily experience one or more periods of disability a year, the total duration averaging nearly twelve days annually per head of population. The losses in other Western countries are similar. Most people in countries that have a high standard of living could easily manage if they were disabled only for that length of time, but some escape altogether perhaps for years, and others have many weeks or months of serious and costly sickness. This is the kind of risk the costs of which can be distributed over or shared by the whole community so that no one is financially crippled.

There are two economic or financial consequences of sickness that involve insecurity. One is the loss of income which many people incur when sickness prevents them from working. The second is the cost of medical, surgical, hospital and other services, often running into hundreds of dollars a family a year, which the sick person must have. The two are inseparable in their effects on the individual or the family, as they both cause financial strain. Social surveys show that they are a frequent cause of poverty, and in consequence many families are burdened with debt and with the anxieties of insecurity which may aggravate illness and retard recovery. Moreover, illnesses are often neglected in their early stages because of the expenses involved in medical care and are therefore more costly to the individual and to the community in the long run.

The effects financially are the same for an individual if as a result of a month's sickness he receives no wages and is therefore worse off by $200, or if he has to pay $200 for medical and surgical care and hospital accommodation. Many people suffer both losses. To avoid undue hardship among people with low or moderate incomes, protection against both these causes of financial difficulty is needed, at least in part. If the social security system provides protection against only one of them, it is a matter almost of indifference to the individual whether it pays him $100 to offset part of his loss of income or provides free medical services which would otherwise have cost him a similar amount.

Sickness is too uncertain and irregular in its onset and too variable in its severity for the cost to be met as it occurs out of the normal family budget. Provision can be made effectively only by saving, but many people do not make adequate savings individually, especially if their means are low, and young people may not have had time to save enough to pay for a severe and costly illness. Moreover, medical care is becoming increasingly costly because of the advances being made in scientific research and techniques. In consequence the difficulty of paying direct for medical care has become much greater and will continue to increase. The remedy is for the risks of sickness to be pooled by the whole community and for medical needs to be met mainly by small regular payments from the family's annual budget.

PRIORITIES

Some methods for the organisation of remedies may be suitable for dealing with loss of income and others for paying the cost of health services. For that reason, these two risks are examined separately in the discussion that follows. In practice, however, they can be dealt with together—the contributions to the health insurance schemes of many countries are used both to finance cash benefits and to provide medical services free or at low rates.

Social security against sickness had small beginnings but has evolved in many countries until cash income benefits and medical care are provided for the whole population (as in Britain and New Zealand) or for a substantial proportion of workers whose incomes are below a specified level. During the course of evolving a plan, each country must decide on priorities. Some provide security, to a greater or less extent, by insurance of both cash income and medical care. Others, Canada and the United States, for example, have hitherto done little, except by public assistance, to provide cash incomes during periods of sickness for the main body of the population.[1] Yet Canada and the United States both have a comprehensive system of unemployment insurance, though the financial insecurity caused by unemployment is often much less than that caused by sickness.

Some countries adopt policies of providing strictly limited medical services while others apply comprehensive schemes. Some of them for reasons of social policy prefer to leave the responsibility for medical care on the individuals themselves. Other countries intend progressively to widen the scope of public medical services, but proceed by stages so that the necessary number of doctors, nurses, and other personnel can be trained and sufficient hospitals and clinics built. In deciding on priorities, these countries are influenced by the cost and the relative urgency of each service, and also by the adequacy at any time of the personnel, buildings and equipment necessary for an efficient service.

Usually first priority has been given to sick persons who because of destitution could not pay for treatment, and who were therefore given free medical care and hospital accommodation.[2] Early free provision is generally made for the institutional care of persons suffering from mental and certain infectious diseases, such as tuberculosis, for the protection of the community as well as for the welfare of the patients. For similar reasons priority has been given to immunisation against smallpox, diphtheria, poliomyelitis and other infectious diseases, and to treatment for venereal diseases. More recently, free mass radiological testing and laboratory diagnostic

[1] Exceptions are provision for veterans, and for special categories—railroad workers in the United States, for example.
[2] In Canada, special arrangements are made by the federal government for the medical care of Indians, Eskimos and seamen, and of immigrants during their first year in Canada.

services have been provided both for infectious diseases and for other prevalent serious illnesses such as cancer and heart strain, where effective treatment may depend on early discovery. Thus, in Canada, there has been a marked tendency for the federal and provincial governments to finance diagnostic services and to provide the necessary equipment. Sickness surveys, including investigations into the adequacy of medical personnel and hospital and clinical facilities, are also financed by governments, as are certain research projects. Government capital grants towards the cost of hospital construction are also often made.

All these special measures by themselves would leave the main part of the population to pay for medical care. Recognising, however, that sickness requiring hospital treatment is often likely to be serious and costly, public opinion in some countries has become increasingly strong in favour of the provision of hospital accommodation free or at low cost. This is the position in Canada, where for some years four of the provinces have provided such accommodation by insurance or other prepayment methods for all or a large part of their people, and where in 1957 Parliament enacted legislation (which will be reviewed later in this chapter) to enable the federal government to share the cost of hospital accommodation with the provinces, with the object of extending this service to the whole of Canada. Since that time, some of the other provinces have instituted hospital schemes. Not only do such arrangements benefit financially people whose sickness requires hospital treatment, but they also provide a sound basis for hospital finances.

Then there is the cost of the services of physicians and surgeons which often equals or exceeds the cost of hospital accommodation. Yet in the United States and Canada for example, payment for these services is mainly left to be made direct by the patient or by voluntary insurance.[3] The absence in these countries of any strong movement for the adoption of social insurance methods to meet these costs is due in part to opposition by the medical profession. The difficulties the profession emphasises have, however, been largely overcome in some other countries, and in Canada and in some states of the United States satisfactory solutions have been

[3] Doctors' fees can often be paid in instalments if the patient's resources are small, whereas hospital charges often have to be paid immediately either by the patient or by the public assistance authorities. This, and also the practice of doctors' charging lower fees to poor patients, may be one reason why there is greater pressure for hospital insurance to cover standard charges than for insurance to cover the cost of physicians' and surgeons' services.

devised, for example to provide medical care for veterans and for victims of industrial accidents under workmen's compensation legislation.

CASH INCOME INSURANCE

The provision of cash income by social security methods to meet the basic needs of people whose income has ceased because of sickness is essentially the same as the provision of income for people whose earnings have stopped because of unemployment or old age. Without sickness insurance, people must rely on the paid sick leave which many business undertakings provide (often as fringe benefits under collective agreements), on voluntary insurance, on their savings or on loans. Running into debt is not, however, conducive to a state of mind which will facilitate recovery; on the contrary, financial strain will retard recovery.

If a great majority of workers, when sick, received cash sick leave payments either from their employers or from voluntary insurance for a substantial part of their earnings, say 40 or 50 per cent, there would be no need to introduce compulsory sickness insurance for this purpose. The rest of the population could apply for public assistance. However, evidence shows that even in countries with a high standard of living, large proportions of the population have little or no protection of this sort and that sickness is a serious cause of poverty, especially among the lower income groups. The more progressive and larger firms often continue to pay for some weeks all or part of the wages of workers who are sick, but many small undertakings do not do so, and casual workers are also unprotected. Highly paid workers may be able to meet their needs for several weeks out of their own resources and thus cover a large part of the cost of their sickness, but unskilled and semi-skilled workers soon suffer privation when their earnings stop.

In the United States in 1954, of 61.2 million workers almost 42 million had some cash income when sick, either from paid sick leave or voluntary insurance. Yet, against a loss of earnings of $6,600 million they received only $1,500 million, or 23.6 per cent, and were, therefore, worse off by an amount of $4,700 million, or more than 76 per cent. At least 20 million, if taken sick, would have had no income either from sick leave payments or insurance. For 27 million persons, the protection was some form of cash income insurance purchased from private insurance companies, a majority

(16.1 million) being under group policies.[4] About 3.6 million were insured under public fund schemes for railroad workers and under the sickness insurance laws of four of the states.[5] The number of persons covered by paid sick leave was estimated to be 10.8 million. Included were federal, state and local government employees as well as those workers in private industry whose wages were continued wholly or in part during limited periods of sickness. Insurance and other forms of protection against loss of income from sickness grew rapidly during the early years after the Second World War, but the expansion slowed down, and after 1952, if allowance is made for increases in the labour force and per capita income, little further advance was made.[6] Paid sick leave, though it covered only part of the loss of earnings, gave substantially more protection than voluntary insurance benefits, which covered only 13 per cent of the total loss of earnings from sickness.

These data show that there are great gaps to be filled in order to establish in the United States a comprehensive system of cash income for the sick. The position is similar in Canada. Many other countries have given the highest priority to programmes that link the provision of cash income with medical care of the sick. Even in various underdeveloped countries cash benefits and medical care have been the first forms of social insurance to be applied. The importance of measures for the health of urban industrial workers has been recognised, for example, in Burma and Venezuela where the first stage in social insurance was the establishment of systems of cash benefits and medical care for sick workers and their dependants.

Compulsory contributory sickness insurance is widespread. Where

[4] The number with individual policies was 14.3 million, which includes some who were also protected by group policies.
[5] Persons covered by private insurance companies under the temporary disability insurance laws of New York, New Jersey and California are included in the 16.1 million.
[6] United States Department of Health, Education and Welfare, Social Security Administration, Division of Research and Statistics, "Protection against Income Loss from Sickness," Note no. 9—156, *Social Security Bulletin,* Jan. 1957. In addition to sick leave payments by government authorities and private undertakings and benefits from voluntary insurance, cash benefits for sickness were provided for railroad workers, by legislation, and the states of New York, New Jersey, Rhode Island and California provided such benefits by legislation. Public assistance benefits based on means tests are available for persons who are permanently and totally disabled, for the blind and for disabled persons responsible for young children.

L

contributory insurance systems are in operation for unemployment, old age or other risks, sickness insurance should be linked with them for reasons of administrative convenience, the contributions being combined.[7] Sickness insurance benefits are usually of limited duration, being paid in many countries for a maximum of twenty-six weeks. This covers a very large part of all sickness, and leaves a small residue of long-term invalidity. It is useful for this distinction to be made between short- and long-term disability, as the latter calls for different measures, including greater emphasis on rehabilitation.[8]

MEDICAL CARE

There is conclusive evidence from many countries, including Canada and the United States, that a major cause of financial difficulty and poverty is heavy expenditure for medical, surgical and hospital care necessitated by serious illness in the family.[9] Such 'catastrophic' illness involving crippling expenditure is experienced by only a relatively small proportion of the population but it hits them hard. This is an ideal risk to be covered by insurance because the cost per family, which is so high for the victims, is quite small if spread over the whole population.

In considering how to provide security against this contingency, three different categories of people claim attention—the poor, the wealthy and the great majority of people who are neither. Already the poor in many countries are given free medical and hospital care, subject to a means test. People who are well off could pay for themselves, but they are relatively few in number, most of them would have private accommodation in hospital and special nursing at

[7] In Canada, the restrictions on federal jurisdiction present difficulties. If these difficulties could be overcome, sickness insurance could be linked with unemployment insurance, or, if flat rate contributions and benefits were preferred, it could be linked with old age pensions in respect of contributions. Alternatively sickness insurance could be associated with the provincial systems of workmen's compensation, which have experience in dealing with medical care and rehabilitation. It could be widened to provide insurance on a contributory basis for widows with dependent children. Five provinces do provide medical and hospital insurance to widows with dependent children who qualify for mothers' allowances.

[8] In France a special system of insurance has been adopted for long-term sickness; the costs of providing income and medical care are higher than for sickness of less than six months' duration, and special attention is given to rehabilitation.

[9] See, e.g., D. V. Donnison, *Welfare Services in a Canadian Community: A Study of Brockville, Ontario* (Toronto, 1958).

higher cost than for standard or basic provision and they are heavily taxed. There are, therefore, administrative and social advantages in including them in any general scheme for health services and in allowing them the value of basic services towards the cost of any more expensive services which they choose to have.

In planning a general scheme for the whole population, it must be emphasised that, except for the poorest section of the population, people can readily afford to pay direct for some portion of their medical costs at the time they are incurred, and this should be regarded as an item of expenditure likely to recur fairly regularly. It could be paid not from an insurance fund but direct by the family as a normal part of its budget, much in the same way as it spends on furniture, clothing and holidays. In Canada and the United States, for example, the great majority of families could meet medical expenses up to $50.00 a year direct, and in Britain up to £10 a year. It is when medical costs run to much larger sums, hundreds of dollars or scores of pounds, that serious financial difficulties and hardships arise and the insurance method becomes essential. A public health service could therefore reasonably require its beneficiaries to pay direct, up to a specified amount, for medical and surgical attention and for say the first three days of hospital accommodation, after which the services would be free or provided for a nominal sum. This principle is adopted in many voluntary health insurance schemes and could readily be applied in a public health service. By this means, some direct payment and responsibility would be borne by the beneficiaries, and the remainder would be pooled by the contributory insurance method or by special or general revenues.

In many countries which have no comprehensive universal medical care services, a substantial part of the population is provided with free medical care from public funds. Protection is also afforded by private insurance, including group insurance by employers, one aspect of which—'fringe' benefits for workers in accordance with collective agreements—has grown in importance since the end of the Second World War. In the United States, however, trade union members are only about 25 per cent of all workers and only a fraction of trade unionists are entitled to these benefits. Private insurance protection is effective for many people with good incomes but not for people in the lower income groups including many aged people who no longer work.

MEDICAL CARE IN THE UNITED STATES AND CANADA

In Canada and the United States the public health services are primarily a responsibility of the provinces or states and of the municipal governments; the federal government facilitates and co-ordinates developments by grants and the promotion of special services. In both countries large sums of public money are spent on health services, but neither country has yet established an integrated system.

In countries with federal constitutions there can be flexibility; different systems can be developed and experiments made in some areas the results of which influence opinion elsewhere. In Canada, with only ten provinces and two territories (the Northwest Territories and the Yukon), there is less diversity and more cohesion than in the United States with its forty-eight state administrations. In both countries the impression is of a patchwork with many gaps, though progress towards a more comprehensive system has been greater in Canada, where there is substantial support for an expansion of public health services, and where federal-provincial systems of hospital care insurance are being established.

Various forms of voluntary health insurance are available in Canada and the United States. The most widely known are the Blue Cross, the Blue Shield (or similar co-operative associations in Canada) and insurance companies.[10] The first two are non-profit concerns. The Blue Cross, which is sponsored by the American Hospital Association and by local hospitals, insures against part of the costs of accommodation in the public ward (or, for an additional premium, semi-private or private accommodation), operating room, radiological, laboratory and anaesthetic services and surgical dressings and drugs. The patient pays any charges in excess of those specified in the plan, and is also responsible for paying the surgeon and physician.

The Blue Shield plans, which are sponsored by the professional medical societies in the various localities, are devised to meet part of these latter costs. Usually the organisation pays the surgeons and physicians their fees at specified rates, but under some plans the patient is given the money to settle his account direct. The patient must pay whatever additional amounts the surgeon and doctor may

[10] In 1955 Blue Cross had 48.6 per cent of the hospital insurance business in the United States and insurance companies 44.1 per cent. Insurance companies had 51.4 per cent of the business of insuring people against surgeons' and physicians' bills, and Blue Shield plans 34.89 per cent.

charge, but many plans provide that the scale of fees in the plan will be accepted as full payment from patients whose incomes are below a specified amount. Some plans provide from $3.00 to $5.00 a day towards the physician's charges while the patient is in hospital.

Blue Cross and Blue Shield plans, in addition to providing insurance against part of the costs of hospital accommodation and medican care, benefit the hospitals and medical profession financially, by ensuring prompt payment of their charges.[11] A substantial majority of those insured are covered under group plans arranged by business firms for their employees and by trade unions for their members. Group insurance has the advantage that the prepayment premiums are lower than they would be for individual insurance, and that protection is given to persons in the group who, because of ill health, would find it difficult or impossible to secure individual insurance.

Insurance companies offer a variety of plans to cover the risks of medical expenses, and the extent of protection depends on the amount of the premium that is paid. The insurance may cover hospital accommodation only, or surgeons' bills only or a combination of these; also physicians' charges for visits to patients in hospital. The most usual is payment for hospital accommodation and surgery. The insurance may provide for hospital accommodation at a daily rate of, say, $10.00, and any additional amount is paid direct to the hospital by the patient. The number of days at the full rate may be limited, for example to twenty or thirty, after which half rates are paid for a further specified period. In some plans a maximum amount of benefit is fixed; also the patient may be required to meet the first $50.00 or $100.00 of the hospital expenses before becoming entitled to insurance benefits.[12] Policies may be designed to insure against major medical expenses, the insured person undertaking to pay a specified amount towards the bills and 20 or 25 per cent of the additional expenses, the insurance company

[11] In the United States in the mid-1950's there were more than 28 million subscribers to Blue Cross plans. More than 100 million individuals had some hospital insurance coverage, and, through the associated Blue Shield plans, more than 85 million had insurance for at least part of the cost of surgical operations. A large proportion of these people are protected by group contracts. The various prepayment plans, however, met only about 15 to 20 per cent of total medical expenses, though the proportion was considerably higher—nearly one-third of medical bills—if institutions for mental care and for chronic sickness were excluded.

[12] For surgery the amount of insurance is set according to a scale of fees covering each of the main types of operation, and the patient pays any amounts over the scale which the surgeon may charge.

paying the remainder. Usually the patient pays the hospital and surgeon's bills and claims from the insurance company the money to which he is entitled under the policy—a different method from the one followed by Blue Cross and Blue Shield, which pay direct to the hospital and surgeon and not to the patient.

In addition to these plans, there are, as already mentioned, compulsory sickness insurance schemes in the states of New York, New Jersey, Rhode Island and California. The people are free to choose between insuring or continuing to insure with private plans and insuring with a publicly operated fund. Reference is made later to the comprehensive hospital insurance arrangements made in several Canadian provinces.

In the United States substantial public programmes for personal health care are applied, but as already indicated, they are far from covering adequately the health risks of the population. Also, voluntary private insurance, although it has expanded considerably since the Second World War, does not provide adequate protection, especially for large numbers of people in the lower income brackets, including the aged, whose need is greatest.[13] The lack of effective protection is due to a combination of factors, prominent among which is over-emphasis on individual responsibility. Other factors are resistance (including opposition by the medical profession) to government schemes, preference for voluntary methods and an unwarranted belief that the need will rapidly be met by voluntary insurance. The wide variations in different parts of the country can largely be accounted for by a desire to maintain state autonomy, and by the consequent opposition to greater unification by extension of federal intervention.

Among the main public health services in the United States are those provided for persons in receipt of public assistance who need medical care, veterans, merchant seamen, railroad workers (under the Railroad Retirement legislation), victims of occupational accidents and diseases, the blind and persons suffering from mental disease, tuberculosis, venereal diseases and poliomyelitis.[14] Public

[13] During the years 1949 to 1955 voluntary private insurance benefits grew more rapidly than public expenditure on personal health services; private benefits rose from 7.4 per cent of the total expenditure on such services in 1949 to 16.6 per cent in 1955, whereas public expenditure rose from 19.4 per cent in 1949 to 23 per cent in 1955.
[14] The federal government makes provision for veterans and merchant seamen. The state and local governments provide for the medical needs of persons in receipt of public assistance, and maintain institutions for the mentally sick and sanatoria for tubercular patients.

funds also provide pre-natal and post-natal clinics for mothers and children, and there are services for crippled children, medical and dental examination of school children, rehabilitation services, immunisation against infectious diseases and mass diagnostic testing. In four states—New York, New Jersey, Rhode Island and California—systems of compulsory insurance have been introduced to provide medical care as well as sickness cash benefits. Most municipalities and other local communities have public hospitals.

In the United States in 1955, private expenditure for personal health services totalled $10,900 million, or about $69.00 for each man, woman and child in the population. Average families spent more than $200 a year for health services, or between 4 and 5 per cent of their income, but 3,500,000 families each spent $500 or more a year[15] Public expenditure on health services in 1955 amounted to $3,300 million, making a combined total of $14,200 million, of which public expenditure represented 23 per cent; it had grown from 9 per cent in 1929, 17 per cent in 1940 and 19.4 per cent in 1949.[16]

Two-thirds of the American population use voluntary prepaid health insurance to assist them in financing a part of their medical bills in advance of sickness. In 1955 they paid $3,150 million for voluntary insurance, $2,540 million of which was paid out to meet their medical bills and the rest to finance the administration of the insurance plans.[17] The amount of the bills covered by voluntary private insurance was about 16.6 per cent of the combined total cost of all personal health services, and this, added to the 23 per cent covered by the public authorities, left a balance of about 60 per cent of the total to be paid direct by the patients. One-third of the population had no health insurance of any kind, and the two-thirds who carried some private insurance had only about one-quarter of

[15] The proportions of family incomes spent on health services in the United States and in Canada are higher than in other parts of the world.

[16] See *Social Security Bulletin*, Dec. 1956, published by the United States Department of Health, Education and Welfare; also a paper on "Trends of Public Welfare and Their Implications" presented by Mrs Ida C. Merriam, United States Department of Health, Education and Welfare, before the American Economic Association, Cleveland, Ohio, Dec. 28, 1956. The figure for public expenditure does not include $761 million for health care for veterans, nor sums spent for medical care under public assistance, workmen's compensation and rehabilitation programmes. If these items are included, the total public expenditure in 1955 was $4,500 million, or about 29 per cent of the combined total of private and public health expenditure.

[17] Thus, for every $100 paid for voluntary insurance, $80.50 was paid toward medical expenditure and $19.50 to meet the costs of administration.

their medical bills covered by this method.[18] The proportion of medical bills covered by private voluntary insurance in 1955 was much higher for hospital services (45.3 per cent) than for physicians' services (25.2 per cent). Though private insurance grew considerably between 1948 and 1955, big gaps were left and a substantial majority of the population were inadequately protected, either by private insurance or publicly financed health services, against the risk of heavy medical expense.

In Canada in 1953, total expenditure on personal health care and treatment was estimated to be $756 million, of which $402 million, or 53 per cent, was for public and private hospital care, including care in mental institutions and in sanatoria for tuberculosis.[19] The average expenditure was over $50.00 for each member of the population, or more than $150 for a family of three persons. About 50 per cent of the total cost was met by direct payments by the patients, about 33 per cent from public funds, endowments and charitable contributions, and the remaining 17 per cent from voluntary insurance funds.[20]

In Ontario in 1954, about 75 per cent of the revenues of public

[18] In 1953 some 60 per cent of families with incomes less than $3,000 a year had no health insurance. A recent sample survey covering 473 families containing 1,657 persons of the lower to upper middle income classes in urban and rural Ohio, Connecticut and Vermont, showed that 28 per cent of families and 35 per cent of individuals had no health insurance. The urban families spent $227 and the rural families $136 on medical care in the year. The average medical expense was $184, and insurance benefits were $35, leaving $149 to be paid direct. Th insured families met about one-quarter of their total medical costs from insurance and paid three-quarters direct. (*Social Security Bulletin*, Nov. 1956).

[19] Department of National Health and Welfare, Research Division Memorandum no. 12, General Series, *Health Care in Canada, Expenditures and Sources of Revenue*, 1953 (Ottawa, Aug. 1955). The total does not include capital expenditure for building hospitals, or costs of administering the public health services and voluntary health agencies. It was estimated that, if these were added, Canada's health bill would have been well over $900 million.   See also: *Canadian Sickness Survey*, 1950-51, reports compiled jointly by the Department and the Dominion Bureau of Statistics; and *The Administration of Health Insurance in Canada*, by Malcolm G. Taylor (Toronto, 1956).

[20] For hospital expenditure only, a higher proportion (56 per cent) came from public funds (including the British Columbia, Saskatchewan, Alberta and Newfoundland hospital schemes), and 28 per cent direct from patients, or 36 per cent direct from patients if federal and provincial hospitals (for which only 11 per cent came direct from patients) are excluded.   Sixty per cent of the cost of physicians' services was covered by direct payments from patients. According to the Sickness Survey in 1951 the cost of medical care (excluding public expenditure) averaged $82.00 per family.

hospitals, clinics and convalescent hospitals came from patients' payments and the remaining 25 per cent from government and municipal grants and from donations. The average cost per patient per day, not including physicians' and surgeons' fees, was $14.64. As the Ontario government indicates in an official statement, 'Each year about 15 per cent of the population incurs over 90 per cent of the costs.'[21] Since hospital needs are so irregular and cannot be budgeted for by each family in the same way as food costs, the conclusion was drawn that the most feasible method of meeting the cost of such care was by insurance. It was also stated that, in 1956, 'the number of persons in Ontario having *some degree* of protection against the costs of hospital care is estimated to be approximately 68 per cent of the population.' For many of these people, however, the protection was seriously inadequate, and nearly one-third had no protection. In 1953, only 7.5 per cent of the Canadian population was enrolled in comprehensive benefit plans covering costs of physicians', surgeons', diagnostic and specialists' services and hospital accommodation.

According to information obtained in the Canadian Sickness Survey,'It appears that approximately 50 per cent of the national bill for personal health care in Canada is still being paid directly by families.'[22] This estimate was related to the early 1950's. Governments provided 33 per cent of the total, and voluntary insurance 17 per cent. In 1950-1, the average expenditure per family was $82.10. People in the upper income group can generally meet medical expenses, even for serious illnesses, without difficulty. People in the middle income group can meet moderate expenses out of current income but experience financial difficulty from serious sickness; however, many of them buy insurance to cover at least part of the risk. People in the lower groups suffer hardship if they become involved in expenditure for medical care beyond quite minor amounts, and they are the least protected by insurance; some of them, in the year covered by the Survey, spent more than 15 per cent of their income on health care. Even when insurance is pur-

[21] *Hospital Care Insurance in Ontario* (Toronto, Jan. 1957), pp. 3, 7, 8.
[22] See Dr C. Lloyd Francis, "Expenditure Patterns from the Canadian Sickness Survey, 1950-51," *Canadian Journal of Public Health,* Aug. 1956, p. 331. It was estimated that in 1951 the amount spent on personal health care, including government expenditure and employers' contributions to prepaid plans, was around $675 million. Expenditure on personal health services in 1953 represented about 4 per cent of the net national revenue at factor cost.

chased by people in the middle and lower income groups, it often covers only about one-quarter of the costs incurred.

The evidence is convincing that a comprehensive compulsory medical service at nominal cost to patients is needed to provide security for large numbers of Canadian families against the financial consequences of sickness. The need in the United States seems to be even greater. There is no likelihood that the problem will be solved by further expansion of voluntary insurance, though this has great value in enabling people to pay for benefits that are not provided by a compulsory standard scheme.[23]

Several Canadian provinces have adopted comprehensive measures for providing hospital services. The Hospital Insurance Act of British Columbia applies to practically all the residents of the province.[24] Public ward facilities are provided for a nominal fee of a dollar a day—less than one-fourteenth of the average cost.[25] The fee does not cover the services of physicians and surgeons, unless they are employed by the hospital, but it does cover bed and meals, nursing, therapy, dressings, drugs and other supplies, radiological and laboratory diagnosis, and operating room and anaesthetic services. Persons who, on the basis of a means test, are receiving social welfare (assistance) benefits do not have to pay this daily charge, nor do aged people who receive provincial assistance to supplement the federal old age pension.

When the scheme was first started in 1949, it was financed by compulsory, direct, annual, flat rate payments made by those insured, the rate being $27.00 a year for a single person and $39.00 for a person with one or more dependants. As a result partly of administrative difficulties of collection, especially in the sparsely populated

[23] State subsidies for voluntary private insurance in non-profit organisations would result in the protection of more people and enable the organisations to provide increased benefits at low cost, but even so, large numbers of people with low incomes would remain unprotected. In January 1954, in a health message to Congress, the President of the United States recommended a limited federal reinsurance service to encourage private non profit health insurance organisations to offer broader benefits to a larger number of families.

[24] Members of the armed forces, veterans, persons employed under the Canadian Shipping Act, those provided with treatment under the Workmen's Compensation Act and some other categories of the population are excluded, as they have special arrangements for hospitalisation.

[25] Some employers provide benefits to supplement the provincial scheme so as to enable their employees to have private or semi-private rooms. Outpatients pay $2.00 per visit for emergency treatment of injuries and minor surgery.

and remote parts of the province, the direct payments were replaced in 1954 by a sales tax.[26]

In Saskatchewan the Hospital Service Plan is a universal compulsory insurance scheme which covers most of the residents of the province and entitles them to accommodation and board in the public ward. It is financed by a tax of $20.00 on all persons eighteen years of age and over, and a tax of a lower rate for each dependant under eighteen years of age; the maximum tax per family is $45.00. The provincial government provides additional funds, as needed, from its general revenue, including since April 1950 one-third of the proceeds of a 3 per cent sales tax. Old age pensioners who formerly had means test pensions or who qualify for provincial supplementary allowances, blind persons and recipients of mothers' allowances are entitled to free hospital and medical care and dental and optical services. In the Swift Current Health Region there is a prepaid medical care plan which provides general practitioners', specialists' and diagnostic services free for all residents, and limited dental services for children. The plan is financed by personal and property taxes and some contributions by the provincial government.

In Alberta a municipal scheme provides accommodation and meals for almost the whole population in the public ward. The patient pays $1.00 a day, the municipality pays the remainder and is reimbursed for half its outlay by the provincial government.[27] Newfoundland has a cottage hospital scheme on a voluntary prepayment basis, in which somewhat less than half the population participates. In most cottage hospital areas the annual rate of payment is $15.00 for the head of a family and $7.50 for single adults. Contributors to the scheme are entitled to free out-patient diagnosis and treatment, to home visits by a doctor and to hospitalisation.

[26] Provincial funds for the Hospital Insurance Service and all provincial government social welfare services are provided by a 5 per cent social service tax (sales tax). Also the provincial and municipal authorities each make grants to the hospitals at the rate of 70 cents a day per patient. The British Columbia Health Insurance Service pays one-half of the cost of constructing hospitals for acute and chronic patients, and one-third of the cost of renovations. The hospitals can obtain federal grants for 40 per cent of the cost of diagnostic, radiological and laboratory equipment; the provincial government pays 30 per cent.

[27] The treatment of venereal diseases, medical examinations for cancer and tuberculosis, care in tuberculosis sanatoria, psychiatric examinations and guidance for mental cases are all free. All victims of poliomyelitis and rheumatoid arthritics under twenty-five years of age receive free hospital and medical care.

In Canada, health is primarily a provincial and municipal responsibility, but the federal government has taken progressive measures for the development of health services, and in particular it has greatly assisted, and shown increasing co-operation with, the provincial governments in their health programmes. Special mention must be made of the programme for paying grants to the provinces. An earlier system of grants was extended in 1948, and the biggest amounts have been made available for hospital construction, general public health, mental health and the control of tuberculosis.[28] In 1953 new grants were introduced for child and maternal health, medical rehabilitation, and laboratory and radiological services. In addition, the federal government undertakes to make direct provision for the health care of special groups, particularly members of the armed forces, veterans, Indians, Eskimos, seamen and newly arrived immigrants, totalling half a million persons. In 1955-6, about 60 per cent of the federal government's health expenditure of $107 million was spent on these groups.

The system of federal grants to the provinces has led to close consultation, co-operation and integration among the different parts of this far-flung country. Federal sharing of costs reduces inequalities in the burden of providing adequate health services and enables the poorer provinces to establish better services than would otherwise be possible.

Health insurance is a live political and social issue in Canada. The greatest support is for hospital insurance and, as outlined below, Parliament enacted legislation on April 12, 1957, to enable the Dominion government to participate financially in provincial hospital insurance programmes. There is, however, substantial demand for more comprehensive insurance measures to cover physicians' and surgeons' services as well.

The 1957 Act provides for the Dominion government to make grants-in-aid for hospital insurance schemes in the various provinces to help with the costs of in-patient accommodation and board in standard or public wards, nursing services, diagnostic services, drugs and biological remedies, the use of operating rooms and anaesthetic facilities, the services of doctors and specialists who are paid by the hospital (as distinguished from those paid by the patient) and certain other services. An amendment of the Act allows

---

[28] The grants for hospital construction account for nearly 40 per cent of the total federal grant, and the grants for the other purposes mentioned account for over 43 per cent of the total.

out-patients the same services except board and room.[29] The
Dominion government's share in the costs for the whole country
amounts to 50 per cent.[30] The Act stipulated that its application was
conditional on the establishment of hospital care insurance schemes
by at least six provinces (that is, a majority of the provinces), con-
taining at least one-half of the population of Canada. This stipulation was a kind of indirect referendum to guarantee widespread
popular support for the use of federal funds for the purpose, and
almost immediately after the Act was passed, a sufficient number
of provinces responded.

The costs of hospital care and diagnosis vary greatly in Canada,
from about $12.25 per person in Newfoundland to around $28.50
in British Columbia, the national average being about $22.85.
For that reason, it was difficult to devise a formula for the Dominion
government's share: if it paid half the costs in each province, Newfoundland would get less than half the amount per patient received
by British Columbia; and if it paid each province half the Canadian
average per patient, Newfoundland and some of the other provinces
where the costs are low would receive 75 to 90 per cent of their
costs, and the provinces where the costs are high would get only
40 to 45 per cent though they would get the biggest amounts. To
meet this difficulty, the Act provided for grants to be made to each
province for (a) 25 per cent of the Canadian average cost per head,
and (b) 25 per cent of the average cost per head in that particular
province, multiplied by the population covered. This formula goes
a long way to meet the problem. Though the richer provinces will
pay more in taxation than they receive in grants and will, therefore,
subsidise the hospital services of the poor provinces, this can be

[29] The Ontario hospital insurance scheme, which was devised by provincial
legislation and came into effect on January 1, 1959, covers out-patients only
in the twenty-four hours immediately following an accident.
[30] The Act provides that the Dominion government will not pay for the
costs of patients in mental hospitals and in sanatoria for tubercular care,
as provincial governments already meet most of these.   Nor does the
Dominion government contribute towards the cost of nursing homes, in-
firmaries and homes for the aged which primarily provide custodian care.
Capital expenditures for hospital building and interest and debt charges are
excluded, as are also the care of veterans, patients under workmen's compensation schemes and persons covered by accident insurance and similar
arrangements. The Act does not provide for accommodation in semi-private
or private wards and any special services other than those given in standard
wards. Furthermore, the federal government will not contribute towards
the costs of administering the hospital care insurance programme.

justified on broad social grounds as a measure of Canadian solidarity.[31]

Various views are held about the part which the medical profession should take in the scheme. The doctors favour control by a semi-autonomous professional commission. Inevitably, the doctors must have substantial responsibilities, especially for determining standards of professional competence. The general control of the policy and administration of a public scheme such as this must, however, be the responsibility of a publicly appointed authority which should work in close co-operation with the profession. The hospital insurance legislation passed in almost every province has had the effect that Blue Cross and private insurance is no longer needed for basic hospital provision, but can be used to cover the cost of additional provision such as semi-private or private accommodation and extra medical benefits.

SOME MEDICAL PROFESSIONAL PROBLEMS

Many complex professional problems require solution in the application of schemes of health insurance. The main ones are how the medical profession is to be properly remunerated and how the services are to be made both efficient and economical. The remuneration of the medical profession can be regulated by negotiation and agreement in much the same way as rates of payment are fixed for other professional and technical groups in the population, for example, the teaching profession. Practicable solutions have been found in countries which have comprehensive medical services, and in other countries, including Canada and the United States, the payments to be made to the many doctors and surgeons who are employed in the public service—by veterans' administrations, Workmen's Compensation Boards or Commissions and as full-time staff members of public hospitals—have been regulated without undue difficulty.

For full-time hospital staffs and other full-time categories the appropriate method of payment is by a scale of salaries which takes account of qualifications, experience and responsibility. For general practitioners and specialists the main alternatives are fees for

[31] The total cost of operating the hospitals of Canada was estimated to be $442 million in 1956. Under the new scheme, the costs to be shared would amount to $365 million, one-half of which would be paid by the federal government. It must be noted that hospital costs are rising, and that the totals are affected by inflation, increases in population and increases in services and equipment.

service and capitation fees. Many members of the medical profession favour the fee for service method combined with the indemnity system: the patient pays the doctor and receives indemnities at specified rates from the insurance scheme, thus maintaining a direct financial relation between patient and doctor, and enabling the doctor to charge more than the indemnity if the patient can afford more or if special services are provided. Some doctors might encourage patients to use their services more freely than was strictly necessary in order to increase their remuneration, but this risk might be controlled in various ways. In the Netherlands, for instance, specialists and surgeons are paid on a fee for service basis, but if they submit bills for more than 22,500 florins in a year a progressively increasing percentage of the surplus is deducted.

In the capitation system each general practitioner receives a specified annual amount for each person registered with him, whether the person uses his services or not. The rate per person is higher in sparsely populated areas than in urban centres, and may be higher for persons over sixty-five years of age because of the probability that they will make greater demands on the doctor's time. Some doctors might register more persons than they could treat effectively, but this danger could be averted by fixing the maximum number a doctor would be allowed to have on his register. In the Netherlands general practitioners on a capitation basis receive reduced fees for patients beyond 3,000.

The methods adopted in different countries do not indicate a clear preference for either of these methods of paying general practitioners. In New Zealand and in France, the fee for service method is applied, this being closer to private practice than the capitation system. In Britain capitation is used in the National Health Service. On balance this method seems to be preferable. The advantage in having the responsible public authority pay the doctor (rather than pay the patient according to a fixed scale and leave him to pay the doctor) is that any direct financial relation between doctor and patient is obviated.

For specialists a system of payments based on qualifications and experience can be devised. Also flexibility can be introduced by leaving specialists and general practitioners free to devote part of their time to private practice. There will always be people in a community who are willing to pay for private service. For the majority of the medical profession, however, public service provides stable and regular remuneration, probably at a higher average level than private practice. Payments in private practice are often uncertain and small, especially for services to the lower income groups.

When a government establishes a public health service it becomes responsible for ensuring that the services are adequate and that they are operated economically. It is therefore of vital importance that the public authority should work in close co-operation with the medical profession to ensure avoidance of waste.

There is a danger that free or heavily subsidised health services may be abused. People who would spend too little out of their own pockets may make extravagant demands on public services and subject doctors to undue pressure. Some will make unnecessary claims for attention to trivial or imaginary ailments, or try to insist on expensive drugs when much less costly remedies would be equally good or even better. If the system provides cash income in addition to medical care, doctors may be under pressure to grant longer absences from work than are necessary. It is easy to accord an extra week of convalescence, and some doctors may do that rather than risk annoyance to a patient who may transfer to another doctor in the hope of gaining easier acquiescence in his demands. These are real dangers, but they can largely be prevented, especially by the use of medical statistics, and some of them can be substantially reduced if small charges are made for medical services as outlined below.

When a national health service is introduced, th. demands on it are often heavy, and it is likely to cost more than was previously spent on health care, no doubt largely because there is an accumulation of needs that were not properly met before. In countries where there is no national health service, there is convincing evidence of great unsatisfied needs. The provision of the additional personnel, equipment and accommodation that are required to meet such needs can lead to progressive improvements in the health, productivity and well-being of the people, and the increased demand may in general be welcomed, as it means that many people will benefit from the treatment of illnesses which they had previously neglected because of the cost.

Often complaints are heard that when a national health service is introduced the standards of medical treatment are lowered. However, the alleged deterioration is likely to be due to a broadening in demand. Previously the upper income groups were able to get all the services they would pay for, but the services available for the lower income groups were much more meagre because of their inability to pay. To say that is not to overlook the extensive services rendered by the medical profession, either free or for a small payment, to people in the poorer sections of the population. To some extent the introduction of a national health service may mean a spreading of medical resources more equally throughout the population, the services to people in the lower income group being better than before and those for people in the middle income groups possibly somewhat more restricted.

Here it must be emphasised that a government, before introducing a comprehensive health service, or a partial service such as hospitalisation, should be satisfied that the medical personnel and facilities available are adequate for the needs of the population. For this purpose, a survey such as that undertaken by the Canadian government is necessary in order to estimate the volume of un-unsatisfied needs, including those of the rural and the poorer urban population. Decisions may then be made on the number of doctors, nurses and technicians to be trained and their distribution throughout the country, and on the number and location of new hospitals and clinics. If there is a shortage of personnel and facilities, the services will inevitably be unsatisfactory, but if there are enough staff and facilities, rich and poor can be provided with adequate treatment, and there is no reason why wealthy people should not pay for additional facilities. A standard service could not ordinarily be expected to send patients to the south of France, to Florida, California or Honolulu for convalescence, but there is nothing to prevent a doctor from recommending such a sojourn to a patient who is well able to pay for it, and from prescribing for him expensive drugs and treatments which may possibly be beneficial, but which are not essential.

SOME FINANCIAL CONSIDERATIONS

Public health services can be financed from the government's general revenues, from special taxes or from contributions paid by the beneficiaries or jointly by them and their employers. Some of these methods can be combined; for example, a government may subsidise a contributory scheme.

In some countries the public health services are financed wholly or largely from the general revenues. Thus about 90 per cent of the cost of the National Health Service in Britain is paid out of the general revenues; the rest comes from the National Insurance Fund (to which the beneficiaries, employers and the state contribute) and from the beneficiaries in the form of payments for certain dental and ophthalmic services and supplies and token payments for pre-

M

scriptions. Where this method is adopted, the view is taken that the state should provide health services free or at little cost to the beneficiaries in much the same way as primary and secondary education are largely free in many countries. There are, however, differences between education and health services which affect the methods of finance. For example, parents are required to keep their children at school often until they reach fifteen or sixteen years of age, and during that time they must meet the cost of their maintenance, though they may be assisted in doing so by children's allowances. The parents therefore bear a large part of the cost of children during the years when they are attending school, and the state can reasonably pay the cost of public education from its general revenues. A substantial part of the cost of public health services should, however, be met by special taxes levied, for the most part, on the beneficiaries, or by direct contributions made by them. In Britain a higher proportion of the cost of the National Health Service, say not less than 20 per cent, could appropriately be paid from the contributory National Insurance Fund, instead of less than 10 per cent as at present. Also, along the lines indicated later, beneficiaries could be required to make direct payments to cover the whole cost of minor inexpensive illnesses and a limited part of the cost of more serious illnesses.

Investigations in many countries yield evidence in support of comprehensive systems to provide both cash income and medical services. For cash income, the contributions and benefits may be set either at flat rates or at rates that vary with wages. In big federal countries in which standards of living vary widely between regions, the system of differential rates has advantages.

Many countries combine cash income benefits and medical services in a single scheme. The medical services are on uniform basic standards, and equal contributions are appropriate. If the contributions vary with wages, the higher-paid workers receive the same services as the others but are paying more for them and are, therefore, in effect, subsidising the lower-paid workers. It is better to finance subsidies from general revenues. Medical benefits can be provided by successive stages as facilities become adequate. It would be illogical and socially unsatisfactory to regard free or low cost hospital accommodation and diagnostic and preventive clinics as the only necessary provision in the medical field.[32] They should

[32] Free or low cost diagnostic and preventive clinics have often proved to be of great value. In some of the lower income districts of New York City, their establishment significantly reduced the demands for accommodation in neighbouring hospitals, and proved to be a considerable economy.

be considered as steps towards comprehensive medical care which would include medical and surgical treatment.

Where cash income and medical benefits are combined, a single contribution or special tax by beneficiaries and their employers can be paid, and this is an administrative economy. For hospital and other medical services, there are advantages in having the responsible public authority do the organising and paying instead of having public or other insurance funds pay cash indemnities to the patient and leave him to pay the hospital and doctor. This does not preclude arrangements, along the lines reviewed below, by which patients may pay direct to the authority an appreciable amount towards the cost of the benefits they receive.

If social insurance methods are to be adopted to cover the costs both of hospital accommodation and of the services of physicians and surgeons, a decision has to be taken on the question whether all the costs, except for sundry token payments, should be covered, or only cases of severe and costly illness; in the latter case the patients would be made responsible for paying for moderate amounts of sickness. So-called catastrophic sickness is a major cause of financial strain; and the claim that it should be covered by a system of social security is strong. This could be arranged on a compulsory contributory basis, or by special or general taxation, with the requirement, however, that individual patients or families would pay some specified amount direct, for example the first $50.00, and that any costs beyond that amount would be met by the social security scheme. Such a policy would be well suited to countries with high standards of living.

There are substantial advantages in adopting a policy which, while distributing the major part of the cost over the whole community, requires a beneficiary, when he uses the health services, to make some direct payment towards the cost of the services he himself receives, in addition to the insurance contributions or tax which he pays in common with all the potential beneficiaries. Usually it is the beneficiary who decides to use the services, and this policy reduces or eliminates the risk of unnecessary demands, tends to reduce the cost of the services and augments the revenues.[33]

This policy is applied to some extent in many countries, in a variety of ways. In France, beneficiaries pay 20 per cent of the costs

[33] Especially in countries with high standards of living, most people who can afford to buy automobiles, television sets and other expensive gadgets can afford to pay appreciable amounts towards the cost of their normal health requirements, though not for serious costly illnesses.

of certain material benefits such as medicines. In British Columbia, patients in hospitals pay a dollar a day, which is less than 10 per cent of the cost of the services provided. In Switzerland, beneficiaries pay from 10 to 25 per cent of the cost of various material benefits, the proportion varying with the fund in which the person is insured. In Japan, an insured person who becomes ill must pay the cost of the first visit to a doctor. In Germany, a voucher, for which a small charge is made, must be presented in order to claim benefits. In the United Kingdom, a small charge is made for each prescription for pharmaceutical supplies, and payments must be made towards the cost of dentures, spectacles and surgical appliances. Some countries require payments when benefits are provided for members of the families of insured persons: in Austria, the charge is 10 per cent of the cost of hospitalisation; in Japan, 50 per cent of the cost of material benefits; and in Germany, in some insurance funds, 20 to 50 per cent of the cost of pharmaceutical supplies.

As already indicated, some private insurance companies cover the costs of hospitalisation and medical care beyond a specified minimum which is borne by the beneficiary. For example, the beneficiary may be required to pay the first £20 or $50.00 of costs incurred by him during a year, and the insurance covers additional costs up to some specified maximum. This is a method which could be applied with advantage in social insurance systems. An alternative would be to require the beneficiary to pay a specified percentage of the cost up to say $200 after which the services would be free. This would solve the problem of catastrophic sickness, and people whose incomes were found by a means test to be so low that payment of the percentage would cause undue privation could be exempted from it.

In Britain, the payments made by patients cover only about 5 per cent of the gross cost of the National Health Service. The charges made could be substantially greater. By making the Service almost free, the British system fails to allow for the fact that, with present standards of living, many patients could afford without hardship to pay a considerably higher proportion of the costs and could quite properly be required to do so.

It is often assumed that the cost of a comprehensive public health service provided at nominal expense to the patients would be much greater than the previous mixture of public and private services, and that it would rise continuously. The evidence from Britain and other countries is that when comprehensive services are introduced, there is a substantial increase in the demand for medical attention, partly because previously many people were unable to afford proper care, but increases in cost for this reason result in an improvement in the health of the population. In Britain, the tendency is towards a gradual but not a large continuous increase in cost. Expressed in terms of constant prices, the cost of the British National Health Service rose by only £11 million, or less than 2 per cent, during the period 1949-50 to 1953-4, and as a proportion of the gross national product, the net cost fell from $3\frac{3}{4}$ per cent in 1949-50 to $3\frac{1}{4}$ per cent in 1953-4.[34]

In Canada, approximately 4 per cent of national income is spent on personal health services, and in the United States, current expenditure is in similar proportion. The adoption of comprehensive health services at nominal direct costs to the patients could be provided for little more public expense than is now being incurred, but the services would be distributed more evenly so as to make more treatment available to people in the lower and intermediate income brackets.[35] Any increase in total costs would be partly due to the provision of more comprehensive services, but mainly to the greater cost of providing more scientific treatment and equipment as a result of medical research, and to growth of population and inflationary factors. There would be likely to be little increase in the proportion of the national income devoted to the health services.

[34] See Cmd. 9663, *Report of the Committee of Enquiry into the National Health Service* (H.M.S.O., 1956); also B. Abel-Smith and R. M. Titmus, *The Cost of the National Health Service in England and Wales* (Cambridge, 1956). In these publications, attention was directed to the need for increased capital expenditure on hospitals. About 45 per cent of all hospitals in England and Wales were built before 1891, and although many of them have been renovated and enlarged, there is need for substantial further modernisation and for the building of new hospitals.

[35] The Truman administration favoured provision of medical care by compulsory insurance; the Federal Security Agency, subsequently merged into the Department of Health, Education, and Welfare, proposed insurance to provide sickness cash benefits for periods up to twenty-six weeks, the scheme to be operated along with the Old-Age and Survivors' Insurance.

CHAPTER X

OTHER CONTINGENCIES

As already indicated, the most costly items of social security are old age pensions, provision for sickness (particularly medical care) and family allowances (especially if they are for substantial amounts and are paid for all dependent children or for all except the first child). Social or public assistance is costly if it is the main form of social security and if it is used to provide benefits for many risks. Even where the main burden is borne by social insurance or state payments without a means test, the costs of public assistance can still be substantial unless the social insurance and state benefits are comprehensive and public assistance is residual.

It is not intended in this survey to attempt to analyse all the elements which comprise an adequate system of social security. This chapter is therefore selective—it reviews provisions for unemployment, industrial injuries and diseases, long-term disability and widows and orphans, and touches briefly on the need for rehabilitation and retraining and on provisions for maternity costs. Effective provision for each of these contingencies can be made from relatively small contributions, since the number of persons who need help at any one time represents only a small fraction of the population. Also, except for unemployment, the number of persons requiring benefit can be estimated fairly closely from statistics and does not vary greatly from year to year. Unemployment is different from other risks because it is likely to vary widely from boom to depression, and for that reason the accumulation of reserves is specially important.

UNEMPLOYMENT INSURANCE

The essential purpose of unemployment insurance is to provide an income for people when they are out of work for short periods, so that they will be enabled to subsist while they look for new employment or until they can go back to their old jobs. Payment of benefits is usually limited to six months, though workers with a long record of continuous employment may have their benefits extended, often up to twelve months. Workers who have exhausted their right to benefit can restore it by obtaining employment and contributing to the unemployment fund for some specified period. Generally, in industrial countries, unemployment schemes should be designed to cover about 6 per cent or at the most 8 per cent of unemployment, though these percentages could be lowered somewhat if the figures on average unemployment over a period of years warranted the change.

A fairly clear line of separation can be drawn between people who are soon back at work and those who suffer from prolonged unemployment. Among the latter are the totally disabled and also people who, because of age or long-term disability, have difficulty in finding new jobs and in keeping them if they do succeed in finding them. Many of these people are in effect unemployable. Still others, including many excellent workpeople, experience long-term unemployment either because their industry is declining or because the economy of the country is suffering from serious prolonged depression. Provision must of course be made for their maintenance, but the appropriate remedies for depression have to be found in credit and other economic recovery policies including public works programmes.

There is need for close co-ordination between agencies that provide for the able-bodied unemployed and agencies that deal with the totally disabled and with persons who cease to be employable because of infirmities associated with approaching old age. The frontiers of these last two categories come close together and there are many people near the borderlines. Moreover, the unemployment, rehabilitation, retraining and health services need to work in close co-operation on behalf of the partially disabled as well as the fit workers who need training for new occupations.

Persons suffering from long-term total disabilities which render them in effect unemployable should be transferred from unemployment insurance to social assistance based on a means test, for the provision of a maintenance income, or else to disability insurance. If, however, they are within a few years of the age at which old age pensions are paid they may be brought under the pensions' administration. The United States Old-Age and Survivors Insurance was amended along these lines in 1956 so that disability benefits could be paid to totally and permanently disabled workers between the ages of fifty and sixty-four, that is, during the fifteen years before qualifying for an old age pension, provided they were fully insured under the scheme. In many countries which have no comprehensive disability insurance, special financial aid, subject to a means test, is given to the blind.

A main difficulty in devising a general system that will deal effectively with unemployment is in estimating the number of persons it will have to provide for at any given time. The incidence of unemployment cannot be calculated as closely as the number of aged or of widows and orphans for example. Any system for unemployment provision must be geared to carry light and heavy loads successively. This usually involves building up funds in good years to meet subsequent severe depressions, in order to avoid having to make hasty and inadequate improvisations when a crisis occurs. Studies of fluctuations in business and employment show that employment may continue at a high level for several years, even for a decade or more, with only minor recessions, but also that poor times may be similarly long, interspersed with a few somewhat brighter years.

Any kind of pay-as-you-go method on an annual basis can be rejected as too uncertain and unreliable. The chaos and hardship in Canada and the United States during the catastrophic economic depression of the early 1930's gave convincing evidence of the need for an extensive, soundly based system of unemployment insurance and for building up reserves in good years. Both countries subsequently introduced such systems.

Difficulties arise in attempting to devise a scheme that will be financially sound however severe the crisis with which it may be required to cope. Depressions are uncertain in magnitude, and it is a problem to decide how great a possible crisis may be. Will it involve 12 or 15 or 25 per cent of unemployment, and for how long —a few months or several years? If a very pessimistic view is taken, it will be necessary to collect high rates of contributions and to accumulate big funds. A usual procedure is to take an intermediate course by setting up a scheme that can be expected to remain financially sound and solvent during substantial fluctuations in unemployment but not expected to cope with an exceptionally severe depression. Measures outside the contributory unemployment insurance scheme would be taken during such an emergency. They would include assistance based on a means test for persons who, because of long unemployment, had exhausted their rights to insurance benefits, the necessary funds being provided by the state. Alternatively the state might extend the period of unemployment insurance benefits, and for this purpose make loans to the unemployment insurance service which would be repaid during years of good employment, or cancelled in whole or in part if, taking account of subsequent levels of unemployment, it would be inexpedient to collect bigger insurance contributions in order to repay the loans. Regardless of the source of the money that is paid out and of its repayment or cancellation, the existence of an organised scheme of unemployment insurance provides a valuable mechanism which can enable systematic provision to be made for the unemployed during a severe depression.

Britain's experience provides useful illustrations of these problems. Throughout the 1920's the widespread system of unemployment insurance worked smoothly and the scheme remained solvent. Early in the 1930's, however, unemployment was so severe that the unemployment insurance funds were exhausted, and the government decided to provide additional funds. There was no need to improvise arrangements for administering them, because two experienced systems—unemployment insurance and public assistance—were available, and their authorities worked closely together in putting the funds to efficient use. As employment improved, the insurance funds were built up again and by 1941 the depression loans were repaid. With much higher levels of employment during the war and for more than a decade afterwards big insurance reserves were accumulated.

When Sir William Beveridge prepared his social insurance report for the government in 1942 he had to take account of the high level of unemployment in Britain during the inter-war years; it had rarely fallen below 10 per cent. At the time of his investigations the financing of unemployment insurance was based on the assumption of an average rate of unemployment, through good years and bad, of about 15 per cent. Sir William based his plan on an average of $8\frac{1}{2}$ per cent of unemployment, assuming that unemployment would be substantially less than in inter-war years, and also taking account of the extension of unemployment insurance to categories among whom unemployment is low. In using this figure he expressed the hope that unemployment would be reduced below that level, but considered that it would not be prudent to base the financing of a scheme on any lower rate.[1] However, his hope was abundantly

[1] It was indicated in his report that when unemployment insurance began in 1913 and 1914, more than 95 per cent of all the unemployment in the insured industries occurred among men who had been unemployed for less than fifteen weeks, and that even if it did not prove possible to get back to that level of employment, it should be possible to make individual unemployment for more than twenty-six continuous weeks a rare thing in normal times. *Social Insurance and Allied Services* (London, 1942), p. 164.

realised and employment was at so high a level during the early post-war years that it proved practicable to reduce to 4 per cent the unemployment percentage on which the scheme was financially based and still build up big reserves.

Estimates of the effects of possible variations in economic and labour conditions on the size and solvency of the New York State Unemployment Insurance Trust Fund were made in 1956 for the six-year period 1956-62. Five alternative estimates were made, ranging from an optimistic to a pessimistic view of the future. On an optimistic view the estimated total of benefits which would be paid by the end of 1962 was $80 million, whereas on a pessimistic view it was $390 million, or nearly five times as much. On the optimistic assumption that expenditure on benefits would be low and income from employers' contributions high, the amount in the Fund at the end of 1962 would be $1,916 million, whereas on the pessimistic assumption that unemployment would be high, expenditure on benefits high and income reduced, the amount in the Fund at the end of 1962 would be $573 million. On the optimistic estimate the number of beneficiaries would be about 300,000 and the average duration of benefit eight weeks, whereas on the pessimistic estimate the former would be 900,000 and the latter fourteen weeks. Even on the pessimistic assumption, the Trust Fund would be solvent at the end of 1962.[2]

In Canada the accumulated reserve in the Unemployment Insurance Fund on March 31, 1958, totalled $743 million. The financial year which ended on that date was the second year in which expenditures had exceeded revenue since the inauguration of the Fund in 1941, the amount of the difference being just over $130 million. Even on the basis of the unusual unemployment in 1957-8 the Fund does maintain a high level of protection against any normal contingencies. The Canadian Fund would be able to support around 5 or 6 per cent of unemployment in the covered occupations out of its annual income without eating into its reserves. In the United States the percentage would be about 4 to 5 at average contribution rates in 1957, though the percentage would vary between states.

Although the financing of unemployment insurance cannot be controlled actuarially, it is desirable that schemes should be com-

[2] New York State Department of Labor, Division of Employment, *Potential Liability of the New York Unemployment Insurance Trust Fund under Various Economic and Legislative Assumptions, 1952-62* (July 1956). The estimates were made on the assumption that no changes in rates, duration and other conditions of benefit would be made in the law.

prehensively reviewed about every five or seven years in order to maintain solvency. Account should be taken of previous rates of unemployment, future prospects and existing reserves, and appropriate adjustments made in the rates of contribution and benefit.

In Britain and Canada the systems are uniform throughout the whole of each country, though in Canada the rates of contribution and benefit vary with earnings, whereas in Britain there is no such variation. In the United States, however, not only do contributions and benefits vary with earnings, but each state has its own legislation with its own rates of contribution, rates of benefit, duration of benefit and eligibility based on each worker's record of contributions. In big countries such as Canada and the United States, with considerable differences in wage levels in different economic regions, there are advantages in having some relation between earnings, contributions and benefits, though three or four categories of earnings would be preferable to double that number or to individual variations. The differences in the United States are a concession to the strength of opinion against federal encroachments and controls, but they give rise to economic and social disadvantages. For instance, the separate state systems tend to reduce the mobility of labour, as a worker who moves from one state to another loses his right to benefit until he has paid sufficient contributions in the state to which he has moved. In Canada the experiences of the depression years led the public to favour placing the responsibility for unemployment on the federal government, and the necessary legislation was enacted in 1941.

In many countries, unemployment insurance schemes to provide benefits without a means test are financed by tripartite contributions. Often, as in Britain, Belgium, the Netherlands, Norway and Canada, the employers' and workers' contributions are equal or almost equal. In almost all countries, both contributions and benefits vary with earnings, though not always in uniform proportion, as the contributions of the lower-paid workers are sometimes less in proportion to their earnings than are the contributions of workers with higher earnings. Then too, the benefits of lower-paid workers are sometimes somewhat subsidised by the contributions of those whose earnings are higher. In Britain, where contributions and benefits are at a flat rate, the lower-paid workers contribute a higher proportion of their wages but they receive benefits which are related to their wages.

Usually a major part of the cost is borne by the employers and the workers, and a much smaller part by the state. In some countries the state's financial participation consists in covering part or all of the costs of administration.[3] In Canada, however, the federal government not only pays the costs of administration but contributes an amount equal to one-fifth of the combined contributions of the employers and workers.[4] In the Federal Republic of Germany, unemployment *insurance* is financed solely by the employers and the workers, their contributions being equal, but, as in many other countries, the cost of unemployment *assistance* is borne wholly by the government. In Switzerland the employers' contributions to joint insurance funds must be at least one-third of their workers' contributions; in addition, payments may be made to the funds in the form of federal and cantonal grants.

In Sweden and Finland there are no contributions from employers, the insurance being financed by workers' contributions and subsidies from the public authorities. State grants in Sweden towards benefits average 50 per cent, but they range from 40 to 75 per cent according to the incidence of unemployment.[5] In Finland the public authorities contribute from one-half to two-thirds of the benefits paid, the proportion depending on the size of the benefits and the family circumstances of the beneficiaries.[6] In Denmark, employers' contributions form only about 5 per cent of the total revenue, workers' over 35 per cent and public authorities' more than 55 per cent.

In some countries, unemployment benefits are financed solely by the employers, for example in Italy and, with some exceptions, in the United States.[7] This method is also used, as in other parts of their social security system, in Soviet countries, where the business undertakings finance unemployment benefits. In the United States,

[3] In Austria the state covers 50 per cent of the administrative expenses, and a part of any deficits not exceeding one-half of the expenditure on emergency aid, which is paid, subject to a means test, to unemployed persons who have exhausted their insurance benefits.

[4] It also reimburses the Unemployment Insurance Fund for certain supplementary benefit payments, and may authorise the Unemployment Insurance Commission to obtain loans to meet deficits.

[5] The Swedish government also refunds 75 per cent of the expenditure for dependants' allowances paid to the unemployed and makes a grant towards costs of administration.

[6] *The Financing of Social Security*: *Report III* (Geneva, 1954), prepared by the International Labour Office for the European Regional Conference of the International Labour Organisation held in 1955, pp. 29, 30. In countries where there is no unemployment insurance the public authorities bear the whole cost of unemployment assistance, for example in France.

[7] In the United States, employers also bear the whole cost of the special Railroad Unemployment and Disability Insurance. In a few states, workers contribute to the unemployment insurance funds.

the federal government uses its powers of taxation to ensure the funds necessary to enable each state to establish a system of unemployment insurance. The standard rate of tax imposed on employers is 3 per cent of pay rolls, of which 2.7 per cent is available to the state governments to provide unemployment benefits; employers can offset against the federal tax any amounts up to 2.7 per cent which they pay in special state taxes used to provide unemployment benefits. Apart from a few general conditions the states have wide freedom in the standards of benefit they fix and the methods they apply. By this nation-wide pay roll tax system the states are enabled to provide insurance benefits for their unemployed workers without the fear of interstate competition which would arise if some states paid substantial benefits and others paid low rates or none at all.[8]

There is considerable merit in the tripartite system. Employers and workers make fairly equal substantial contributions, and the government pays the costs of administration and a small subsidy of 10 or 20 per cent of the cost of the benefits. It has advantages over less broadly based financing, and ensures that the beneficiaries contribute appreciably. A residual responsibility should rest on the state to provide cash benefits and organise public works and relief works outside the insurance system to meet severe and prolonged depressions.

Where the cost is borne by employers, as in the United States, the assumption seems to be made that employers are responsible for unemployment. Yet the main cause of unemployment is the varying impact of economic conditions; individual employers have only secondary opportunities to reduce unemployment, and the extent to which they can reduce it varies greatly from industry to industry. Moreover, employers usually transfer a large part of the cost of their contributions to the consumers by increasing prices, or to the workers by paying them less in wages, the proportions transferred being determined mainly by the economic conditions in each industry.

In the United States, which is one of the few countries (other than the Soviet countries) where employers pay the whole cost of unemployment insurance, a system of 'experience rating' is applied

---

[8] See: United States Department of Labor, "Twenty Years of Unemployment Insurance in the U.S.A., 1935-1955," *Employment Security Review*, Aug. 1955; and United States Department of Labor, Bureau of Employment Security, Unemployment Insurance Service, *Comparison of State Unemployment Insurance Laws as of December*, 1955 (Washington, 1956).

in all the states. In this system the pay roll tax which each employer pays may be higher or lower than the 2.7 per cent, mainly according to the amount of unemployment benefits drawn by workers previously employed by him.[9] He therefore has an inducement to keep his employment as stable as possible so that his tax rate may be reduced, but the possibilities of his doing so vary greatly from industry to industry. Though experience rating is to some extent a 'tax' on dismissals of workers, the gains to employers in securing lower rates are slight in practice and seem to have only minor effects in stabilising employment. Moreover, the system may deter employers from providing short-term jobs for unemployed people, and from taking on additional workers if the prospects of retaining them are uncertain. Also, employers have inducements to secure restrictions of benefits both in amount and duration, thereby providing reduced protection for the unemployed. One consequence has been that benefits and methods vary greatly between states. Yet proposals that federal standards should be set are opposed as constituting interference with the freedom of state legislatures to regulate their own affairs. The results of unemployment experience rating in the United States are not such as to commend the system.[10]

In the United States the intention of the legislation was that benefits should be 50 per cent of wages, but in practice the maximum benefits allowed have not been adjusted rapidly enough to keep pace with wages, and in the middle 1950's the average benefits were only about 34 per cent of earnings. In the fiscal year 1956 the average weekly benefit, including dependants' allowances, was $26.33; in 1955 the lowest average in any state was $17.06, the highest was $32.27 and the average for all states was $25.05. In 1956, the maximum duration of benefits for about 25 per cent of the covered work force was a uniform twenty-six weeks (thirty in Pennsylvania), and for 48 per cent the duration was variable, with a maximum of twenty-six weeks (twenty-six and a half in Wisconsin).

[9] The maximum rate varies from state to state; usually it is 2.7 per cent, and is nowhere more than about 4 per cent. The rate for each employer is frequently calculated on the basis of the relation between the benefits paid to his workers and the amount of his contributions. Most states fix minimum rates. In New York State the rates in 1955 ranged from 0.5 per cent of pay rolls to 2.7 per cent, the average being 1.53 per cent. The United States average in 1956 was 1.3 per cent, and the average benefit was 33.7 per cent of wages.

[10] The complexities of unemployment experience rating are reviewed by Eveline M. Burns in *Social Security and Public Policy* (New York, 1956), pp. 165-71, 184-8.

For the remaining 27 per cent the maxima were lower.[11]

In Canada the rates of contribution and benefit vary with earnings, as shown in Table VIII. The employers' contributions are equal to the workers', and the rate of their combined contribution is in the order of 2 per cent of wages, or 2-2/5 per cent if the federal government's contribution is included. This is substantially above the average rate of the pay roll tax paid by employers in the United States. A small reduction in the amount of benefit replaces a previous provision for five waiting days at the beginning of a worker's benefit year. The duration of a worker's benefit depends on his record of employment and contribution up to a maximum of thirty weeks' benefit. Because unemployment is high in some occupations during the winter, supplementary benefits are paid in those months to certain categories of workers whose rights to benefit have been exhausted. The rates of benefit for most categories are much higher than the old age pensions, but the latter are non-contributory and are paid from the age of seventy onwards.

TABLE VIII

Workers' Weekly Earnings, Contributions and Benefits, Canada, Unemployment Insurance Act, 1955*

Earnings (Dollars)	Contributions (Cents)	Benefits in Dollars No Dependants	One or more Dependants
24.00	30	11.00	15.00
30.00	36	13.00	18.00
36.00	42	15.00	21.00
42.00	48	17.00	24.00
48.00	52	19.00	26.00
54.00	56	21.00	28.00
60.00	60	23.00	30.00

In Britain, unemployment insurance benefits are paid at a flat rate and do not vary with earnings, and the ordinary adult rate is

[11] United States Department of Labor, Bureau of Employment Security, Unemployment Insurance Service, *Summary Tables for Evaluation of State Unemployment Insurance Benefits Provisions, as of October 15, 1956* (Washington, Nov. 1, 1956).

* The contributions are related to ranges of earnings. Thus workers earning $21.00 but under $27.00 a week contribute 30 cents. Benefits are also related to the same ranges of earnings. Workers who become sick while unemployed can continue to draw benefit. Few men in Canada would earn below $36.00 a week, and most women would earn more than $24.00. About 75 per cent of all insured workers are men.

the same as for sickness benefits, retirement pension and widows' pension.[12]

Unemployment insurance systems are supplemented in many ways. For example, a business undertaking may introduce systematic short time, that is, it may spread partial unemployment over all the workers instead of having some on full time and the rest totally unemployed. In some systems of unemployment insurance, workers on systematic short time may draw benefits to augment their reduced earnings. Another link has been made by the inclusion of a guaranteed annual wage or supplementary unemployment benefits in some collective agreements, notably in the steel and automobile industries in the United States. In such agreements, business undertakings guarantee minimum annual payments to defined categories of permanent workers, and the unemployment insurance benefits paid to workers temporarily laid off are regarded as constituting part of these guaranteed payments. Another form of provision by legislation or collective agreements in some countries is 'severance pay' for a worker who is dismissed, the amount varying with his length of service with the firm.

In the early stages of unemployment insurance, various classes of workers, agricultural workers for example, are usually excluded. As experience is gained, categories of workers initially excluded for administrative or other reasons are progressively brought into the system. Agricultural workers have been included in some countries but agriculture has some special features which differentiate it from industry. Thus, farmers and farm labourers alike may suffer distress akin to unemployment because of crop failure due to droughts, floods, unseasonable frosts, and other vagaries of nature. Often farmers, even though they are self-employed, have an income similar to that of employees in business and industry, and when their income is greatly reduced by causes such as those mentioned they need support. Those who cannot borrow from banks or other credit organisations may be given loans or grants to buy livestock, seeds, fertilisers or equipment, or may be provided with other forms of credit. These measures correspond somewhat in their purposes with unemployment insurance benefits for employed persons, but may be of greater assistance to farm families than cash payments for the purchase of food and clothing; moreover, they promote self-support. Public assistance and free medical care can be provided

[12] The new ordinary adult rate introduced in 1958 was 50s. a week, to which additions were made for dependants.

where necessary. Programmes of farm security, farm relief or prairie farm assistance are important in the United States, Canada and other countries where agriculture is a big element in the economy.[13]

Though cash benefits for the unemployed are an essential part of a comprehensive social security system, they are less fundamental than economic measures to sustain high levels of employment, the organisation of employment exchanges to bring together with a minimum of delay workers seeking jobs and employers needing workers, and the retraining of workers from declining industries for occupations in which the prospects of employment are good. The maintenance of unemployed workers should always be regarded as a temporary expedient to cover transitional periods of adjustment.

The establishment of employment exchanges is one of the first measures that should be introduced to deal with unemployment. The system of exchanges should be nation-wide, to ensure the fullest opportunities for movement from localities and industries where there is unemployment to localities and industries where workers are in demand. Employment exchanges are also essential for the administration of unemployment benefits. In the United States it is a condition of federal approval that any state system of unemployment insurance must pay benefits through public employment offices or other appropriate agencies. A co-ordinated national network of public employment offices has been built up through federal co-operation with state-administered employment services.[14] The services given involve a thorough study of the qualifications of each applicant for the requirements of the vacancies available.

Increased emphasis has been placed, especially since the Second World War, on training schemes. Workers may become unemployed because of a permanent decline in demand in their occupa-

[13] Under the Prairie Farm Assistance Act, passed in Canada in 1939, the federal government makes direct monetary payments to farmers in areas of low crop yields in the Prairie Provinces and in the Peace River District of British Columbia. Assistance is granted at a rate of $2.50 an acre on not more than one-half of cultivated land up to a maximum of 200 acres. The act is designed to assist municipalities and provinces, in years of crop failure, to meet relief expenditures which otherwise would be too great for them. The scheme is financed partly by a levy of 1 per cent of the purchase price of the grains marketed, and this levy covered about one-half of the expenditure up to 1953.
[14] An account of the development is given by the United States Department of Labor in "The Public Employment Service System, 1933-1953: A Brief History," *Employment Security Review*, June 1953.

N

tions, or because of technical changes in processes which call for new skills. For such workers training for new jobs is necessary. Often this training is given by business undertakings when they introduce new processes and techniques, and their workpeople can therefore be kept on. However, for many firms this is not practicable, and there is great value in the establishment of training centres by the public authorities to prepare workers for new occupations. This was done on a big scale for war service personnel on their return to civilian life, and has been continued as a permanent method of adjusting manpower to economic and industrial changes. Such re-training of able-bodied unemployed workers is the equivalent of, and is just as essential as, the rehabilitation of the victims of industrial and other accidents and of workers who, because of the effects of sickness, are unable to return to their former occupations. The schemes have so much in common that they should be closely co-ordinated.

WORKMEN'S COMPENSATION

In the early days of modern industry many processes were highly dangerous, and safeguards by means of factory legislation and inspection were meagre or non-existent. No system of workmen's compensation was in operation. When accidents occurred the workers were often blamed for them. Some employers, for humanitarian reasons or to avoid legal action, would pay something to injured workers or to the families of workers who had been killed, but the amounts were only a small fraction of the loss involved. Injured workers had the right to bring actions under common law and were entitled to damages if they could prove liability on the part of the employer. But they were ignorant of legal procedures, the procedures often proved to be costly because difficult questions of fact were involved, and there was a risk that the damages would be reduced or refused if the employer could prove contributory negligence by the worker. The right to sue was therefore of little value as a safeguard. When legislation properly extended the right to include compensation for industrial diseases the difficulties were increased, as it was often difficult to prove whether a worker's illness was a consequence of industrial processes or of some weakness or disease which would have resulted in a breakdown no matter where he had been employed.

Provision for the victims of industrial injuries was so seriously inadequate that towards the end of the nineteenth century and early in the present century workmen's compensation laws were passed in some of the leading industrial countries. These made employers responsible for paying compensation, at specified rates, for temporary disability, for permanent injuries according to the degree of incapacity (total or partial) and for fatal accidents. Some acts required employers to insure their risks so that small scale employers with insufficient funds of their own to pay compensation for a serious accident at their works would be able to meet their obligations. Employers who could satisfy the competent authority that they were in a strong enough financial position to pay compensation out of their own resources could be granted exemption from insurance. Some laws, however, left employers free to decide whether or not they would insure, and in consequence it frequently happened that injured workers could get little or no compensation.

The insurance companies varied from small ones with high administrative costs to big efficient undertakings, but, as the evidence from many countries shows, the average premiums charged for insurance were (and still are) high in relation to the compensation paid. Because industries and business undertakings vary widely in their risks of accidents, the insurance companies set the premiums higher or lower accordingly. Also, they would alter the rates charged to each employer within an industry, raising them if he had experienced a bad year and had involved the insurance company in heavy compensation payments, and lowering them after a good year. It is claimed that 'experience rating' offers a big financial incentive to employers to make every effort to reduce accidents. No doubt it was an important consideration half a century ago before factory acts, factory inspection and other industrial safety procedures were widely applied. Nowadays, however, these procedures exert increasing pressures on employers, and it seems unlikely that variations in premiums on the basis of accident experience do much to promote greater industrial safety. Indeed, the policy of varying the rates is being challenged.

What methods may be used to provide the money from which compensation is paid? In relation to the cost of a general system of old age pensions, public health services or family allowances, the cost of providing an adequate system of compensation for industrial injuries is comparatively small. Also, whether it is financed by employers only or by the joint contributions of employers and workers supplemented by the state, workmen's compensation is generally recognised as being a cost of production.[15] The work during which injury occurs is undertaken to provide goods and services for consumers, so the cost is more fairly borne by them (in the form of increased prices) than by employers. Yet though the cost is relatively small and the right of injured workpeople to compensation is undisputed, the systems in force in many countries are seriously inadequate. Workmen's compensation was one of the first aspects of social security to be regulated, but it was regulated in accordance with principles that are now out of date. The old laws and the administrative systems that were based on them have often not been brought into line with the widely accepted social policies of today.

The main requirements of a satisfactory system include safety and preventive measures in which labour representatives should participate, fair compensation for the injured worker and an effective system of rehabilitation to ensure that he is restored as quickly as possible to as high a degree of productive efficiency as can be effected by modern medicine and therapy. Litigation and other costs should be reduced to a minimum so that a high percentage of the amounts contributed will go to the injured worker. For permanent injury, whether total or partial, or for the death of a breadwinner, compensation should be in the form of a pension, not the lump sum that is still so often customary. Except in rare special circumstances, compensation should be given in a lump sum only for minor permanent injuries that involve only a 10 per cent or at the most a 20 per cent loss of capacity.

In Britain the system of financing benefits for persons injured at work, set out in the National Insurance (Industrial Injuries) Act of 1946 and put into operation in 1948, represents a new conception of social responsibility and a big advance in social solidarity, and the principles on which it is based are likely to gain support in other countries. One of its special features is that the same rates of contribution are paid in respect of a worker whether he is in a safe or

[15] In most countries the cost of workmen's compensation is borne solely by employers but in Britain it is financed by employers, workers and the state. In Greece the cost is covered by employers and workers. In some countries, including Germany, workers pay part of the cost through their contributions to sickness insurance funds from which benefits are paid for the first few weeks of sickness resulting from industrial accidents. In Denmark the state pays part of the industrial accident premiums due from small scale employers whose incomes are below a specified amount. In a few countries the state bears the administrative expenses of industrial injury schemes.

in a dangerous industry. This feature is socially sound. It is based on the argument that the industries with high accident risks are vital for the whole community—that their workers and employers produce goods and render services that are essential to workers and employers in safe occupations, and to consumers. Industries and occupations are interdependent, and it is fair and reasonable that the risks of dangerous industries should be pooled with those of safe industries.

A second special feature of the present British system is that it is not financed by the employers only, but by the joint contributions by all employers and workpeople and by a state subsidy.[16] This feature was largely consequent on the decision to pool the risks of the dangerous industries with those of the safe ones. As Sir William Beveridge pointed out in his report, 'There is no reason why the employer of a bank clerk or of a domestic servant, rather than the clerk or the domestic servant himself, should contribute to the cost of accidents in mines and ships. Insofar as there is community of interest between different industries, making it fair that all industries should share equally in providing for a risk which affects them unequally, this community of interest applies to the employees as well as to the employers.[17] Another argument in favour of this feature is that if workers make contributions themselves, they have a greater interest in the system than they would if the funds were provided only by their employers. Not infrequently, where social security schemes are financed only by employers, policies and administrative methods are applied which are less favourable to the workers than where there are joint contributions. A further argument in favour of joint contributions is that they remove the implication that industrial accidents are the fault of the employer.

A third feature of the British system is that, as in other parts of British National Insurance, both the contributions and the benefits for industrial injuries are at flat rates. They are the same for unskilled workers with low wages as for skilled craftsmen with high

---

[16] In 1958 the rate of contribution of an employed man for industrial injuries insurance was 8d. a week, his employer paid 9d. a week, and the state added one-fifth of the combined contribution of the worker and his employer. A woman employee paid 4d., her employer 5d., and the state added one-fifth of the joint contribution.

[17] *Social Insurance and Allied Services*, pp. 41, 42. Sir William Beveridge, however, favoured a special levy on employers in specially dangerous industries as an incentive to prevent accidents and diseases, and to that extent he deviated from the policy of the complete pooling of risks which was adopted by the government and enacted by Parliament.

wages.[18] In this respect the British system is different from the workmen's compensation systems in all other countries. It leaves employers and workers free to make additional provision, and the National Coal Board and the National Union of Miners by agreement have introduced a joint contributory scheme for the coalmining industry to supplement the National Insurance scheme. A scheme in which contributions and benefits varied with earnings, risks were pooled among all industries and contributions were made by workers as well as employers would be practicable and could, if desired, be devised.

In Canada, workmen's compensation systems are regulated by provincial legislation and financed solely by employers, higher contributions being made by employers in the more dangerous industries. In the Ontario system, which has many excellent features and has served as a model in other provinces, the industries are divided into twenty-six classes, each with one or more subdivisions or groups. The employers are assessed or rated for contributions according to the 'accident experience' of each class and group. In effect, each industrial class is a mutual insurance association for the employers of that class, but there is also a reserve to provide funds in case a disaster in any one class should cost more than that class alone could meet. To that extent the accident fund is one and indivisible, and liability rests on all industry collectively.

The Ontario Workmen's Compensation Board makes the assessments and administers the accident fund. This method has great advantages over the method of leaving employers to insure their liabilities independently with private accident insurance companies. The Board can operate at much lower administrative costs and can apply co-ordinated policies. In particular it is responsible for medical care and rehabilitation, and its administration in this field, in which it has established effective co-operation with the medical profession, has been remarkably successful. The number of persons permanently disabled has been reduced until it forms less than 4 per cent of those temporarily disabled, a proportion which must be one of the lowest anywhere in the world. The Board is responsible for decisions on compensation, and its decisions are final. Because cases do not go before the courts, heavy litigation costs and delays in reaching decisions are avoided.

In the United States, the position is less satisfactory in most states than it is in Britain and in some of the Canadian provinces. Adminis-

[18] As is indicated later there are various supplementary benefits to provide equitable compensation for persons in special circumstances.

trative costs are unduly high, medical care and rehabilitation services are inadequate and litigation is excessive. Many state laws provide for compensation for total disability at a maximum of two-thirds of loss of earnings but in practice much less is received. Dr and Mrs Somers state that 'Overhead costs—insurance, legal fees, and administration—consume about half of the total costs of compensation. This means that employers are paying out about twice as much as their employees obtain in benefits. The cost of insurance is the major element in this overhead.'[19] They also say that 'It is doubtful whether average compensation benefits now replace as much as one-third of wage loss. In many States compensation payments do not compare favorably even with ordinary poor relief standards.' Their investigations showed that the problem is especially acute for the permanently injured and for the survivors of those killed on the job, the indemnity in these cases being even lower proportionately than for temporary cases, 'probably not exceeding 20 per cent of wage loss on the average, with death cases faring worst of all.'[20] Yet the total cost of workmen's compensation to American employers in 1955 was estimated to be about $1,500 million a year, or 1.0 per cent of the·covered pay roll.[21] Dr and Mrs Somers note further that 'Most States pay lip service to rehabilitation as a basic principle of workmen's compensation, but few, if any, do much about it. Indeed, present workmen's compensation practices are frequently alleged to be a deterrent to effective rehabilitation.'[22] As responsibility for providing and controlling medical care is divided. in most states, between the employers and the insurance companies there is lack of a constructive policy.

There is also a lack of co-ordination among the various social security agencies, so that although compensation for industrial injuries is often only a small fraction of the loss involved, 'It is possible, for example, that survivors of a fatally injured worker, who are eligible for workmen's compensation death benefits, OASI survivor benefits, and benefits from one or more collectively bargained group insurance plans, may be entitled to considerably

[19] Herman Miles Somers and Anne Ramsay Somers, *Workmen's Compensation* (New York, 1954), p. 269.
[20] *Ibid.*, p. 273.
[21] A total of $920 million in payments for wage loss and medical benefits was spent under the workmen's compensation programmes in 1955. The number of covered workers in an average week was estimated to be between 39 million and 40 million.
[22] *Workmen's Compensation*, p. 269.

more than the total wage loss suffered."[23]

Under the Federal Employees' Compensation Act the rates of compensation are usually much higher in practice than under state laws, the total disability rate being two-thirds of loss of earnings for persons without dependants, and three-quarters for those with dependants. Under the Federal Employees' Liability Act, railway workers and seamen, who can claim in the courts against their employers, have frequently been awarded large amounts in recent years, but the payments are made as lump sums.

Various problems are encountered in deciding what should be paid to an injured worker and to the dependants of a worker who has been killed in an industrial accident. Injuries range from minor temporary ones to major permanent or fatal ones. Often over 90 per cent of injuries are temporary and within a few weeks or at most a few months the workers concerned are back at work and suffer no permanent consequences. For such cases, what is needed is medical care and income maintenance during the period of recovery. The basis for income maintenance in almost all countries has been compensation for loss of earnings while the workers are away from their jobs.

The problems of compensation are more complex when injuries are permanent and involve either partial or total incapacity. A worker may have lost one eye or both, an ear, hands, a foot or leg, or may have sustained internal injuries which permanently undermine his health and efficiency. There is first the difficulty of deciding the degree of incapacity, and this decision must often be somewhat arbitrary. Then the same physical injury may be much more serious for workers in some occupations than for others: the loss of a finger would prevent a pianist from continuing his career whereas it would be little handicap to a tram conductor or an elevator attendant. Loss of hearing would exclude a piano tuner from remaining in that occupation but might have little effect on a textile weaver.

Not only is there the question whether an injured worker can continue in his occupation and the loss of efficiency if he does so, but, if compensation is to be paid for reduced earning capacity, consideration must be given to the amount he will be able to earn in a new occupation. It happens not infrequently that a man compelled by injury to give up his occupation is so successful in a new one that he earns much more than before. It is on record that a skilled British industrial worker, unable to resume his job because

[23] *Ibid.*, p. 288.

of an accident at work, turned to lecturing and writing, from which his income was substantial, and, entering politics, became prominent in public life. In such circumstances, should no compensation be paid for the permanent disability sustained?

The difficulty of assessing loss of earning capacity has led to abuses. Employers and insurance companies have offered an injured worker a job at wages equal to or only slightly below his former earnings and have then argued that little or no compensation was necessary; but had the worker been dismissed some months after the compensation claim had been settled, perhaps at a time of slack trade, he would have found it impossible to prove that he had been dismissed because his efficiency had been reduced by the injury. Another consequence of this abuse was that an injured worker had little incentive to co-operate with rehabilitation services for fear of reducing his compensation. In these circumstances, workmen's compensation became a happy hunting ground for lawyers, and legal expenses often cut heavily into compensation payments.

Employers and insurance companies have greatly preferred to pay compensation for permanent disability in a lump sum rather than have to find resources for pensions which might continue for many years. However, payment in a lump sum is usually seriously unfair to the worker concerned, though he himself may be attracted by a lump sum equal to say three years' earnings: it may seem big money to him, and he may think he can use it as capital to start a retail business. However, even if he does not lose his money in that way or by wasteful spending, he is likely to find himself quickly in serious need. He may be a man in his twenties or thirties, with a young family to support, and a lump sum, which will probably be used up in three or four years at most, is gravely inadequate as compensation for total or serious permanent incapacity. His future can be safeguarded only by a pension to cover basic needs, and even this should be increased periodically in times of inflation to compensate for the declining value of money.

As has already been indicated, the fact that in almost all countries workmen's compensation has been based on employers' liability has resulted in excessive litigation, inconsistent decisions and costly administration. It was largely to get rid of the nuisance of litigation with its uncertainties and perplexities that Ontario, followed by all the other Canadian provinces, adopted the system of placing the adjudication of compensation claims in the hands of a board instead of the courts. The British system also removes burdensome litigation from the great majority of claims.

In some systems, including those in the United States and Canada, the workmen's compensation laws provide that the granting of compensation rights under those laws is accompanied by the withdrawal of the workers' right to claim damages under the common law by court action based on employers' liability due to negligence.[24] One of the purposes of this abolition of common law claims was to reduce litigation. This aim has been achieved in Ontario, where final decisions are taken by the Workmen's Compensation Board, but not in the United States, where within the workmen's compensation system there is 'prodigious litigation.'[25]

The question must be considered whether the obtaining of rights under workmen's compensation laws should involve the giving up of all other rights to compensation. The answer depends on the adequacy of the payments made under workmen's compensation laws, and especially on the extent to which the system is flexible enough to deal equitably with the many variable circumstances which can arise; for example, it ought to be able to adjust its rate of compensation for the loss of a hand according to the effect of that loss on the earnings of a particular worker. Then many workmen's compensation laws specify maximum rates of compensation for various degrees of injuries, and these may be seriously inadequate. It would seem, therefore, that rights under workmen's compensation laws should not deprive workers of other rights if they have a case for additional compensation. Naturally employers wish to know the extent of their liabilities, and are in favour of restricting workers' rights to those provided in the workmen's compensation laws. However, even if the right to claim additional compensation in the courts is retained, the great majority of cases will be settled within the system established by the workmen's compensation laws and action for additional compensation will be taken in only a relatively few cases because of special circumstances for which that system is inadequate.

In the British system until 1948, injured workers or the dependants of workers who had been killed had to choose between claiming under the workmen's compensation legislation and making direct claims for damages against the employers. They could not

[24] Workmen covered by these laws have no right of action against their employers for injury from an accident that occurs during employment. Workpeople not covered by workmen's compensation laws, and railway workers and seamen under their special legislation in the United States, retain the common law right of court action.

[25] Somers and Somers, *Workmen's Compensation,* Preface, p. ix.

do both, and many preferred the greater certainty of the former to the risks of the latter. Since 1948, however, compensation has been payable under the industrial injuries insurance system, but workers also have the additional right to court action for damages.

Compensation may be based on loss of earnings at the rate at which they were being paid during a period shortly preceding the accident, on loss of potential earnings, on need or on the degree of physical injury—the loss of an arm or leg, for instance. There can therefore be considerable differences in rates of compensation. Most systems fix the rate on earnings before the accident, which are usually readily ascertainable. Potential earnings are difficult to estimate, though it is fair (especially in the case of young workers) that accounts should be taken of the future earnings which workers would have been likely to gain had it not been for a handicap caused by an accident. Compensation based on need tends to result in similar flat rates of benefit for skilled and unskilled workers alike. Compensation based on degree of physical injury also results in flat rates of payment for skilled and unskilled workers alike, without allowance for differences in earnings.

The British system of industrial injuries insurance has departed from the usual method of compensation for permanent disability based on loss of earning capacity, and applies flat rates of compensation according to 'loss of faculty', that is, degrees of incapacity measured by physical loss such as loss of feet, hands, eyes and so on.[26] Proportionate pensions are paid for disability of 20 per cent and upwards, whereas for disability of less than 20 per cent the compensation is a lump sum. Since it is paid at flat rates, the compensation is generally the same for a similar physical injury irrespective of differences in earnings. Compensation for total disability caused by industrial accidents is paid at a higher weekly rate than sickness and unemployment benefits. Industrial injury pensions and other payments are granted to persons who are still disabled after twenty-six weeks during which injury benefits in cash and medical care have been provided.

There are important supplements to the basic compensation. If an injured worker is still sick or is unemployable he receives a supplement, and additional amounts for his wife and other dependants. Additional payments may also be made where there is special hardship, and this provision enables some allowance to be

---

[26] Compensation is paid even if there is contributory negligence on the part of the worker. If, however, there is wilful misconduct, compensation is paid only if the injury results in death or serious permanent disablement.

made where injury prevents a worker from continuing in his occupation and involves his going into a less remunerative one; in effect, some account is taken of loss of earnings. Supplements are also paid to workers whose injuries necessitate constant attendance. The pensions are paid, as already indicated, at a flat rate regardless of the beneficiaries' former earnings, but it is of interest to show them as percentages of wages. The basic pension would come to about 50 per cent of the former wages of an unskilled worker, but if he were entitled to supplements for unemployability, and for a wife and one child, the total would amount to about 80 or 90 per cent of his former wages; for a skilled worker, the basic pension would come to about $33\frac{1}{3}$ per cent, and the pension and the same supplements to about 50 or $66\frac{2}{3}$ per cent of former wages.[27] Compensation for loss of faculty is set without any consideration of future earnings, so workers who receive it are entirely free to earn whatever they can without affecting their pension.

The rates have been increased from time to time to compensate for the effects of inflation. It must be emphasised that in countries where workmen's compensation rates vary with the earnings of the injured workers and where, also, maximum rates of compensation are fixed, the effect of inflation is to make the system of compensation approach progressively towards a flat rate system, unless the maxima are frequently adjusted to make allowance for the fall in the purchasing power of money. The effect is particularly severe on the more highly paid workers.

In the British system all medical costs are covered by the National Health Service. Here the question may be considered how medical care and rehabilitation can best be provided for victims of industrial accidents. Results show that if the responsibility is left to employers, the insurance companies and the injured workers, there will be no clear co-ordinated policy and the insurance companies will be mainly concerned with paying the medical bills. Where responsibility rests with boards or institutes appointed by the government, excellent work has been done in rehabilitation.

In some countries, particularly in South America, social security institutes set up to provide cash benefits and medical care for victims of industrial accidents and also for sickness among workers

---

[27] In 1958, the basic pension for total disability was 85s., the unemployability or sickness supplement 50s., for special hardships up to 34s., for constant attendance up to 35s. or for the most serious cases 70s., for wife 30s, and for the first child 20s. For widows, the pension during the first thirteen weeks was 70s a week and thereafter 56s.

have often found serious shortages of hospital and clinical accommodation to meet the needs of their contributors. They have, therefore, used some of their financial resources to provide such accommodation and also rehabilitation centres. However, the treatment
of victims of industrial accidents and diseases is only a part of a
larger problem which includes those who suffer injuries on the
roads or at home. There are good grounds for the special organisation of medical care by workmen's compensation authorities and
social security institutes if there is a shortage of facilities or if there
is not an adequate public health service, but as soon as practicable
all services dealing with the same problems should be brought under
unified control. This is necessary in order to avoid duplication, confusion and discrimination. In particular, the best possible rehabilitation services should be available without distinction for all victims
of accidents, not only for the sake of economy in organisation, but
for the welfare of the individuals and the productivity of the
community.

LONG-TERM DISABILITY

From the standpoint of social security, long-term disability, whether
partial or total, presents a difficult problem. Some cases of total
disability are clearly defined, but many are near the border that
separates the employable from the unemployable. The line between
those for whom there are prospects of recovery after long treatment
and those whose disability from ill health is likely to be permanent
is often blurred. People whose disability is caused by premature
ageing are on an ill-defined boundary between sickness and old age.
Some people are born with physical or mental disabilities or become
disabled in childhood or youth, and are either unemployable or are
handicapped in varying degrees as workers. Some are disabled by
accidents or by war service.

Social assistance is the main method of providing for disabled
persons, except for those disabled by industrial accidents or war
service, or those so near pensionable age that they can be granted
old age pensions at somewhat reduced rates. Sickness and unemployment insurance schemes are not applicable as their benefits
are of limited duration, usually three or six months and rarely
more than a year. Consequently persons suffering from long-term
disabilities exhaust their rights to insurance benefits. Long-term
disability can, however, be covered by social insurance.

In the United States, totally and permanently disabled persons who are fifty years of age or more and are qualified for benefits because of their contribution record can be granted pensions under the Old-Age, Survivors, and Disability Insurance Program which was extended in 1957 to cover such persons. Pensions are paid only where the disability is severe and the person is virtually helpless and in need of continued attendance and supervision. They are paid till the person reaches sixty-five years of age and becomes entitled to an old age pension. The Program was also extended to enable monthly benefits to be paid to disabled persons over the age of eighteen who are unable to support themselves by working, provided they were totally disabled before reaching that age.[28] Disabled people not covered by this system because they are under fifty years of age or have not qualified by their contributions may receive public assistance, and almost all the states administer assistance programmes for persons who are permanently and totally disabled. The federal government makes substantial grants to the state governments towards the cost.

In Canada totally and permanently disabled people who are eighteen years of age and over may obtain regular public assistance under the Allowances for Disabled Persons Act, 1954. As in the United States the test of disability is stringent. By agreement between the federal and provincial governments, the federal government pays 50 per cent of allowances of $55.00 a month, or half the amount paid, whichever is the less. A maximum annual income that includes the allowance is fixed, and grants are paid only to persons whose incomes are less. Once allowances have been granted they are in effect pensions, and the only supervision needed is to determine whether there have been changes in income or a substantial improvement in health, the latter probably being rare in view of the stringent standards of disability applied.

Various countries make special provision for the blind. Thus, in Canada, the provinces pay allowances to blind persons. Subject to certain limits, each province is free to fix the maximum allowance and the maximum income, and to adjust them to changes in the cost of living if it wishes to do so. The federal government has power to contribute 75 per cent of $55.00 a month or of the allowance paid, whichever is the less, to each blind person aged twenty-

---

[28] The cost of the total disability benefits is financed by an additional contribution of $\frac{1}{4}$ per cent on the earnings of employees, to be paid both by employer and employee, thereby raising their total contributions to $2\frac{1}{4}$ per cent; for self-employed persons the addition is $\frac{3}{8}$ per cent on earnings, making their total $3\frac{3}{8}$ per cent.

one or over.[29] In Australia and New Zealand, payments, subject to a means test, are made to persons who are blind or totally and permanently incapacitated for work. In the United States the federal government makes substantial payments to the states towards the maintenance of the blind.

WIDOWS AND ORPHANS

Older workers become increasingly concerned about provision for their old age, whereas young married workers and those in early middle life are anxious for the security of their wives and children. The breadwinners desire assurance that if they die early or become seriously incapacitated their dependants will not be destitute. As a great majority of widows with dependent children, and of orphans, are likely to be in need, the most satisfactory method of provision is by contributory insurance or by the method used in Canada for old age pensions and family allowances. Generally a means test should not be applied, the essential conditions being the fact of widowhood and of children below the age for leaving school.

In Britain and the United States, insurance systems provide protection for large numbers of widows and orphans to whom benefits are paid without means tests. Those who are not eligible under the insurance system may be given public assistance benefits on the basis of a means test. In Canada, Australia and New Zealand public or social assistance benefits subject to a means test are paid.

In the British system of National Insurance, widows are paid an allowance during the first thirteen weeks of widowhood, plus an allowance for each dependent child. Afterwards, a widow with one or more dependent children receives the widowed mothers' allowance together with allowances for the children.[30] The widows' pension is paid to older or infirm widows without dependent children. Guardians' allowances are paid in respect of orphan children. There

[29] This power is accorded by the Blind Persons Act, 1952. A residence qualification of at least ten years is required. Some provinces make supplementary payments to blind persons: in Saskatchewan the supplement in 1957 was $2.50 a month without a means test; in Alberta and British Columbia it was $10.00 a month, subject to a means test.
[30] In 1958 the rate of widows' benefit for the first thirteen weeks was 70s. a week, plus 20s. for the first child and 12s. for the second and each further dependent child. After the first thirteen weeks a widowed mother received 56s. a week together with the allowances for children until the youngest child living with her reached eighteen years of age. These allowances for children are higher than those under the Family Allowances Act. The pension for older and infirm widows is the same as the retirement pension.

are national assistance grants for those whose essential needs cannot be met by the insurance benefits. The care of children without normal homes is provided specially by the Children's Act, 1948, including care in foster homes and institutions, and adoption.

In the United States, widows, their dependent children and orphans are protected on the death of the breadwinner under the Old-Age, Survivors, and Disability Insurance Program if the contribution record of the breadwinner satisfies the conditions. The amount of benefit depends on the number and age of the children and also varies with the earnings of the deceased worker. Monthly allowances are payable to children under eighteen years of age, to their mothers, and to aged widows. No benefit is paid to a mother who remarries, or after the youngest child reaches eighteen years of age. Widows and children of persons not qualified for benefits under the Program, or under the special system for railroad employees, may obtain public assistance based on a means test as administered within each state, the federal government making financial contributions.

In Canada all the provinces have laws which provide for needy mothers and their children.[31] The total cost is borne by the provincial governments except in Alberta, where a part of each allowance is charged to the municipality where the beneficiary resides. There is no federal subvention. The conditions of eligibility vary from province to province, but means tests are applied in all of them. Allowances are paid only to those whose incomes are below specified amounts, and in some provinces private assets may be controlled by the administrative authority for the benefit of the mother and children. The maximum allowances that may be paid are regulated. The system is essentially a special form of social assistance, as all applicants must prove need. In various provinces, the beneficiaries may obtain free medical care. Allowances may be paid to foster mothers and to mothers who have adopted children.

In New Zealand the main provision on the death of the breadwinner is the payment of benefit to widows who are mothers of one or more children under sixteen years of age, or who, having been

---

[31] See Department of National Health and Welfare, Research Division, *Mothers' Allowances Legislation in Canada*, Memorandum no. 1, Social Security Series (Ottawa, Jan. 1955). In the early stages provision was mainly for women whose husbands were dead or incapacitated, but it has been extended to cover desertion, and may extend to families where the husbands are serving penal sentences, and to divorced and unmarried mothers. In 1955, more than 40,000 families with some 109,000 children were assisted at a cost in allowances of over $22 million.

married for not less than fifteen years have had one or more children, or, having been married for not less than five years were widowed after reaching fifty years of age. The rate of benefit is subject to a means test, and benefit ceases if the widow remarries. Benefits without a means test are payable in respect of all children. Orphans' benefit, subject to a means test, may be paid instead of family allowances for children who have lost both parents.[32]

In Australia provision is on similar lines to that in New Zealand and payments are subject to a means test.

MATERNITY

Many systems of social insurance provide maternity benefits for women workers for a specified number of weeks beginning some time before confinement and continuing afterwards. These serve to compensate in part for loss of wages. In Britain allowances are paid for eighteen weeks, starting from the eleventh week before confinement, to those who are eligible by their insurance contributions.[33] Other women are paid smaller allowances for thirteen weeks. In addition, a maternity grant of £12 10s. is paid for each child born.[34] In Australia maternity grants of £15 are paid for the first child born, and somewhat larger grants for the others. In New Zealand free services are available at state maternity hospitals, and payment is made from the Social Security Fund to the hospitals, medical practitioners and nurses for their services in maternity cases.

Social insurance in Canada and the United States makes no provision for maternity grants or allowances before and after confinement. In these and many other countries public moneys are used to provide advice and services at pre-natal and post-natal clinics for mothers and infants.

GENERAL

The infinite variety of human needs makes it inevitable that no system of social security can be devised that will anticipate and provide in specific terms for every possible contingency. The history of industrial development in a particular country, the nature of its predominant industries, the cultural attitude to state action in

[32] *New Zealand Official Year Book.*
[33] In 1958 the rate for insured women workers was 50s. a week.
[34] An additional grant of £5 is payable as a home confinement grant where the mother does not make use of free or assisted institutional confinement under the National Health Service or otherwise at public expense.

O

providing social protection and many other factors will determine which contingencies are recognised as appropriate for inclusion in its social security system. For example, it will be appropriate for a country which has a relatively high proportion of older people in its population to place emphasis on homemaker services, and for a country with a high proportion of children and young adults to place emphasis on effective training and employment services. It would not be possible within the confines of a single book to explore all the various additional contingencies which can be provided against or to assess the relative weight of different parts of a social security system in one country as against another. The major risks of an industrial society have been dealt with in this and earlier chapters of this book. Other contingencies are likely to affect only relatively small fractions of the population and compared with the major risks are not likely to involve large financial costs. In so far as these risks are not included specifically in a social insurance system they must be covered by an adequate system of public or general social assistance.

CHAPTER XI

SOME ECONOMIC CONSIDERATIONS

Although social security is primarily humanitarian in purpose, it has significant economic aspects of which the public is not sufficiently aware. In previous chapters, incidental references have been made to some of these features, but they will now be examined somewhat more fully. What is said is in the nature of comment and the raising of problems. Much more information and experience of social security will be needed before firm conclusions can be reached.

In all countries high levels of employment and high standards of health and education are recognised as vital elements in security and social welfare. In some countries, particularly Canada and the United States, special emphasis is placed on progressive expansion of the economy, including large-scale capital investment, as the best way to raise standards of living, thereby increasing the capacity of the people to provide to a greater extent for their own security and reducing their dependence on social security measures introduced by the state.[1] In these countries there is wide support for free enterprise and personal incentive, and anything that hampers them is opposed. Economic prosperity and higher standards of living will result in high levels of employment, and it follows that the cost of unemployment benefits will be small, more people will be able to provide for their own needs by saving and therefore fewer people will need public assistance; moreover, a high demand for labour will provide more opportunities for older people to continue working and might make it possible to raise the age at which old age pensions are payable. Similarly a good health programme can increase the fitness and productivity of the population and reduce the cost of sickness benefits; adequate housing is also a big factor in health and security. Better education and vocational training

[1] This point was emphasised by Professor Harry M. Cassidy in an unpublished memorandum written in 1947 on "The Premises and Principles of Social Security," p. 1: "It is a truism that jobs for all represent the best kind of economic security. To the extent to which there is economic prosperity, the pressure of demands for social services, particularly income-maintenance services, will be greatly reduced."

result in greater efficiency and productivity and diminish the risks and costs of unemployment.

Both preventive services and constructive economic policies are, therefore, closely linked to social security. 'Social progress and economic progress are interdependent, each making its distinctive positive contribution to the general development and to the improvement of levels of living. Social programmes cannot, on the one hand, be regarded merely as devices for exploiting the gains from each new economic advance by distributing more equitably the fruits of joint labour and ensuring a minimum level of living for everyone in the midst of life's vicissitudes. Nor can they be considered merely as a means of improving the "human capital" required for production, for that would be tantamount to regarding human betterment as a means to a materialistic end, whereas it is in fact the end of all collective social endeavour.'[2]

In public discussion attention is often directed to the economic costs of social security but much less frequently to the economic costs of insecurity. The reason is largely that the former are immediate and definite whereas the latter often appear only in the long run and are difficult to evaluate. It is argued that a country's power to compete in world markets will be weakened if its social security costs are greater than those of its rivals in trade. Little account is, however, taken of the gains in efficiency which a country derives from its expenditure on social security, and there is no evidence that any country has been hampered in its international trade by the costs of social security at current standards. It is much more likely to gain in competitive power because its human resources are protected against deterioration and because its production is benefited, especially by health and rehabilitative services and children's allowances. A large part of social security expenditure, probably as much as 70 or 80 per cent, pays for itself, and some parts of it yield handsome dividends. Programmes of health and child welfare are indeed valuable investments in a country's human capital.

The amount available for social security is determined in relation to other demands on the national income, including capital for in-

[2] From a report on a co-ordinated policy regarding family levels of living submitted to the United Nations by a group of experts under the chairmanship of Dr George F. Davidson, Deputy Minister of Welfare in the Canadian Department of National Health and Welfare, and jointly sponsored by the United Nations and the International Labour Organisation in co-operation with other specialised agencies of the United Nations. See United Nations document E/CN. 5/321, Feb. 28, 1957, Appendix.

vestment and expenditure on defence. In circumstances of international crisis an increase in expenditure on defence may be more vital for social security than bigger old age pensions and unemployment benefits. Within social security itself some items are more urgent and vital than others, and decisions must be taken on priorities. Such decisions are necessary because resources are usually scarce in relation to the demand for them. Economics is built on the fact of scarcity of resources. There may be plentiful supplies or even surpluses of some commodities, but a nation's income is never sufficient fully to meet all needs. Consequently, if more is spent for one thing, less is available for others, and therefore priorities must be established and limitations imposed.[3] Such priorities are determined by public opinion and political pressures. Opinions and pressures result from people's preferences, and many people choose expenditure on immediate enjoyment and neglect provision for such uncertainties as illness and unemployment. To young people, the satisfaction of present needs has a more powerful attraction than the laying aside of funds to meet the distant and uncertain needs of old age. This attraction is indeed the basis of instalment buying or hire purchase which is in effect a mortgage on the future and makes the need for stability of employment and other forms of social security all the greater.

UNDERDEVELOPED COUNTRIES

One of the most difficult decisions which must be taken by governments of economically poor, underdeveloped countries is to determine the proportion of the national income that should be set aside for capital investment. A sufficient amount must be used for that purpose to increase productivity and thereby raise future standards of living, but present standards are so low that substantial diversions from immediate consumption may cause hardship and privation and weaken by poverty the productive efficiency of large numbers of people. It has been estimated that an underdeveloped country with a typical rate of population increase of $1\frac{1}{2}$ to 2 per cent a year should save for capital investment at least 10 to 12 per cent of its net national income if it is to sustain a process of economic development that will give reasonable assurance of a

---

[3] When labour and capital are idle during a depression, they can be brought into productive use without causing a reduction in output elsewhere. When, however, there is full employment, an increase in expenditure on camps, airfields and military equipment means a reduction in the building of houses, hospitals, schools, motor cars and television sets.

long-term rise in standards of living.[4] Yet many underdeveloped countries in recent years do not appear to have been saving more than about 5 per cent of their national income.

In favourable circumstances appreciable amounts of foreign capital may be available, but generally countries must rely largely on their own resources for investment funds. Unless, therefore, stagnation is to persist, priority for development is essential, and social security schemes should be restricted to meeting the most urgent needs. Also, since in over-populated countries there is usually much under-employment and concealed unemployment, plans involving relatively small capital costs but using these idle reserves of labour are specially suitable for increasing productivity.

Because resources in relation to population are so meagre in economically poor, over-populated countries, decisions on social security priorities are particularly difficult and painful. There is so much to be done and so little to do it with. The experts who in 1956 undertook for the United Nations a study of a co-ordinated policy regarding family levels of living indicated priorities for underdeveloped countries.[5] In their report, while emphasising that each country has its own special problems and priorities, they were generally in favour of giving priority to preventive measures and the organisation of social services which would promote economic development, and expressed preference for benefits in the form of goods and services. Inevitably they recommended absolute priority for assistance in the form of food and other goods to persons in urgent need. They advised that the establishment of institutions to provide welfare services for mothers and children be given priority over family allowances, and that health, rehabilitation and social advisory services be given priority over social security systems that would provide cash benefits.

A main difficulty in countries with large populations and low wages is that so many people are near or even below subsistence level. Comprehensive schemes of cash benefits are impracticable because resources are limited and because the number of poor people is large in relation to the funds available. Social security benefits fixed substantially below current wages would be at starvation levels. Shortages of trained administrative personnel and social welfare workers in these countries also limit the adoption of extensive social security programmes. The main practicable solu-

---

[4] See United Nations document 11.B.2, *Measures for the Economic Development of Underdeveloped Countries* (1951), p. 76, Table 2.
[5] U.N. document E/CN. 5/321, App., esp. paragraphs 69-74, 120.

tion under such conditions is the one already indicated of providing benefits in the form of goods and services (free meals particularly) to specially necessitous people.

In some underdeveloped countries, for example Burma and Venezuela, contributory schemes of social insurance against sickness and occupational accidents have been introduced among industrial workers in the cities. Cash benefits are paid but great emphasis is placed on medical care and rehabilitation services. Except for compensation payments to permanently disabled workers, the financing of these schemes is relatively easy since it is mainly concerned with immediate and short-term requirements and is free from the complexities of long-term liabilities such as are involved in systems of old age pensions and unemployment insurance. At the same time valuable experience is gained in administering sickness and accident rehabilitation services and cash benefits.

SOCIAL SECURITY AS A FACTOR IN ECONOMIC STABILITY

Social security is sometimes described as a 'built-in' economic stabiliser. It has frequently been supported not only for the benefits it brings to individuals and their families, but also because it increases the stability of the economy. In Canada this was one of the reasons for the introduction of the family allowance system shortly after the end of the Second World War, as it was thought that there might soon be a severe trade depression similar to that which followed the First World War and that its severity would be mitigated by the regular payment of allowances for each dependent child in a family.

A distinction must be drawn between the stabilising effects of benefits which will remain fairly constant in total amount during boom and depression and those which are relatively small when trade is good and are much greater in bad times. Among the former are children's allowances, allowances for widows and orphans, sickness benefits, industrial accident benefits and old age pensions. The constancy of these payments is in itself a stabilising factor, but it is largely neutral to fluctuations in prosperity. Sickness benefits may increase somewhat in a period of depression and so may old age pensions because of the earlier retirement of aged people who find increased difficulty in retaining or securing employment, but the changes would be slight.

The two main benefits that fall in prosperity and rise in depression are unemployment insurance and public assistance payments. They put a brake on booms and reduce the severity of depressions. Unemployment insurance funds grow in booms and are reduced in depressions, both movements exerting a stabilising tendency. The larger amounts paid to the unemployed when trade is bad are almost entirely spent immediately on food and other consumers' goods and prevent the industries that produce these goods from being as depressed as they otherwise would be. Also the sustaining of these industries reacts favourably on the industries that produce capital goods.

However, the beneficial effects in curbing the fluctuations of the trade cycle must not be exaggerated. The decline in purchasing power in a depression is much greater than the increases in social insurance and assistance payments to the unemployed. If, for example, Britain were to suffer a severe depression in which unemployment rose to about 12 per cent compared with the low levels of less than 2 per cent in the years of good employment in the middle 1950's, the additional numbers unemployed would total about 2 million and their loss of wages would be at a rate of over £1,000 million a year, not including the loss caused by short time and reduced overtime. Not more than about a third of the loss would be compensated by unemployment benefits, leaving a deficit in the purchasing power of workpeople of something in the order of £700 million, some of which, however, would be met by drawing on savings or by running into debt.[6] In Canada there was a steady increase in the size of the Unemployment Insurance Fund until at March 1957 the Fund stood at over $874 million. In 1957-8 the amount paid in contributions was substantially less than the amount paid out in benefits, so that the Fund fell to a little over $744 million in March 1958 and has fallen still further in the most recent year.[7] With a total unemployment of well over 500,000, the probable loss in earnings would be at a rate of perhaps $1,500 million a year, of

[6] Workpeople who exhausted their right to unemployment insurance benefits because of prolonged unemployment, usually of six months or more, would generally receive public assistance benefits.

[7] The figures for the operations of the Unemployment Insurance Fund in Canada for the years 1955-8 are as follows:

	Total	Paid in	Paid out
1955-6	$854,198,518	$228,711,745	$215,205,543
1956-7	874,574,651	251,671,851	231,295,718
1957-8	744,200,124	254,701,803	385,076,330

This trend has continued into 1959, when the Fund took in during the first eleven months to February 1959 some $216 million and paid out some $412 million.

which about $385 million was covered by unemployment insurance payments. This means a loss of about three-quarters of the purchasing power of the group affected by unemployment.

Unemployment insurance and assistance benefits are of considerable value as an economic stabiliser, but are only one of the means by which the severity of depressions could be limited. In many countries unemployment benefits average only 30 to 40 per cent of wages, and unemployment therefore involves a heavy fall in workers' purchasing power.[8] The lower the percentage of benefit in relation to wages the smaller the effect on economic stability. Also a large part of the decline in production and trade during a depression can be accounted for by the fact that many companies reduce their demand for new machinery and other capital goods while faced with economic uncertainties and financial stringency.

Proposals have been made for strengthening the stabilising effects of social security by increasing rates of benefit and reducing contributions during depressions and by reducing rates of benefit and increasing contributions during booms. These proposals are attractive in theory, as they would increase the stabilising effects of unemployment insurance, but would be difficult to apply in practice. In a severe depression there would probably be considerable resistance to increasing the rates of benefit and reducing the contributions, because the accumulated funds would be declining rapidly and, unless the funds were very big, changes of the kind proposed would endanger the solvency of the scheme. A reduction in the rates of benefit during periods of prosperity would be unfair to those who happened to be unemployed during such times, and an increase in the rates of contribution would be opposed because the reserve funds would already be growing rapidly. The most practicable course would be to ensure adequate funds for public assistance to supplement the unemployment insurance scheme, especially by paying benefits to workers who had exhausted their insurance rights. The additional amounts required could be financed mainly by borrowing instead of by higher taxation, the loans being repaid in years of prosperity. This method would have the effect of stabilising the economy.

The adoption of 'experience rating' in unemployment insurance in the United States somewhat reduces the value of the system as

---

[8] In some systems where unemployment benefits vary with wages, they may be as much as 60 or 70 per cent of the wages of low-paid workers if benefits for dependants are included. For highly paid workers without dependants the benefits may be only 20 to 30 per cent of the wage.

an economic stabiliser. Rates of contribution are reduced in periods of good employment, with mildly inflationary consequences, and are increased in periods of depression, with some deflationary consequences. These results are the opposite of what is required for purposes of stabilisation. This disadvantage and the fact that much unemployment is due to causes beyond the employers' control more than outweigh the value of the inducement of experience rating to employers to reduce the turnover of labour.

If social security benefits are paid, business will not decline as far as it otherwise would. They provide a psychologically valuable influence by lessening the feeling of insecurity which can aggravate an economic depression. It has been indicated, however, that even where unemployment benefits are relatively high and the system most extensive, payments to the unemployed fill only a small part of the gap in spending which is experienced in a depression. Since the time when fairly comprehensive unemployment insurance schemes were adopted, their effectiveness as an economic stabiliser has not been tested by severe depressions, except in a few European countries. In such circumstances, many other major measures would be needed, including an easy money policy, a big public works programme and other emergency schemes to stimulate recovery. Social security is only one of the many measures needed to sustain economic stability.

THE REDISTRIBUTION OF INCOME

Social security systems are instruments for redistributing or transferring income among different sections of the community. If they are financed largely from the general revenues by progressive taxation, there is a substantial transfer from rich to poor in countries where the range of wealth and incomes is wide.[9] The lower income groups pay less in taxation and receive more in benefits. In countries where the range of income among different sections of the community is relatively narrow, the money needed for social security comes broadly from the same classes of people who will benefit, and schemes are financed either by contributions of considerable amounts from the class of beneficiaries, or by earmarked taxes paid

[9] It has been advocated that measures of social progress should be directed towards reducing inequalities in incomes earned, so that less redistribution would be necessary through taxation and the provision of social security and welfare benefits. See, e.g., A. G. B. Fisher, *Economic Progress and Social Security* (London, 1945), p. 132, and Ronald Mendelsohn, *Social Security in the British Commonwealth* (London, 1954), p. 284.

by them in substantial proportions. The aged are supported from contributions by people of working age in their own class. Similarly, the fit support the sick, large families benefit from contributions from bachelors and those with small families, the unemployed by those who retain their jobs, while widows, orphans and victims of industrial accidents are aided by the more fortunate. Resources are transferred from the economically active to those in need. The costs are largely borne by the main body of the population who are also the beneficiaries, since they are protected against risks. The transfers are generally among the beneficiaries, as the risks are pooled among themselves, but in some schemes the higher-paid workers subsidise the lower-paid because the latter receive relatively bigger benefits in proportion to their contributions. This does not apply where contributions and benefits are at flat rates for high- and low-paid workers alike.

There are similarities between redistribution in social security and redistribution in the financing of internal national debts. It is sometimes argued that the payment of interest on internal debt is not a burden on the economy as the money is merely transferred and remains in the .country. Social security also effects transfers. Yet the conclusion that the financing of the internal debt or of social transfers is 'neutral' because the money is kept in the country is not necessarily true. Whether there will be a gain or loss to the economy and also to social welfare depends on the effects on those who pay the taxes or contributions and those who receive the benefits.[10]

It is psychologically effective to link contributions or earmarked taxes to benefits. They seem to the contributors to be not so much a form of taxation as a price they pay for specific individual benefits.[11] People do not regard as a tax the price they pay for bread and milk, the premiums they pay to private insurance companies or the contributions they make to group sickness benefit and retirement schemes organised at their places of employment. Similarly the contributions made to the state for unemployment insurance or old age pensions are essentially a subsidised price paid to cover a risk or to buy a benefit.

[10] For a review of the effects of social security transfers on social welfare, see A. C. Pigou, *The Economics of Welfare* (London, 1948), chap. XII.

[11] The attitude taken to increased taxes which are to be paid into the general revenue is quite different because, even though some of the money is used for social welfare benefits, the revenues are spent for a wide range of general purposes of which most taxpayers are only vaguely aware and which do not seem to be closely related to their own needs.

For this reason it is unsound to argue that special taxes or contributions by workers are a form of taxation which is inequitable because it is regressive. Even if it be accepted that the contributions are in effect regressive taxes, they have to be considered not by themselves but as part of the whole structure of the tax system in which inequities in some taxes are offset by high rates of progression in others to make the system as a whole equitable. But if, as seems reasonable, the contributions are more akin to a price than a tax, the question of inequity does not arise. Also the benefits are usually subsidised to a greater or lesser extent by the contributions of employers and the state.

The effects of social security on productivity depend mainly on the influence of transfers on incentives, savings, efficiency and mobility of labour. The effects on those from whom income is transferred and on those who, on balance, are the recipients must be considered separately.

The effect of high taxation, especially if it is heavily progressive, is to reduce the incentive and effort of the more highly paid members of the community upon whom economic efficiency and progress so greatly depend. The effect is similar whether the revenues obtained are used for social security or for any other purpose, for example national defence. High taxation also reduces the ability of these people to save and to provide resources for capital investment. It is not possible to separate the effects of taxation for social security purposes from the effects of taxation for other purposes.

The economic effects of social security payments on the recipients vary widely from one category to another. The benefits paid to the aged, the totally and permanently disabled and others incapable of work yield no direct returns in productivity. They are humanitarian payments. Yet before social security benefits were paid or when they were inadequate, many of the aged and infirm people were supported by relatives and this involved privation for the relatives and their children. Indirectly, therefore, even the payment of benefits to persons incapable of work can have favourable indirect reactions on the health and well-being of the next generation of workers.

It used to be argued more than it is today that social security payments reduce the desire to work and to save, and that they injure the economy by encouraging idleness and malingering and by sapping self-reliance and initiative. There is no evidence that this is true for the great majority of the population, though it may be valid for a small shiftless minority. The beneficiaries are generally in real need, and are anxious to support themselves again so far as possible. Because the principle of less eligibility is applied, social security benefits are relatively meagre, being much below the wages most workers can earn. Therefore, there is great inducement to return to work, and also to save in order to have supplementary resources. The amount of saving by the lower-paid workers is, however, small, but the contributions they make to social security funds are a form of compulsory or disciplined saving and amount to more than they would save voluntarily.

If there is loss in productivity it is due largely to defects in the application of social security and can be remedied. The methods adopted and the regulations applied should be designed to encourage and facilitate return to work. There is economic loss to the community if compensation paid to a workman injured in an industrial accident is not accompanied by systematic arrangements for rehabilitation and training for suitable work. Moreover his return to work must be accompanied by the right to receive compensation payments again if the effects of the injury recur and he again ceases to be able to work.[12] Without this right an injured worker may prefer the security of continued compensation payments to the risk of losing them if he returns to work and subsequently has a breakdown from the after effects of the injury. For war veterans this guarantee usually operates, and it should do so equally for victims of industrial accidents.

There is loss to the economy if sickness insurance to provide cash benefits is not associated with medical care and hospital services to ensure early recovery and return to work. Services such as these, and rehabilitation schemes, are also needed for many people suffering from long-term disability caused by sickness or accidents other than industrial injuries. They are needed for elderly workers who are not fit to continue heavy work but could be efficient in lighter jobs. Productivity is reduced if retirement is compulsory at a specified age, as many of the workers would still be efficient producers, sometimes for many years longer. The loss may be particularly heavy if the retirement age is early.

Unemployment insurance benefits tend to reduce the mobility of labour, and in some circumstances this can be a disadvantage to the economy. A distinction is necessary between temporary unemployment or lay-offs after which workers are likely to be needed

[12] In the British system of industrial injuries insurance, where compensation is for loss of faculty and is not linked to future earning capacity, this problem does not arise to the same extent.

again in the same business undertaking or industry, and long-term unemployment involving a change of location, industry or occupation. In the former case, the reduction in mobility effected by unemployment benefits is advantageous, as the workers will be available when they are needed and will avoid the dislocation and expense of moving. In the latter case the effect in reducing mobility is an economic handicap and the unemployment insurance system should be linked with an efficient employment exchange service and retraining facilities. The payment of benefits must be conditional on unemployed workers' accepting suitable jobs offered to them by the employment exchange; the condition that they must show evidence of genuinely seeking work has often proved impracticable. In order to facilitate mobility, unemployment insurance systems should be nation-wide. If benefits can be drawn in any part of the country, the unemployed will feel free to move about to find jobs; otherwise they will be more likely to stay in their own region rather than lose their right to benefit. Here it may be noted that unemployment insurance and assistance benefits tend to increase the bargaining power of trade unions with the result that wages may be raised somewhat higher than they otherwise would be. Such workers as become unemployed owing to the higher wages will receive unemployment pay and this will reduce the risk of their being compelled by poverty to undercut the wage scale.

The means test if used extensively is a deterrent to saving. That is one reason why public assistance should be limited as far as practicable to providing for a relatively small minority of people who for one reason or another are not protected by social insurance. Also, applicants who have moderate savings and own their home should be allowed to retain them and still receive assistance grants.

The weaknesses in some aspects of social security which have been outlined can readily be remedied. If they are remedied, and if social security cash payments are administered so as to encourage and facilitate resumption of work and are linked to rehabilitation services, and if deterrents to saving are removed, the system can make a positive contribution to productive efficiency. Rehabilitation services are expensive but can result in economic gains that more than cover the costs, as is shown by the results achieved in a number of countries. In these and other ways investment in human beings can bring even better returns than investment in machines and other material capital. Investment in human beings is primarily a function of the state even more than of industry as individual business undertakings retain the material capital in which they invest but lose some of the value of their investment in workpeople because of the turnover of labour.

INFLATION

In previous chapters reference has been made to inflation. Here it may be repeated that the intention of social security schemes and especially of social insurance is to provide specified benefits which can be used to buy goods and services. Contributors support the schemes politically and make their contributions in good faith with the expectation that the benefits will be paid to them in money that will buy as much as the money they contributed or was contributed on their behalf. To be paid benefits in depreciated money is morally a breach of contract.

The problem is particularly important for old age pensions because of the length of time during which contributions are paid and the effects of inflation when the pensions are paid. Equity requires that the value of all past contributions shall be adjusted to allow for changes in the value of money since the contributions were made. Thus, in principle, if a contribution of $50.00 were made in 1930 and the cost of living had trebled by 1955, the person concerned should be credited with $150 and given compound interest on this amount, and appropriate adjustments should be made for other years. In practice these detailed calculations will not be made; nevertheless when the time comes for the pension to be paid it should be adequately adjusted to allow for changes in the cost of living, and throughout the period when it is being paid, further adjustments should be made. Workmen's compensation pensions should be adjusted similarly.

Such adjustments involve departures from ordinary methods of bookkeeping and accountancy and involve dislocations in actuarial computations. This is a special version of a much discussed accountancy problem. In periods of inflation, accountancy must be flexible enough to supplement bookkeeping standards which are appropriate only on the assumption that the value of money is stable. If benefits are increased to compensate for inflation, much more may be paid out in monetary units than the bookkeeping equivalent of the contributions, but not in real terms, and that is what matters.

Pensions and other benefits should also be adjusted to allow for substantial changes in the productive efficiency of the economy. Twenty-five or thirty years ago the human effort required to produce a given quantity of goods and services was greater than it is today.

Therefore, in terms of effort, the cost of contributions was greater in the past than it is today for an equivalent amount. More generally the past generation of workers should, after their retirement, benefit from the progress made in efficiency of production and in standards of living.

From time to time rates of pension and other social security benefits, and also contributions, are raised to allow for increases in the cost of living, and even also to some extent in a rough approximate way for changes in productive efficiency. These adjustments are often made at irregular intervals and are influenced by political forces. There are, however, good grounds for considering more regular and systematic changes, and interesting experiments along these lines are being made. Thus in Sweden in 1950 the system was adopted of adjusting the flat rate pensions to changes in the cost of living. In 1956 the government of West Germany devised a scheme by which the amount of a worker's pension would be fixed in relation to the average wage in industry at the time his pension was due to be paid. The average wage at any time reflects the changes in the cost of living, productivity and prosperity up to that time: the pension of a particular worker, being calculated on the basis of his position in the wage scale during his working life, reflects his individual position in relation to that of his fellow beneficiaries. The two factors together ensure that the worker's pension reflects both the general changes in average wage levels and the previous individual position of the pensioner in the wage scale.[13] The principle applied has much merit, and the relating of the pension to the average or general level of wages at the time pensions become due and subsequently during the life of the pensioner could be applied equally to flat rate pensions or to those which vary with the wages the worker had earned.

FEDERAL, REGIONAL AND LOCAL RESPONSIBILITIES

An important economic problem is the distribution of the costs of social security among central, regional and local authorities. In countries with unitary constitutions the costs are shared between the central and local governments, whereas in countries with federal constitutions they are distributed among the federal government, the provincial or state governments and the municipal councils. Two

[13] This method was incorporated in a national superannuation scheme considered by the British Labour Party in 1957.

main questions to be considered are the aspects of social security that are primarily matters of local responsibility and those that are essentially of wider concern, and the economic resources available at each level to finance the various services.

In reviewing the first question, distinctions must be drawn between services financed and administered by municipal or other local authorities, those financed partly by the central government but administered by local authorities, and those financed and administered wholly by the central government. In countries with federal systems of government, the constitution defines the limits of federal and provincial or state responsibility.

When social security consisted only of public assistance, the responsibility both for financing and administering assistance was local. An early example was the British Poor Law of 1601 which made the parishes responsible for relief of the indigent. The law worked fairly well when labour was relatively stationary, but became ineffective when, as a result of modern industry and greatly improved transportation, there were nation-wide movements of capital and workpeople. A parish or municipality generally gave assistance only to needy people who had been born there or had lived there for a considerable number of years. In consequence some people would not leave their parish and lose their right to maintenance even though there were good prospects of employment elsewhere, and those who did leave might find themselves destitute in a distant parish that would refuse assistance. Gradually, however, the assistance areas were widened, first by grouping neighbouring parishes into poor law districts, and subsequently by establishing assistance on a regional or national basis.

One of the clearest trends in social security has been a shifting of financial responsibility from smaller to bigger units of government, from municipalities to provinces or regions and from them to central governments. Thus in Canada in 1913, municipal expenditure on assistance, social welfare and public health was nearly double that of the provinces; by the mid-1920's the two were almost equal; and by 1937 the expenditure of the provincial governments for these purposes was nearly double that of the municipalities. Federal financial responsibility became even greater, and by the middle of the century about three-quarters of all social security payments were financed by the federal government and one-quarter by the provincial governments and municipalities.[14] The trend was

14 The federal government's expenditure included benefits for veterans, for which it was responsible.

P

similar in other countries. By the middle of the century, in Great Britain and New Zealand for example, the central governments had become fully and directly responsible for all social security payments for income maintenance, whether by insurance or assistance.

In the United States, though the same trend is well defined, there has been a stronger preference for maintaining considerable local and state responsibility and a reluctance to increase the power of the federal government. However, during the depression years of the 1930's the municipalities could not cope with the many millions of people who were in need, and the federal government was forced to improvise measures of relief and to finance a large part of the cost of public assistance; the state governments also took an increased share of the burden. The arrangements for greater federal and state participation were established more permanently in the United States by the Social Security Act, 1935, which provided for Old-Age and Survivors Insurance and Unemployment Insurance as well as for payments towards public assistance. In 1954, the federal government bore slightly more than 50 per cent of the total cost of public assistance and the states paid 37.4 per cent, leaving only about 12 per cent to be financed by the municipalities.

The responsibility of central governments for social security increased partly because many of the problems were seen to be nation-wide and to require national solutions, but also because municipal and even provincial resources were inadequate. Central governments have greater powers of taxation, including income tax, corporation taxes and customs and excise. Some social security programmes are both financed and administered by the federal or central government. This is the method in Canada for old age pensions, which are paid from seventy years of age, and for family allowances, and in the United States for Old Age, Survivors, and Disability Insurance. Other kinds of social security, where close personal contact must be maintained with the beneficiaries, must be administered locally, though the systems may be financed wholly cr partly from central funds. Public assistance and health services require local administration, though the responsible officers may be appointed by either the central or the local government.

For unemployment insurance a national organisation is preferable, as unemployment is often widespread in its impact and labour is nation-wide in its mobility.[15] There must, however, be local offices to control applications for cash payments and to organise

[15] A national system is also preferable to provide aid for farmers and farm workers who are suffering because of crop failures or economic depression.

employment exchanges so that unemployed workers can be put in touch with employers who have jobs to offer. This method is applied in Canada, where the Unemployment Insurance Commission is responsible throughout the country for finance and administration.[16] In the United States, as indicated earlier, unemployment insurance is applied by separate legislation in each state, subject to certain general conditions set by the federal government; the employment exchange services are co-ordinated federally. Workmen's compensation for industrial accidents and associated rehabilitation services is organised in Canada on a provincial basis in accordance with provincial legislation, and this method is also adopted in the United States, each state having its own legislation.

Where legislative control over social security rests with the states or provinces but substantial contributions are made from the central government's funds, two problems arise. The first is to decide on what principle the central government should allocate the funds, and the second, closely related problem is to encourage the local authorities to establish adequate standards of social security and to promote reasonable uniformity. One method is for the central government to pay amounts in proportion to the population of each province or state. That would be sound enough if there were no great differences in the wealth and standards of living of the various areas. If, however, some are much poorer than others, they cannot provide reasonably high standards of social security unless they receive bigger grants than the richer areas. In the United States in the 1950's the average income per head in some of the poorer states was considerably below half that in the richest states. The range was wider than that between some countries in Western Europe. To provide reasonable compensation for such big differences by federal grants involves complex political and economic considerations which can only be settled periodically in each country on the basis of experience.

If central government grants vary according to the amounts which the state or provincial governments spend, there is no certainty how much the central government will be called upon to provide, though with experience this can be estimated fairly closely. A state or province that is more liberal in its benefits or has greater

[16] In order that this system could be applied, it was necessary to amend the British North America Act, and in 1940 it was amended to give the federal government exclusive jurisdiction over unemployment insurance. Constitutional rigidities can hamper federal governments in undertaking greater responsibility for social security made desirable by changes in economic and social conditions.

need may draw more from the central government than one that is less liberal or has less need. Such variations in amount are preferable to fixed sums for public assistance and for the development of public health services. In financing social insurance schemes, however, the government's contribution should be either a specific sum or a clearly defined proportion of the contributions of employers and workers. The regular revenues should be enough to provide reserves sufficient to meet ordinary fluctuations in expenditure from year to year. The limitation on the government's regular contributions does not, however, mean that in an exceptionally critical period it would not have to meet deficits, perhaps by making loans repayable after the crisis had passed. The draining of reserves calls special attention to the severity of the crisis and the need for additional remedies.

Differences in central government grants to states or provinces arise according as the purpose is to secure equal or uniform standards of benefits in each area, or to ensure similarity in the tax burden in each. Equality of standards might be secured by making a grant of 50 per cent of the cost, and yet the tax burden in a rich province to provide its share of the cost might be much lighter than in a poor province. A method that would enable allowances to be made for differences between rich and poor provinces would be to vary the grants on the basis of average income per head, making the biggest per capita grant to the poorer regions. Where the differences in wealth and income are as great as those between rich and poor states in the United States, it is impracticable to ensure uniform standards of monetary benefits, as a rate of benefit that would be reasonable in relation to average standards of living in a rich state would be too high in the poorest states. In Canada, although there are considerable differences in standards of living between the maritime provinces and the richer ones (particularly Ontario and British Columbia), they have not proved too wide to prevent the application of uniform flat rate pensions and family allowances without means tests to the whole country. These equal monetary payments are, however, of considerably higher real value to people, for example, in small ports and rural areas in Newfoundland and Nova Scotia than to people in Toronto and Vancouver. The Canadian unemployment insurance system in which contributions and benefits vary according to wages has the effect of providing lower average benefits in the poorer than in the richer provinces. Such differences in benefits also result in the United States under the Old-Age, Survivors, and Disability Insurance Program and

Unemployment Insurance, in which contributions and benefits vary with wages. Indeed, as indicated earlier, an argument in support of this system of varying contributions and benefits in accordance with wages is that it is better adapted than uniform flat rate benefits to a country with big differences in average standards between rich and poor states. Uniform national standards of benefit are practicable only where economic conditions and average incomes per head do not vary greatly from region to region.

The central government may either require the state or provincial governments to observe fairly rigid conditions if they are to obtain grants, or allow them much flexibility. Thus in the United States the federal government, which contributes substantially to public assistance, leaves to each state the responsibility for setting its own means tests and its own standards of benefit. Also, for unemployment insurance the federal government neither specifies standards nor duration of benefits. Each state therefore has freedom to adapt the system to its own conditions. Some states, however, may be over generous and others unduly parsimonious; in such circumstances more guidance by the central government is desirable, yet it may not be given because of opposition to central control and authority.

Flexibility in administration by state or provincial governments gives opportunities for experiments to be made, and in the early stages of social security it is desirable that they should be made. The results of experience with hospital insurance, particularly in British Columbia and Saskatchewan, were of value to the Canadian government in planning a country-wide scheme. In the United States, four of the states—New York, New Jersey, Rhode Island and California—have adopted sickness insurance systems. Similarly, experiments can be tried in limited areas within provinces or states, for example, the experiment of free medical care in the Swift Current area of the province of Saskatchewan.

INTERNATIONAL STANDARDS AND RELATIVE COSTS

During the inter-war years the conventions on social security adopted by International Labour Conferences laid down principles considered suitable for application in different countries, but did not set any standards of benefit. After the war, however, various minimum standards were specified in the Draft Convention on Seamen's Pensions, 1946, and the Draft Convention concerning

Minimum Standards of Social Security, 1952. In devising the standards it was recognised that it would be quite impracticable to fix the same rates of monetary benefits to be paid in all countries because of the wide differences in standards of living. What was done was to define the benefits for the sick, unemployed, aged and other categories at a uniform proportion of certain average wage standards in each country. Thus the rate of old age pensions in Canada or the United States, if fixed in conformity with the Draft Convention concerning Minimum Standards of Social Security, would be 40 per cent of the average wages of specified grades of workers in those countries, while the rate in India would also be 40 per cent—but 40 per cent of the much lower average of wages prevailing there. This is the only feasible basis for regulating standards internationally.

The Draft Convention on Seamen's Pensions requires payment of pensions on the basis of premiums or contributions of not less than 10 per cent of the total remuneration of the seamen. Thus, while defining a standard proportion, the Convention allows for different rates of pension to be paid as determined by the levels of remuneration in each country. Considerable flexibility is allowed in the Draft Convention concerning Minimum Standards of Social Security in order to enable countries with different systems of social security to ratify it. The condition of ratification is that a country must apply the standards to at least three of the following nine elements: medical care, sickness, unemployment, old age, employment injury, family allowances, maternity, invalidity and widows and orphans. If a country were to select the less expensive elements such as maternity, widows and orphans and employment injury, it could meet the requirements of the Convention at a cost of only 1 or 2 per cent of its national income, whereas for a country that selected the most expensive ones (old age pensions, medical care and family allowances) the cost would be 6 or 7 per cent.

It might be supposed that if each country were to base its levels of social security benefits on the wage levels of the country, equality of the burden of costs would thereby be ensured between one country and another in relation to the capacity of each country to provide social security. This is not so. Especially in the case of old age pensions and family allowances, costs based on standard percentages of average wages may vary substantially from country to country, largely because of differences in age distribution. The costs in any country depend mainly on how great a proportion of the whole population is composed of people of working age. In a country that had large numbers of young children, low expectation of life and few old people, the cost of children's allowances would be higher and the cost of old age pensions lower than in countries with relatively more older people. Thus according to calculations based on demographic data around 1950, the cost of old age pensions, if paid from sixty-five years of age at 40 per cent of the average income of the population in the age group from fifteen to sixty-four years, would have ranged as a percentage of that income from 1.8 per cent in Venezuela to 7.1 per cent in France.[17] In the United Kingdom it would have been around 6 per cent, and in Canada and the United States about 5 per cent.

For family allowances the range would have been similarly wide, from under 1 per cent of the income of people of working age in some Western European countries and as high as 2.4 per cent in Puerto Rico where the proportion of children was much higher.[18] Such differences influence the decisions made on social security policy.

The Draft Convention concerning Minimum Standards of Social Security also provides that a country whose economy and medical facilities are insufficiently developed may, if and for so long as the competent authority considers necessary, avail itself of temporary exceptions. In particular, temporary ratification of the Convention is allowed if its terms are applied to 50 per cent of the industrial workers in business undertakings that employ twenty persons or more, instead of to 50 per cent of all employees as required of other countries. This is an important concession to countries in which agriculture and small scale industry form the basis of the economy. In Burma for example, which has a population of 20 millions, the total number of gainfully employed may be 6 or 7 million, but of these some 90 per cent are in agriculture or in small scale industry and only a few hundred thousand in undertakings that employ twenty persons or more. Thus if Burma ratified the Draft Convention by applying it to industrial injury, invalidity and widows and orphans, the risks of perhaps only about half a million workers would be covered, whereas in Britain and other highly industrialised countries the numbers covered in proportion to the population might be fifteen times greater, and ratification of the

---

[17] Pierre Laroque and Antoine Zelenka, "International Balance of Social Security Costs," *International Labour Review*, vol. LXVIII, July-Dec. 1953.
[18] These percentages were calculated on the basis of an allowance for every child under fifteen years of age of 3 per cent of the total income of the population in the age group fifteen to sixty-four.

Draft Convention by those countries might be based on more costly forms of protection[19]

[19] The Draft Convention normally requires benefits to be paid for sickness for a period of not less than twenty-six weeks, but in underdeveloped countries a temporary exception could be made that would require them to be paid for a maximum period that would work out, on an average, to ten days of incapacity per year per worker protected.

CHAPTER XII

CONCLUSIONS

The progressive advance of the machine age has drawn more and more people away from agriculture, with its direct resources of food and shelter, its relative stability and the mutual supports of rural community life, and has made them dependent on industry, which provides them with higher standards of living and the amenities of urban life but also increasingly confronts them with the insecurities of specialisation, changing fashions, competition and the great swings from boom to depression. Specialised goods and skilled services may be in keen demand today and unwanted tomorrow. Automation may change the pattern of the demand for labour and, while increasing the welfare of the many, may cause hardship and distress to those who are discarded by its use. Modern life is being geared for increasingly rapid change, and the stabilities and securities of mutual support and interdependence formerly found in the family and in local integrated communities have given place to the isolations of urban life.[1] Vast city areas 'are becoming victims of their very bigness and the high mobility of people within them. The lack of the basic elements of neighbourhood and community in many sections is frightening. Many areas exist, peopled by thousands of families who are rootless, restless and temporary.'[2]

The needs of progress often disturb long-established communities, and large numbers of individuals and families, if left to cope with the upheaval themselves, would encounter distress which they could

[1] In 1934, when the United States was faced with the distresses of the great depression, President Franklin D. Roosevelt said: "Security was obtained in the earlier days through the inter-dependence of members of families upon each other and of the families within the small communities upon each other. The complexities of great communities and of organised industries make less real these simple means of security. Therefore we are compelled to employ the active interest of the nation as a whole through Government in order to encourage a greater security for each individual who composes it."

[2] Professor Stuart K. Jaffary of the School of Social Work, University of Toronto, in his article in the *Social Worker*, April-June 1957. The quotation is related particularly to the San Francisco-Oakland and Los Angeles regions of California. New residents were moving into the latter area at a rate of some 4,200 a week.

not remedy. Thus the St Lawrence Seaway and hydro-electric scheme involved the flooding of large areas hitherto occupied by towns, villages and smaller communities. However, the interests of the residents have been safeguarded by compensation, the building of new houses and the moving of old ones to new community sites on higher ground. Only by comprehensive organisation and public responsibility can security be guaranteed.

Into the upheavals and contingencies of modern life, social security introduces one necessary element of stability and protection, and contributes to a somewhat more equitable distribution of income between the fortunate and the unfortunate. In the present century, it has evolved from relief for the indigent to a basic system of protection for whole populations. Before it came into operation the risks of life had been borne somehow, often at the cost of great distress and hardship, with meagre assistance mainly from local authorities, relatives and private charity. The cost of social security to the state is, therefore, not entirely a new charge. Much of it is a more equitable sharing of the burden. The public will, however, demand that provision by the state shall meet better standards than the former meagre ones. The cost will therefore be greater, but the additional cost is for better provision and services, and will be offset by gains in social welfare and productive efficiency.

Social security is much more than a charitable and humanitarian device. It is a constructive policy which promotes industrial efficiency, and against its costs must be set substantial economic returns. The provision of health services especially increases the economic productivity of the present generation of workers, and family allowances and welfare services for children and young persons raise the efficiency of the next generation. Even pensions for the aged whose productive years are over can benefit workers by relieving them of a substantial part of the burden of maintaining aged parents, which used to involve privation for the workers and their children.

In all countries, the need for social security is no longer an issue between political parties. What is still controversial is the rate of expansion to protect more people and cover more risks, together with methods of financing and standards of benefit. Social security is essentially a means used by the present century to meet the rapid changes of industrial and economic life. The first half of the century saw the progressive acceptance in country after country of basic principles of social security. Largely because this was a new territory of public responsibility, systems were designed bit by bit.

Priorities had to be established, tentative experiments made, administrative organisations built and personnel trained. Social security was applied piecemeal, and there were many gaps, some overlaps and many anomalies and administrative complexities.[3] Vast experience has, however, been steadily accumulated, and the present mid-century years are appropriate for taking stock of what has been done and what needs to be done.

During the second half of the century gaps will be filled, anomalies removed and more consistent patterns woven. Periodic reviews are valuable for the purpose of planning to combine separate systems where practicable, and to simplify administration both for the collection of revenues and the payment of benefits. They may also enable resources to be better distributed among the different contingencies. Since the Second World War, the tendency has been growing to look at social security as a whole instead of considering each contingency separately, and also to extend it progressively to larger sections of the population. These trends are already evident in many advanced countries. Britain and New Zealand have made the greatest progress. In Canada and the United States, because of their size and federal constitutions, the problems are more complex. Yet in these countries the same trends can be seen. In the United States the scope of Old-Age and Survivors Insurance has been progressively enlarged to include farm workers, self-employed persons, domestic servants and others who were originally excluded, and in 1957 its scope was enlarged to cover totally and permanently disabled people over fifty years of age. In Canada, unemployment insurance, old age pensions and family allowances without means tests have all been introduced since 1940. In almost all countries, there has been a marked tendency for the financial responsibility of local or municipal authorities to diminish and that of regional and national authorities to increase.[4]

'It is not necessary,' Professor Cassidy said, 'to build the house of social security all at once, but so much of it as is built should have all its parts related and coordinated, and there ought to be provision

[3] Gaps in the Canadian system of social security and welfare caused by its piecemeal development are referred to by Professor John S. Morgan of the School of Social Work, University of Toronto, in *The New Look in Welfare* (Toronto, 1955), p. 12.
[4] In Ontario, for example, out of a total of $7.27 per head spent on provincial public welfare including public assistance during the year ended March 31, 1956, the municipalities paid $1.64, the provincial government $4.20 and the federal government $1.43. Before the war, the municipalities paid a much higher proportion.

for building the rest of it according to an all-over plan.'[5] He also emphasised the need for efficient administrative machinery and professional personnel. The lack of them is one of the reasons why underdeveloped countries have yet been unable to establish extensive systems. Even in countries such as Canada that have a high standard of living, progress towards more adequate medical care for all has been delayed by shortages of hospital, clinical and diagnostic facilities and doctors, nurses and administrators, and these are still being increased in number to meet the needs of the population. To introduce hastily devised schemes without having built up the necessary organisation often does more harm than good. During the early and intermediate stages of growth there is a strong case for limiting schemes to particular areas, categories of workers and risks so that experience can be accumulated and personnel trained. Limited schemes should, however, be planned so that they can gradually be extended to more occupations and sections of the population and schemes for different risks integrated in their administration, contributions and benefits.

Though human needs are similar in all countries, differences in size, economic and demographic conditions, standards of living and political and social philosophies, traditions and experience result in varying methods for the provision of social security. Countries cannot all adopt a uniform pattern. Each country will shape its system in its own way, and will adapt the system in different periods to meet new conditions. Even major changes may be necessary in the course of time.[6] Although all social security programmes have the common objective of meeting human needs the methods are appropriately adjusted to the economic circumstances and social attitudes of the people of each country. Some broad general principles and policies may have universal validity, but their application in any country must be flexible. Methods which have proved successful in one country may not necessarily be suitable for another. Variety is appropriate and inevitable.

There are differences both in attitudes and methods. In the United States and Canada, public opinion is strongly in favour of economic

---

[5] From a privately circulated memorandum.
[6] Outstanding examples of such major changes are the introduction of wage-related social insurance in the United States under the impact of the depression in the 1930's, and the adoption in Britain after the Second World War of basic insurance covering all risks and a National Health Service for the whole population instead of the former system limited to people in the lower income groups.

expansion, but increasing production and prosperity alone do not remove the need for comprehensive measures of social security. Even in the most prosperous countries, substantial numbers of people are in need because of the inevitable risks of life. There is an unfounded belief, held by many people in the United States and Canada, that voluntary methods of private insurance, especially for sickness, will be extended so widely that social insurance measures will not be required. A wealthy country can more easily make provision for those in need, and a sound social security system as a foundation for voluntary methods can contribute towards economic expansion and not retard it. 'The abolition of want in the United States is no longer a problem of economic capacity. It is solely a problem of our ability and willingness to organise to do the job. A high level of production, though necessary for the abolition of want, does not accomplish the goal automatically. It is necessary as well to have the institutional arrangements for making sure that all continue to share in consumption when income from earnings stops, and to have as well arrangements for meeting need which arises from other causes.'[7]

People in some countries and regions are more favourable to public services than people in others. Where public opinion supports substantial government participation for achieving economic and social objectives and regards it as a convenient and efficient instrument for these purposes, the adoption of extensive systems of social security is more likely than in countries where government intervention is viewed with distrust and is, therefore, kept at a minimum and only tolerated as a last resort when other solutions prove impracticable. In some circumstances, the method of government subsidies to private bodies is preferred. Thus, in the province of Quebec, it is the policy of the government to grant subsidies to religious and private institutions rather than establish public services. These institutions assist widows, orphans, the blind, aged and other indigent persons and share the cost with the municipality of residence and the provincial government, the assistance including maintenance, accommodation, medical care and welfare services. In the western Canadian provinces, community responsibility in the form of organised public services is more readily accepted, perhaps partly as a consequence of the need for mutual aid which was characteristic of the early pioneering days.

[7] "Social Security Today" by Robert M. Ball, Assistant Director, Bureau of Old-Age and Survivors Insurance, *Journal of the American Public Welfare Association,* July 1957.

There are wide differences in method from country to country. In Britain the social insurance system is based mainly on flat rate contributions and benefits. This is an application of the fundamental principle that the state should provide basic security but leave freedom for voluntary provision above that level. Though it provides benefits for all without a means test, it otherwise resembles assistance methods which, in effect, provide flat rate benefits for persons without resources. In the United States the opposite policy has been applied in insurance schemes for aged persons, widows and orphans, the unemployed, victims of industrial accidents and certain totally and permanently disabled persons. For all these, the contributions and benefits vary with wages, subject to specified maxima and minima. Canada stands in between, with flat rates for old age pensions and children's allowances, and variation with earnings for unemployment and workmen's compensation. The financing of old age pensions in Canada is distinctive, as the benefits are paid from the yields of special earmarked taxes. Canada also has a nation-wide system of unemployment insurance, whereas in the United States, where insistence on state rights is strong, each state has its own system, subject, however, to the pressures of the federal pay roll tax. In the United States there are no government contributions to the social insurance systems, which are financed either jointly by employers and workers, or by employees only.

These differences are illustrative of wide variations in practice. Some of them are specially suited to the conditions of a particular country. Others are experimental or the results of temporary political attitudes and are likely to be amended.

Underdeveloped countries are in special difficulties in providing social security because of lack of funds and shortages of experienced personnel to operate the services. They suffer from the dilemma that their needs are so great and their resources so small. Comprehensive systems suitable for advanced industrial countries with high standards of living and education are inappropriate for underdeveloped countries which are mainly rural and agricultural and have large numbers of illiterate people. Underdeveloped countries are compelled by these circumstances to begin with a limited programme concentrated on the most serious needs. These include provision for workers who because they have moved into urban and industrial centres have been uprooted from their traditional ways of living in rural communities. Many schemes start in a few of the main cities and organise mainly short-term provision such as sickness benefits and compensation for industrial accidents. At the same time, such countries can gradually develop, both in urban and rural areas, community and health services which do not involve payments in cash to maintain income, but are designed to improve health and efficiency and promote better standards of community living.

In the introductory chapter to this volume, various questions were raised to which tentative answers can now be given. On the question of voluntary methods, experience shows that they are not effective in providing basic security especially for the lower-paid sections of the community, though they are attractive in their freedom and flexibility and are of great value in enabling people to make supplementary provision appropriate to their varying circumstances. Adequate provision for sickness, unemployment, disability and old age competes with television sets, tobacco, alcohol and other items of expenditure for the distribution of the family income. There is no doubt which have the stronger claims to priority. Left to themselves, however, many people will take risks and fail to attain security, and only the discipline of compulsory contributions can secure effective basic provision for them. It is not practicable to draw a distinction between these people and those who, left to themselves, would make provision. The systems must, therefore, apply to all, or at least to all workers or all those with an income below some specified amount. In the freedom-loving democracies, however, the state should restrict the use of its compulsory powers to measures essential for the general welfare which many individuals would not undertake voluntarily, and to services which the state can administer substantially better at a given cost than private concerns. In the field of social security, this implies that the standard of cash benefits and other services provided by the state should be relatively low, leaving freedom for the voluntary provision of additional benefits; otherwise, the state, whether from motives of paternalism or in the exercise of power, would unduly restrict individual initiative and responsibility.

Experience of the working of social security systems during the first half of the present century provides a valuable fund of information which indicates some trends and general conclusions, and also reveals new problems; much more experience and research are needed in order to determine the effects of different policies and methods on productivity and on the welfare of those in need. The answers will not depend exclusively on economic and financial factors, but also on the balance of political forces and on social and psychological considerations.

Experience shows that reliance on public assistance with a means test and payments varied according to need is becoming outmoded as the main system of social security, notwithstanding the many improvements made in its operation. Preference has grown for the paying of benefits as a right without means tests, and for financing them either by contributory social insurance or from special or general taxes, leaving public assistance to meet a residue of needs.

The payment of defined benefits without reference to private resources to all who encounter specified risks can greatly reduce the place of social assistance in the social security system. It can relegate poor relief and assistance based on means tests to a residue of people who, because of special circumstances, are not covered by general schemes, or for whom standard rates based on community averages are inadequate, or who have exhausted or not acquired the right to benefit from them. This plan has several advantages. Means tests are still disliked, their use penalises the thrifty and they are costly to administer as the circumstances of individuals and families must be thoroughly investigated by experienced social workers. The residue to which means tests are applied should be kept as a small proportion of the whole, and if, except for special temporary reasons, the proportion of people on means test benefits increases substantially, ways should be found of reducing it. In Britain in 1953, about 26 per cent of all old age pensioners were receiving supplementary assistance; this percentage was too large and was subsequently reduced by increasing the rates of insurance pensions to allow for the higher cost of living. In the United States, the extension of the coverage of Old-Age and Survivors Insurance and the provision in 1956 of insurance benefits for totally and permanently disabled persons between fifty and sixty-five years of age will reduce the proportion of people receiving means test assistance. It must be added that means tests are now applied in many countries with sympathy and human understanding, and need no longer encounter the opposition rightly directed against the harsh and severe inquisitions of former poor relief days.[8]

Statistics show that a great majority of the people of any country have only a low or moderate income and are in need to at least some extent when they become victims of risks, and this evidence lends support to the idea of providing benefits for all. Thus, data from many countries show that a large proportion of aged people

---

[8] People who pay income tax must submit to means tests every year for the less attractive purpose of paying taxes than of substantiating claims for social security benefits.

no longer able to work are reduced to poverty, and the proportion is so great that there is merit in providing old age pensions for all without a means test (as is done, for example, by the Canadian federal government), even though a minority do not need them. As is noted by Professor John Morgan, 'the need of persons over seventy for income maintenance beyond their own resources was found to be an almost universal one.'[9] Similarly, a great majority of people with large families suffer from reduced standards of living, and there is a strong case for paying allowances to families with children over the average number. Most of the unemployed, most sick people, and most widows and orphans are in financial need, and it is preferable to pay benefits for all, even though a small number could do without them. Only small minorities of people are so well off that benefits would not be of substantial use to them in providing necessaries, but they would be entitled to draw benefits nevertheless.[10] There are advantages in social solidarity and administrative convenience in treating all alike, and the wealthier people contribute much more than the benefits they receive by the taxes they pay at progressive rates.[11]

The working of social security systems has revealed various gaps, and a general trend has been to include groups of people and risks not previously covered. Benefits are, with rare exceptions, generally set substantially below the wages of people in employment. The proportion varies considerably in different countries. There is wide agreement that benefits should be below wages, partly to keep the cost down, but also to avoid the danger of malingering. How much below wages the benefits should be is still highly controversial, and

[9] "Social Welfare Needs of a Changing Society: The New Canada," *Social Service Review*, Dec. 1954. Professor Morgan indicates that it would be administratively wasteful to use the elaborate procedure of detailed means test investigation when a large proportion of persons over seventy years of age need full benefit.

[10] In New Zealand, benefits are paid only to those with incomes below specified levels, though all contribute.

[11] Proposals have been made, for example by Lady Rhys-Williams, that greater use should be made of the method of income tax reliefs to provide social security. It has been applied in reliefs for dependent children and in the deduction of certain medical expenses from gross income. If almost everyone paid substantial amounts in income tax, it would be practicable to use tax reliefs to meet many social security needs. However, many of the people in the greatest need are below or only a little above the income tax level, and the method is therefore impracticable unless the tax system is radically revised. See: Lady Rhys-Williams, *Income Tax Reform* (London, 1948); and the Liberal Party memorandum, *The Reform of Income Tax and Social Security Payments* (London, 1950).

Q

in future benefits may be proportionately increased as standards of living rise, though they will need to be kept below the levels at which malingering might become serious.

Countries have not yet reached a concensus on the question whether social security should be restricted to providing for basic needs, with benefits set at uniform flat rates, or whether it should be differential, with benefits related to wages. As a result of further experience, a system with two or more tiers may possibly evolve, one providing basic security towards which the state would make substantial contributions from public revenues, and the others financed mainly by the beneficiaries and their employers, their contributions varying with wages. Another unsettled issue is whether benefits should vary according to the kind of risk; some countries favour variation and others prefer all risks to be treated alike. In many countries, the benefits for industrial accidents are better than those for other misfortunes. A greater measure of agreement may be reached on these and many other questions as more experience is gained, but there will remain many variations in policies and methods from country to country.

From the experience of various countries, it would seem that basic security in fairly advanced countries can be provided at a cost of about 10 per cent of national income, though the cost would be two or three per cent more in a prolonged period of severe depression and heavy unemployment. The costs of social security should be measured not merely in money totals, but in relation to changes in the value of money, the size and distribution of the population and growth in national productivity. Frequently, voices are raised in condemnation of increases in the amounts spent on social security without making proper allowance for such changes. An increase of several million dollars in the cost of social security may seem a matter of grave concern, and yet it may represent a lower real cost when related to growth in population, productivity and prices. The most effective test, therefore, of the cost of social security is its relation to national income.

A cost of 10 per cent can provide only meagre standards of subsistence in present conditions of productivity. These limited resources must be distributed among the various risks in order to achieve maximum security and welfare. In economic terms, they should be used to give, as far as possible, equimarginal returns from each risk. Thus, better results may be obtained by increasing the facilities for medical care where they are inadequate than by paying substantial sums as allowances for the first child in each family.

Experience in many countries shows that the most appropriate method of financing many social security schemes is by contributory insurance on a tripartite basis. Contributions by beneficiaries should generally not be less than one-third of the total, and if, because of inflation or any other reason, the rates of benefit are raised, there should be a corresponding increase in contributions. In countries where incomes are unevenly distributed and the proportion of wealthy people is large, the contributions of the state from general revenues can suitably be a bigger part than in countries where incomes are more equally distributed. However, wherever schemes are limited to specific categories of workers forming only a relatively small part of the whole population, the funds should come entirely or largely from the workers and their employers. State funds should be used only sparingly, if at all, to subsidise benefits which only limited sections of the population enjoy. As schemes become comprehensive, the state may more reasonably bear an increased proportion of the cost.

A suitable alternative to financing by tripartite contributions is by earmarked taxes, which should be raised when benefits are increased. The yields of such taxes can appropriately be augmented by subventions from general revenues. In federal countries where some social security schemes are administered under state or provincial legislation, substantial grants-in-aid by the federal government are desirable and should be used to ensure the universal application of essential minimum standards.

Schemes should generally be financed so as to be able to meet their obligations out of their regular revenues without relying on the government to meet deficits of varying amounts, though this general rule may be qualified for paying unemployment benefits during periods of severe and prolonged depression. Loans can be obtained to meet moderate short-term deficits and should be repaid, if necessary by raising the rates of contribution. For ordinary fluctuations reserves should be used. In financing old age pensions the special problem arises whether to accumulate large funds, the interest on which will help substantially in meeting the growing expenditure of the future, or to adopt a pay-as-you-go plan. The best method is to compromise by establishing funds which, together with successive increases in rates of contribution at intervals of, say, ten or twelve years, will meet the cost of future benefits.

Benefits should be concentrated where they are most needed. Thus, in unemployment and sickness schemes there is often a waiting period of three days before benefits begin. Countries with high standards of living could give consideration to a waiting period of a week, as most workers would be able to meet their needs without hardship for that length of time. Then, the cost of the scheme could be reduced or bigger benefits could be paid to those who were without earnings for longer periods. Similarly, individuals and families could be required to pay up to a specified amount each year for medical treatment they received, and beyond that amount they would be given treatment free or at nominal cost. By this means the more serious cases would be relieved of heavy expenditure. The same principle is appropriate for family allowances, which might be paid only from the second or perhaps the third child. If old age pensions start at the age of sixty-five, they might be lower for the first five years and then increase from the age of seventy when a much smaller proportion of the pensioners would be able to continue to work and when their own resources from private savings would probably be less.

There is a tendency in various countries to fix too young a normal age for retirement pensions. This is largely because sufficient account is not taken of improvements in the health and efficiency and of the expectation of life of older people during the past half-century, the increasing use of mechanical methods for heavy work that used to be done manually and the contrast between labour shortages in the post-war years and heavy unemployment in the inter-war years, when older people had great difficulty in finding jobs. In many countries the normal pensionable age for men is sixty-five, and this involves a much heavier cost than if the age were sixty-eight or seventy,[12] and a loss of the substantial productivity of large numbers of people who are fit for work for several years longer. If pensions are paid only on retirement, the great majority of workers experience substantial reductions in their standard of living and lose the satisfactions derived from work and from daily association with their fellow workers. The system should be flexible, so as to provide the incentive of suitably increased pensions for those who work beyond normal pensionable age, and lower pensions for those who retire earlier because their infirmities make them unfit for work.

The provision of basic standards of pension leaves individuals, particularly those in the higher income categories, responsible for making additional provision by saving or by arrangements with employers. Security plans at the place of employment, whether on

[12] In 1954 a committee appointed by the British government recommended a gradual raising of the pensionable age from sixty-five to sixty-eight years.

the employers' initiative or by collective agreements, have become widespread, and call for some regulation.

The serious illness of a breadwinner or of the members of his family is a major cause of poverty. These people need both cash income to compensate in part for loss of earnings, and the means of meeting heavy expenses for medical care, though most people should pay some specified amount towards the cost. For persons who become permanently incapacitated as a result of industrial accidents or diseases, pensions and not lump sums should be paid.

Along different lines but with disastrous effects, inflation is a serious cause of insecurity and distress. It eats up savings, weakens the incentive to save, and leaves large numbers of people in poverty, often when they are aged and unable to cope with the losses forced upon them. It is one of the urgent tasks of government to remove this insidious evil.

The collection and distribution of money to provide cash incomes is relatively easy to organise, except for means test payments, but health, rehabilitation and welfare services, including the care of orphan children, the sick and the aged, require personal attention by specialists—doctors, nurses and trained social workers—as well as equipment for diagnosis and therapy. Much of the work involved in the administration of cash benefits can be done by electronic and other machines, but the services not only involve direct contact with individuals, each with varying physical, psychological and emotional needs and problems, but must be carried out locally. Such services claim high priority, they are constructive and can contribute greatly to national productivity and human welfare. Health services are particularly valuable and can pay big dividends in efficiency and well-being. For many welfare services there is scope for close co-operation between government and voluntary agencies.

Although systems and standards of social security differ considerably from country to country there has been a growing trend since the Second World War for reciprocity agreements to be concluded between countries that are neighbours or are closely associated economically. These agreements enable workers from one country who go to work in another to be granted some of its social security benefits. Even without reciprocity Britain has extended the benefits of her National Health Service to visitors from abroad whether they are there as workers, on business or on vocation.

Reciprocity agreements have been concluded or are under

negotiation between Britain and several Western European countries. The Scandinavian countries have agreements among themselves. Progress along these lines has been made by the countries associated in the European Coal and Steel Community, and the measures to bring about the closer economic integration of Western Europe by establishing a common market and removing barriers to trade give promise of further impetus to reciprocal agreements on social security.[13] Moreover, the member states of the Council of Europe have given consideration to plans for a social security code for Western Europe which, while not aiming at uniformity, would reduce differences and facilitate reciprocity. International reciprocity is likely progressively to extend during the later decades of the century.

Social security in the future will be based on a strong sense of public responsibility for the prevention of poverty, an attitude which has grown rapidly throughout the world during the second quarter of the twentieth century. It will continue to grow. Social insurance will increasingly become the method, with substantial direct contributions by those who draw the benefits. They will thereby join together in mutual support of the less fortunate among themselves, and the title to security will depend largely on their own participation and productivity.

[13] The European League for Economic Co-operation has taken an unofficial lead in this work and its conferences and reports have been influential with the governments.

SELECTED REFERENCES

The documentation on social security, including legislative texts, reports of Government commissions and committees, and private publications is vast. A short list is given below of some recent books, reports and other documents in the English language which deal with the broader issues and policies.

GENERAL

Abel-Smith, Brian: *The Reform of Social Security.* London, 1953.

Ball, F. N.: *National Insurance and Industrial Injuries.* London, 1948.

Ball, Robert M.: 'What Contribution Rate for O.A.S.I.?' *Social Security Bulletin.* Washington, D.C., July 1949.

Barber, Clarence L.: *The Cost of Public Welfare Expenditures to Canadians.* Toronto: distributed by Gilbert Jackson and Associates. October, 1955.

Beveridge, Sir William: *Report on Social Security and Allied Services.* Cmd. 6404. London, 1944.

Burns, Eveline M.: *The American Social Security System.* Boston, 1951. 'How Much Social Welfare Can America Afford?' In *Proceedings of the National Conference of Social Work.* New York, 1949. *Social Security and Public Policy.* New York, 1956.

Canadian Welfare Council. *Canadian Welfare.* Ottawa, (Periodical).

Cassidy, Harry M.: *Social Security and Reconstruction in Canada.* Toronto: The Ryerson Press, 1943.

Clarke, C. E.: *Social Insurance in Britain.* Cambridge, 1950.

Fisher, A. G. B.: *Economic Progress and Social Security.* London, 1945.

Friedlander, W. A.: *Introduction to Social Welfare.* New York, 1955.

Grauer, A. E.: Monographs on 'Public Assistance and Social Insurance' and 'Public Health.' In *Report of Royal Commission on Dominion-Provincial Relations.* Ottawa, 1939.

Haber, William, and Cohen, Wilbur J.: *Readings in Social Security.* New York, 1948.

International Labour Office: *Approaches to Social Security.* Montreal, 1942. *The Financing of Social Security.* Geneva, 1957. *International Survey of Social Security,* Geneva, 1950. *The Investment of the Funds of Social Security Institutions.* Geneva, 1939. *Objectives and Advanced Standards of Social Security.* Geneva, 1952. 'Post-War Trends in Social Security.' *International Labour Review.* Geneva, June-September, 1949. *Systems of Social Security: Great Britain.* Geneva, 1957. *Systems of Social Security: New Zealand.* Geneva, 1949. *Systems of Social Security: United States.* Geneva, 1954.

Kapp, K. William: *The Social Costs of Private Insurance.* Harvard, 1950.

Liberal Party: *Reform of Income Tax and Social Security Payments.* London, 1950.

Marsh, David C.: *National Insurance and Assistance in Great Britain.* London, 1950.

Marsh, L. C.: 'Social Security in Canada.' In *Report of the Advisory Committee on Reconstruction of the House of Commons Special Committee on Social Security.* Ottawa, 1943.

Mendelsohn, Ronald: *Social Security in the British Commonwealth.* London, 1954.

Meriam, Lewis, Schlotterbeck, Karl and Maroney, Mildred: *The Cost and Financing of Social Security.* Washington, D.C., Brookings Institution, 1950.

Merriam, Ida C.: 'Social Welfare Programs in the United States.' *Social Security Bulletin.* Washington, D.C., February, 1953. 'Social Security Financing.' *Social Security Administration, Report No. 17.* Washington, D.C., 1952.

Mushkin, Selma J. and Crowther, Beatrice: *Federal Taxes and the Measurement of State Capacity.* U.S. Public Health Service, Washington, D.C., May, 1954.

Myers, Robert J.: 'Actuarial Aspects of Financing O.A.S.I.' *Social Security Bulletin.* Washington, D.C., June, 1953.

Myers, Robert J. and Rasor, Eugene A.: 'Long Range Cost Estimates for O.A.S.I.' *Social Security Administration, Actuarial Study 36.* Washington. D.C., June, 1953.

National Council of Social Service: *Public Social Services: Handbook of Information on Services Provided by the State.* 9th Edition. London, 1950.

Niessen, Abraham M.: 'O.A.S.I. and Its Relation to the State Assistance Plans.' *Social Service Review.* Washington, D.C., September, 1952.

Parker, James S.: 'Financial Policy in O.A.S.I.' *Social Security Bulletin.* Washington, D.C., June, 1951.

Peacock, Alan T.: *The Economics of National Insurance.* London, 1952. (ed.) *Income Redistribution and Social Policy.* London, 1954.

Pigou, A. C.: *Economics of Welfare.* London, 1948.

Potter, D. and Stansfield, D. H.: *National Insurance.* London, 1949.

Robson, W. A.: (ed.) *Social Security.* 3rd Edition. George Allen and Unwin, London, 1948.

Rowntree, B. Seebohm, and Lavers, G. R.: *Poverty and the Welfare State.* London, 1951.

Russell, James E.: (ed.) *National Policies for Education, Health and Social Services.* New York, 1955.

Siegfried, Charles A.: 'Why Pay-as-you-go?' *American Economic Security, Conference Issue.* 1953.

Swan, Eliot J.: 'Economic Aspects of Social Security.' In *Housing, Social Security and Public Works.* Washington, D.C.: Board of Governors of the Federal Reserve System. 1946.

United Nations: *Report on Maintenance of Family Levels of Living: Social Policy Relating to Social Insurance, Social Assistance and Related Social Services.* E/CN.5/321. February, 1957.

Williams, Gertrude: *The Price of Social Security.* London, 1944.

Witte, Edwin E.: 'Twenty Years of Social Security.' *Social Security Bulletin.* Washington, D.C., October, 1955.

GOVERNMENT REPORTS

CANADA

Department of National Health and Welfare: *Government Expenditures and Related Data on Health and Social Welfare, 1947-1953.* Ottawa, June, 1955.

Social Security Expenditures in Australia, Canada, Great Britain, New Zealand and the United States, 1949-1952. A Comparative Study. Ottawa, 1954.

Province of Ontario, Minister of Public Welfare. *Annual Reports.* Toronto. · · ·

UNITED KINGDOM

Government Actuary, *Report on the First Quinquennial Review: National Insurance Act, 1946.* London, 1954.

Ministry of Reconstruction: *Social Insurance.* Cmd. 6550. London, 1944.

National Assistance Board: *Annual Reports.* London.

National Assistance Advisory Committee: *Reports.* London.

National Insurance Fund: *Accounts,* published annually. London.

Treasury: *Estimates of National Income and Expenditure.* Annually. London.

UNITED STATES

Committee on Labor and Public Welfare: *Final Report on Welfare and Pension Plans Investigation.* Washington, D.C., 1956.

House Committee on Ways and Means: *Analysis of the Social Security System.* Hearings before a Sub-Committee. 83rd Congress, 1st Session. Washington, D.C., 1953.

Social Security Administration. Bureau of Public Assistance. *Characteristics of State Public Assistance Plans.* Report No. 21. Washington, D.C., 1953.

Handbook of Public Assistance Administration. Washington, D.C. Division of Research and Statistics. *Social Security Programs and Economic Stability.* Washington, D.C., 1954.

Social Security Yearbook. Washington, D.C. *Some Basic*

Readings in Social Security. Report No. 28. Washington, D.C. 1950.

AGE AND RETIREMENT

American Statistical Association: *What is Actuarial Soundness of a Pension Plan?* Proceedings of a Panel Meeting, Chicago, December, 1952.

Bers, Melvin K.: *Union Policy and the Older Worker.* Institute of Industrial Relations, University of California. Berkeley, 1957.

Bond, Floyd and Associates: *Our Needy Aged. A California Study of a National Problem.* New York, 1954.

Clark, F. Le Gros: 'Physical Problems of the Employment of Ageing Men.' *International Labour Review.* Geneva, October, 1957.

Cohen, Wilbur J.: *Retirement Policies Under Social Security.* Institute of Industrial Relations, University of California. Berkeley, 1957.

Corson, John J. and McConnell, John W.: *Economic Needs of Older People.* New York: The Twentieth Century Fund, Inc., 1956.

Community Chests and Councils of America, Inc.: *Community Organisation for the Aged in 1953.* New York, 1953.

Crook, G. Hamilton, and Heinstein, Marten: *The Older Worker in Industry: A Study of the Attitudes of Industrial Workers Towards Aging and Retirement.* Institute of Industrial Relations, University of California. Berkeley, 1958.

Donahue, Wilma T.: *Planning the Older Years.* Ann Arbor, 1950.

Gordon, Margaret S.: *Employer Policies Toward the Older Worker.* Institute of Industrial Relations, University of California, Berkeley, 1958.

Govan, Elizabeth S. L.: *The Needs of the Aged.* Ottawa: Canadian Welfare Council, 1951.

Havighurst, Robert J. and Albrech, Ruth: *Older People.* New York, 1953.

Huntington, Emily H.: *Employment Problems of Women Aged 40 and Over.* Institute of Industrial Relations, University of California. Berkeley, 1958.

Labour Party (U.K.): *National Superannuation.* Policy Document. London, 1957.

MacGregor, D. C.: 'The Old Age Pension Legislation.' In *Report of Proceedings of the Fifth Tax Conference.* Toronto: Canadian Tax Foundation, 1951.

Myers, Robert J.: 'Bases and Background of the Retirement Test.' *Social Security Bulletin.* Washington, D.C., March, 1954.
'Old Age and Survivors' Insurance. Retirement Test under the 1954 Amendments.' *Social Security Bulletin.* Washington D.C., December, 1954.

National Council of Social Service, Inc.: *The Care of Old People*. In Report of National Conference. London, 1950.

Nuffield Foundation: *Old People*. London, 1947.

Parker, James S.: *Social Security Reserves*. Washington, D.C.: American Council on Public Affairs, 1942.

Preston, George Heinrichs: *Should I Retire?* New York, 1952.

Shenfield, B. E.: *Social Policies for Old Age: A Review of Social Provision for Old Age in Great Britain*. London, 1957.

Steinhans, H. W.: *Financing Old Age*. New York: National Industrial Conference Board. 1948.

Steiver, Peter O. and Dorfman, Robert: *The Economic Status of the Aged*. Institute of Industrial Relations, University of California. Berkeley, 1957.

Stieglitz, Edward J.: *The Second Fifty Years*. Philadelphia, 1946.

Tibbitts, Clark (ed.): *Social Contribution by the Aging*. Committee on Aging and Geriatrics, American Academy of Political and Social Science. Philadelphia, 1952.

Vaughan-Morgan, John; Maude, Angus and Thompson, Kenneth: *The Care of Old People*. London: Conservative Political Centre. 1952.

Wallace, Elisabeth: 'Old Age Security in Canada; Changing Attitudes,' *Canadian Journal of Economics and Political Science*. May, 1952.

Welford, A. T., and others: *Skill and Age*. London, 1951.

GOVERNMENT REPORTS

CANADA

Department of National Health and Welfare. *Old Age Income Security*. Memoranda on New Zealand, Australia, Great Britain, United States and Selected European Countries. Ottawa, 1950.

Senate and House of Commons Joint Committee. *Report on Old Age Security*. Ottawa, 1950.

UNITED KINGDOM

Committee on the Economic and Financial Problems of the Provision for Old Age. *Report*. Cmd. 9333. London, 1954.

Report on Taxation Treatment of Provisions for Retirement. Cmd. 9063. London, 1954.

Occupational Pension Schemes. London: H.M. Stationery Office, 1958.

UNITED STATES

Department of Labor, Bureau of Labor Statistics. *Employment and Economic Status of Older Men and Women*. Bulletin, 1213. Washington, D.C., 1957.

Joint Committee on Railroad Retirement Legislation, 83rd Congress, 1st Session. *Economic Problems of An Aging Population*. Washington, D.C., 1953.

Social Security Administration. 'Age of Population and Per Capita Income, by States, 1953.' *Social Security Bulletin*. Washington, D.C., December, 1954.
'Financial Policy in Old Age and Survivors Insurance, 1935-1950.' *Social Security Bulletin*. Washington, D.C., June, 1951.

HEALTH

Abel-Smith, Brian and Titmuss, R.M.: *The Cost of the National Health Service in England and Wales*. Cambridge: The National Institute of Economic and Social Research. 1956.

Anderson, Odin W. and Feldman, Jacob J.: *Family Medical Costs and Voluntary Health Insurance*. New York: Health Information Foundation, 1956.

Canadian Welfare Council. *Health Insurance. What are the Issues?* Ottawa, 1956.

Davis, Michael Marks: *Medical Care for Tomorrow*. New York, 1955.

Dickinson, F. G. and Raymond James: 'The Economic Position of Medical Care, 1929-1953.' *Journal of the American Medical Associations*. Bulletin 99, 1954.

Heagerty, J. J.: 'Health Insurance.' *Report of the Advisory Committee on Health Insurance to the House of Commons Committee on Social Security*. Ottawa, 1943.

International Labour Office: *Vocational Rehabilitation of the Disabled*. Report IV (2) to the International Labour Conference, Geneva, 1954. *The Cost of Medical Care*. Geneva, 1959.

International Social Security Association: *Rehabilitation and Assessment of Benefit*. Report to Xth General Meeting. Geneva, 1951.

Kessler, Henry H.: *Rehabilitation of the Physically Handicapped*. New York, 1953.

Roberts, F.: *The Cost of Health*. London, 1952.

Ross, James Sterling: *The National Health Service in Great Britain*. New York, 1952.

Taylor, Malcolm G.: *The Administration of Health Insurance in Canada*. Toronto, 1956.

GOVERNMENT REPORTS

CANADA

Department of National Health and Welfare: *Canadian Sickness Survey, 1950-1951*. Ottawa, 1953 to 1955.
Health Insurance. Memorandum on New Zealand, Denmark, Sweden, Great Britain, Norway and The Netherlands. Ottawa, 1950-52.
Selected Public Hospital and Medical Plans in Canada. Social Security Series, No. 15. Ottawa, July, 1955.

Voluntary Medical Care Insurance: A Study of Non-Profit Plans in Canada. General Series No. 4. Ottawa, April, 1954. *Voluntary Medical and Hospital Insurance in Canada.* General Series No. 9. Ottawa, August, 1955.

UNITED KINGDOM

Committee of Enquiry into the Cost of the National Health Service. *Report.* Cmd. 9663. London, 1956.
Ministry of Health. *Annual Reports.* London.

UNITED STATES

Building America's Health. A report to the President by the President's Commission on the Health Needs of the Nation. Washington, D.C., 1952-53.
Social Security Administration. 'Voluntary Health Insurance and Medical Care Costs, 1948-1955.' Social Security Bulletin. Washington, D.C., December, 1956.

FAMILY ALLOWANCES

International Social Security Association: *Family Allowances.* XIth General Meeting. Report II. Geneva, 1954.
Myrdal, Alva: *Nation and Family.* London, 1945.
Rathbone, Eleanor: *Family Allowances.* George Allen and Unwin, London, 1949.
United Nations, Department of Social Affairs. *Economic Measures in Favour of the Family.* New York, 1952.

GOVERNMENT REPORT

UNITED KINGDOM

Ministry of National Insurance. *Family Allowances.* Cmd. 8517. London, 1952.

UNEMPLOYMENT

Burns, Eveline M.: *British Unemployment Programs, 1920-1938.* Washington, D.C., Social Science Research Council, 1942.
Clague, Ewan: 'The Economics of Unemployment Compensation.' *Yale Law Journal.* December, 1945.
Lester, Richard A. and Kidd, Charles V.: *The Case Against Experience Rating in Unemployment Compensation.* Industrial Relations Monographs, No. 2. New York: Industrial Relations Counselors, Inc., 1939.
Myers, Charles A.: 'Experience Rating in Unemployment Compensation.' *American Economic Review.* June, 1945.
Tillyard, Sir Frank, and Ball, F. N.: *Unemployment Insurance in Great Britain, 1911-1948.* London, 1949.

Waytinsky, W. S.: *Principles and Cost Estimates of Unemployment Insurance*. Washington, D.C.: Department of Labor, Bureau of Employment Security, 1953.

GOVERNMENT REPORTS

UNITED STATES

Department of Labor, Bureau of Employment Security. *Adequacy of Benefits under Unemployment Insurance Laws, as of August, 1954.* Washington, D.C., 1954.

'Review of Experience Rating.' In *Labor Market and Employment Security*. Washington, D.C., July, 1952.

Unemployment Insurance Legislative Policy: Benefits, Eligibility. Washington, D.C., 1953.

WORKMEN'S COMPENSATION

Potter, D. and Stansfield, D. H.: *National Insurance (Industrial Injuries)*. London, 1950.

Reede, Arthur L.: *Adequacy of Workmen's Compensation*. Harvard, 1947.

Samuels, H. and Pollard, R. S. W.: *Industrial Injuries*. London, 1950.

Somers, Herman Miles, and Somers, Anne Ramsay: *Workmen's Compensation*. New York, 1954.

GOVERNMENT REPORTS

CANADA

Province of Ontario, Workmen's Compensation Board. *Annual Reports*. Toronto.

UNITED KINGDOM

Accounts of the Industrial Injuries Fund. Annual. London.

Social Insurance. Part II. Workmen's Compensation. Cmd. 6551. London, 1944.

INDEX

Accident rates, 65; 108 *n.*

Accumulation-of-funds system, and "pay-as-you-go", 69-84; in financing old age pensions, 126-7, 243; during depression periods, 217

ADMINISTRATIVE COSTS
hypothetical expenditure on, 90-3; of Canadian old age pensions system, 132; of unemployment insurance, 188

Adoption of children, 207

Aged, welfare services for the, 136-8

AGRICULTURE
price fluctuations, 16; farm relief and price maintenance, 28-9; assistance to farmers, 192, 226 *n.*; farm workers' unemployment insurance, 192, 226 *n.*; farm relief in Canada and U.S.A., 192-3

Almshouses and institutions for the aged, 137, 138

Anderson, W. M., 11

Annuities in pension schemes, 126-8

Atlantic Charter, the, social security as an objective of, 20

AUSTRALIA
10; uniform benefits system, 43; causes of lack of co-ordination, 53 *n.*; differences in wages of skilled and unskilled workers, 60; as a "middle-class-only" country, 64; percentage distribution of receipts for social insurance and family allowances, 67 (table), 68; expenditure as percentage of national income, 87 (table), 88 (table); percentage distribution of expenditure, 94 (table); percentage distribution of income maintenance payments, 95 (table); official pensionable age, 114; life expectation, 114 *n.*; family allowances, 147-51 (*passim*); family allowances as proportion of social security benefits, 154 (table); aid for disabled and blind persons, 206-7; provision for widows and orphans, 207-8, 209; maternity grants, 209,

AUSTRIA
financing of sickness and maternity benefits, 66; percentage distribution of receipts for social insurance and family allowances, 67 (table), 68; expenditure as percentage of national income, 87 (table); percentage distribution of expenditure, 94 (table); hospital patients' payments, 180; financing of unemployment insurance, 188 *n.*

Automation: *see* Labour-saving machinery

Ball, Robert M., 11, 237 *n.*

Band, James, S., 11

BELGIUM
family allowances costs distribution, 65 *n.*; percentage distribution of receipts for social insurance and family allowances, 67 (table), 68; expenditure as percentage of national income, 87 (table); percentage distribution of expenditure, 94 (table); family allowances, 142; employers' equalisation-fund system, 144; unemployment insurance, 187

BENEFITS
distribution problems, 24; classes of, 34; variable and uniform flat-rate systems, 39-46; standardisation of public assistance, 50; advantages of cash benefits, 51-2; anomalies, 52-4; linked to contributions, 56, 60; workers' unequal shares of payments, 62; dependence on annual votes, 73; effect of inflation, 78-9, 85; hypothetical expenditure on, 90-3; for retirement, 120-5; relation of wages to, 120-1; health services systems of, 178-9; in unemployment insurance, 187, 190-1; in workmen's compensation, 203, 245; in kind, in underdeveloped countries, 214, 215; as economic stabilisers, 215-17; and inflation periods, 223; local variations, 228; international standards, 229-32; relation of, to wages, 238, 241, 242; concentration of, for greatest need, 243

BEVERIDGE REPORT
on benefits anomalies, 52; on need for reviewing systems, 53; on retirement ages, 115 *n.*; on unemployment insurance, 185-6; on workmen's compensation, 197

Bisson, J. G., 11

BLIND PERSONS
as efficient workers, 109 *n.*; special aid for, 184, 206-7

Blue Cross, the (Canada and U.S.A. health scheme), 164-5, 166, 174

Blue Shield, the (U.S.A. health scheme), 164-5, 166

Bodmer, Laura, 89 *n.*

BRITAIN
expansion of services in World War II, 19; demands for correlation of state and private schemes, 41-2; flat-rate benefits challenged, 45; Unemployment Insurance Fund deficit (1934), 48 *n.*; public assistance, 50; co-ordination measures, 53; regulations for contributions for different groups of workers, 56; employers' and workers' contributions, 60 *n.*; Lloyd George scheme, 62; workers' unequal shares of payments, 62; contributions system reforms, 65; family allowances financed by state, 65; state's share of health service costs, 66; percentage distribution of receipts for social insurance and family allowances, 67 (table); old age pensions payments, 71 *n.*; financing systems for family

allowances, 73; special contributions method of financing, 74; variation in interest rates, 78 *n.*; expenditure as percentage of national income, 87 (table), 88 (and tables), 89; percentage distribution of expenditure, 94 (table); percentage distribution of income maintenance payments, 95 (table); proportions of national income spent on old age pensions and family allowances, 95-8; retirement-age workers in light and heavy industries, 108 *n.*; old and young workers' accident rates, 108 *n.*; increased employment of the elderly, 109, 110; statistics of persons of retirement age, and their potential earnings, 109-10; official pensionable age, 114; life-expectation in England, 114 *n.*; earnings regulations for pensioners, 116; increased old age pensions for those working beyond pensionable age, 116; population percentages of pensionable-aged persons, 118; relation of wages to benefits, 121; Labour party and supplementary pension schemes, 122; proposals for wage-related pensions, 123-4; civil service pensions, 125 *n.*; occupational pensions schemes, 133-4; financing of civil service superannuation schemes, 135; poor-law institutions, 137 *n.*; family allowances, 147, 148, 150, 154; health services, and costs, 158, 177-8, 180, 181; doctors' payments system, 175;

unemployment insurance, 185, 187, 191; workmen's compensation, 195 *n.*; 196-7, 202, 203-4, 221 *n.*; provision for widows and orphans, 207; maternity benefits, 209; industrial injuries system, 221 *n.*; early parish relief system, 225; responsibility of central government, 226; most progressive country in social security, 235; basic all-risks insurance, 236 *n*; adoption of flat-rate system, 238; supplementary assistance for old age pensioners, 240; raising of pensionable age, 244 *n.*; benefits extended to foreigners, 245. *See also* Beveridge Report

BRITISH GUIANA
pensions, 48; proportion of elderly poor, 112 *n.*

BURMA
limitations of early scheme, 33; sickness and maternity benefits, 66, 161; investment of government funds, 76; introduction of contributory scheme, 215

Burns, Dr Eveline, M., 11

CANADA
workmen's compensation, 28, 41, 56, 156, 198, 201-2; old age pensions, 34-6; strong sense of individual responsibility, 37, 236-7; operation of uniform benefits, 43; flat-rate benefits challenged, 45; public assistance, 50-1; difficulties of coordination, 53; family allowances, 34-5, 36, 41, 59, 65, 73, 147, 148-151, 154, 155 *n.*; per-

R

centage distribution of receipts for social insurance and family allowances, 67 (table), 68; financing of old age pensions and unemployment insurance, 66, 74-5, 129, 238; wage-related benefits, 74; special contributions scheme, 74; family expenditure survey, 82; expenditure as percentage of national income, 87 (table), 88 (and tables); hypothetical expenditure, 92-3; percentage distribution of expenditure, 94 (table), 95; and of income maintenance payments, 95 (table); old age pension increases, 95; official pensionable ages, 114, 117; life-expectation, 114 n.; old age assistance, 117; old age pension scheme, 130-2, 226, 238, 241; occupational pensions, 132-3, 134-5; relation of income tax to family allowances, 153 (table); family allowances as proportion of social security benefits, 154 (table) and n.; health services, 158-60, 161, 162 n., 181; individuals' inability to meet medical costs, 163; medical care systems and costs distribution, 164-74; payments to doctors, 174; hospital patients' payments, 180; advance measures to combat effects of depressions, 184; unemployment insurance, 186-8, 216-17; assistance to farmers, 192; disabled and blind persons' allowances, 206; provisions for widows and orphans, 207, 208; maternity schemes, 209; family allowances

as economic stabiliser, 215; expenditure by federal, municipal and provincial authorities, 225; financial and administrative systems, 227; benefits affected by local variations in living standards, 228; problems and progress, 235; gaps in system, 235 n.; shortages of facilities and trained personnel, 236; subsidy grants, 237; flat and variable-rates systems, 238

Capitation system for doctors' fees, 175

Cassidy, Prof Harry M., 19, 211 n., 235-6

CEYLON
percentage distribution of receipts for social insurance and family allowances, 67 (table), 68; expenditure as percentage of national income, 87 (table)

CHILDREN
as economic asset, 16; income tax allowances for, 152-4; medical care of, in U.S.A., 167; disablement benefits for, in U.S.A., 206; adoption of, 207; allowances for, to widowed mothers, 207-8. See also Family allowances; Widows and orphans

Children's allowances: see Family allowances

CIVIL SERVICE (Britain)
employment of older workers in, 110; pension schemes policy, 125 n.; financing of superannuation schemes, 135

Cohen, Dr Wilbur J., 11

CONTRIBUTIONS
types of, in relation to benefits,

46, 56; role of, in Britain, 56; varying rates for different groups of workers, 56; as factor in social security, 57; distinction of, from taxes, 58-9; by workers, 58-9; by employers, 62-3; under Lloyd George scheme, 62; by public authorities, 63; tripartite system, 64, 187-91, 243; for old age pensioners beyond pensionable age, 116; in wage-related schemes, 122-6, 187; pooling system, 128; for unemployment insurance, 187-91; for workmen's compensation, 197; as form of compulsory savings, 221; systems compared, 243

Co-ordination of schemes, 52-4, 235

COSTS
19-20; problems of, 24, 25; difficulty of international comparisons, 32; distribution of, 64-8; almost wholly met by employers in Soviet countries, 64; accumulation-of-funds system versus "pay-as-you-go", 69-84; cost policies for health services, 162-81; sharing of, by federal, regional and local authorities, 224-9; and international standards of benefits, 229-32

CZECHOSLOVAKIA
family allowances costs borne by employers, 65; expenditure as percentage of national income, 87 (table)

Davidson, Dr George F., 11, 19 n., 140, 212 n.

Davis, Richard E. G., 11

DENMARK
waiting period for sickness benefits, 39 n.; state aid to employers for industrial injuries costs, 65 n., 196 n.; sickness and maternity benefits, and old age pensions, 66; expenditure as percentage of national income, 87 (table); percentage distribution of expenditure, 94 (table); life-expectation, 114 n.; unemployment insurance contributions, 188

DENTAL SERVICES
Britain, 177, 180; Canada, 171

DEPRESSIONS
and public assistance, 48-9; and family allowances, 145; social security measures as stabilising factor in, 155; as cause of unemployment, 183; build-up of funds for, 184; state's responsibility for unemployment relief in, 189; effect of, on unemployment insurance, 216

DISABILITY
long-term, 205-7; percentage distribution of income maintenance payments for, 95 (table); efficiency of blind workers, 109 n.; and U.S.A. occupational pensions, 133; public assistance for, in U.S.A., 161 n.; and unemployment insurance, 183; financing of insurance, in U.S.A., 188 n.; in Canada, 198. See also Workmen's compensation.

Dixon, W. G., 11

Doctors: *See* Medical profession

Earthquake victims, 29
Economic stabilisation,
social security as factor in, 215-18

EMPLOYERS
and pay-roll tax (U.S.A.), 34; contributions by, in variable benefits schemes, 40; role of contributions by, 62-3; contributions by, in Soviet countries, 64; contributions systems, 65, 74; industrial injuries and family allowances costs borne by, 65-6; and financing of sickness and maternity benefits, unemployment insurance and old age pensions, 66; and wage-related pensions, 123; and provident funds method for pensions, 126; and occupational pensions, 135; early family allowances schemes by, 143-4; and sickness benefits, 160, 163, 165; contributions to unemployment insurance, 187-90; and workmen's compensation, 194, *et seqq.*

Employment exchanges, 193, 222

Equalisation funds, 144

European League for Economic Co-operation, 246

Expectation of life: *See* Life-expectation

Experience rating (in unemployment insurance), 189-90, 195, 217-18

FAMILY ALLOWANCES
139-55; Canada, 34-5, 36, 41, 59, 65, 73, 147, 148-51, 154, 155 *n.*; first experiments in, 141-3; France and Belgium, 142-4; equalisation-fund system, 144; introduction of state scheme, 146 *et seqq.;* no U.S.A. scheme, 146-7; Australia 145-54 (*passim*); New Zealand, 145-54 (*passim*); as a proportion of social security benefits, 154 (table); as economic stabiliser, 215

Famine relief, 29

Farmers, aid for,
192, 226 *n.* farm relief in Canada and U.S.A., 192-3; *See also* Agriculture

Feudal system, 17

Financing of schemes: *See* under individual entries— Family allowances; Workmen's compensation, etc.; and under individual countries

FINLAND
sickness and maternity benefits, and unemployment insurance, 66, 188; percentage distribution of receipts for social insurance and family allowances, 67 (table), 68; expenditure as percentage of national income, 87 (table); percentage distribution of expenditure, 94 (table)

Flood victims, 29

Fisher, A. G. B., 218 *n.*

Foster homes,
for the aged, 137; for children, 207, 208

FRANCE
family allowances, 65-6, 142, 143, 147; percentage distribution of receipts for social insurance and family allowances, 67 (table), 68; sickness and maternity benefits, 66, 162 *n.*; expenditure as percentage of national income, 87 (table); percentage distribution of expenditure, 94 (table); equalisation fund system, 144; doctors' fees, 175; health-service beneficiaries contributions, 179-80; financing of unemployment insurance, 188 *n.*

Funeral payments (Britain), 66 *n.*

Germany, West: *See* German Federal Republic

GERMAN FEDERAL REPUBLIC
wage-related pensions, 45, 125, 224; benefits for sickness, maternity, old age pensions and unemployment insurance, 66; percentage distribution of receipts for social insurance and family allowances, 67 (table); expenditure as percentage of national income, 87 (table); percentage distribution of expenditure, 94 (table); adjustable pensions scheme, 122; health service beneficiaries' payments, 180; financing of unemployment insurance and assistance, 188; financing of workmen's compensation, 195

Gold Coast, 16

GOVERNMENTAL FINANCING
methods, 72-7; by central, regional and local government, 224-9; trend towards increased responsibility, 235

Government employees, 29-30

Great Britain: *See* Britain

GREECE
financing industrial injuries insurance, 65 *n.*; financing of workmen's compensation, 195 *n.*

Group insurance (in health schemes), 165

GUATEMALA
percentage distribution of receipts for social insurance and family allowances, 67 (table), 68; expenditure as percentage of national income, 87 (table)

HEALTH SERVICES
156-181; general measures and benefits to individuals compared, 31; advantages of benefits in kind, 51; contributions, in Britain, 66 *n.*; financing systems, 69; expenditure as percentage of national income, 88 (table); estimated payments by beneficiaries, 89; percentage distribution of expenditure, 94 (table); medical care in Canada and U.S.A., 164-74; doctors' payments, 174-5; use and abuse of, 176-7; financing policies, 177-81; local administration, 226; scope for voluntary and government co-operation, 245. *See also* Sickness benefits

Hendry, Prof Charles E., 10, 18

HOSPITALS
Britain's need of new hospitals, 181 *n.*: *See also* Health services

Housing schemes, 32

Howery, Dr Victor, 11

ICELAND

family allowances costs distribution, 65 *n.*; expenditure as percentage of national income, 87 (table)

Indemnity system for doctors' payments, 175, 179

INDIA

and wage-benefit relation, 230

Industrial injuries insurance: *See* Workmen's compensation

Industrialisation,
as factor in need for social security, 39

Inflation, effects of,
38, 42, 44, 48, 52, 78-9, 85, 223-4, 245; changes necessitated by, 57-8; state responsibility in combating, 63; on private savings, 72, 112; measures to counteract, on pension rates, 124-5, 128; on workmen's compensation benefits, 204

Insurance companies, 195, 201, 204

International Labour office,
adoptions and recommendations, 31 *n.*, 33, 44-5, 118-19, 188 *n.*

INVESTMENT

by private savers and companies, 72; in governmental financing, 73-7; variations in interest rates, 78 *n.*; productive investment of funds, 80-4; problems of, in underdeveloped countries, 214

IRELAND

old age pensions financing, 66; percentage distribution of receipts for social insurance and family allowances, 67 (table), 68; expenditure as percentage of national income, 87 (table); percentage distribution of expenditure, 94 (table)

ISRAEL

percentage distribution of receipts for social insurance and family allowances, 67 (table), 68; expenditure as percentage of national income, 87 (table); percentage distribution of expenditure, 94 (table)

ITALY

family allowance costs borne by employers, 65; financing of unemployment insurance, 66, 188; percentage of distribution of receipts for social insurance and family allowances, 67 (table), 68; expenditure as percentage of national income, 87 (table); percentage distribution of expenditure, 94 (table)

Jaffary, Prof Stuart K., 233 *n.*

JAPAN

percentage distribution of receipts for social insurance and family allowances, 67 (table), 68; expenditure as percentage of national income, 87 (table); percentage distribution of expenditure, 94 (table); health service beneficiaries' payments, 180

Kariba hydro-electric scheme,

and investment of government funds, 76

Keynes, John Maynard, 142

King, W. L. Mackenzie, 20 n.

Labour-saving machinery, 18, 19; as factor in employment of the elderly, 102-4

Laroque, Pierre, 231 n.

LIFE-EXPECTATION
statistics, 114; as factor in pension systems, 126 n., 128; effects of increase in, 156

Lincoln, Abraham, 37

LIVING STANDARDS
as factor in need for social security, 38-9, 244; as factor in sharing of costs, 64; relation to social security standards, 80, 83-4; and retirement pension rates, 120; and tax system of financing pensions, 129; relation to health service contributions, 179; effects of raising, 211-12; effects of, on financing of systems, 227; effects of, on benefits, 228, 230

Lloyd George scheme (Britain), 62

LUXEMBURG
family allowances costs distribution, 65 n.; expenditure as percentage of national income, 87 (table); percentage distribution of expenditure, 94 (table)

MacGregor, Prof D. C., 128

Malaya, 16

Malingering, 241, 242

MATERNITY BENEFITS
financing of, 66, 66 n., 69; schemes for, 209

MEANS TESTS
in non-contributory schemes, 40; and I.L.O. public assistance standards, 44; evolution of, 45-6; improved application of, 49-50; for old age pensions, 112-13, 117, 120; as deterrent to private saving, 120, 222; avoidance of, in family allowances schemes, 147; in special aid for the blind, 184; in widows' and orphans' schemes, 207, 208; disadvantages of, 240-1; in Canada and U.S.A., 21 n., 37, 130-2, 161 n.; in Australia, 206-7; in New Zealand, 50, 117-18, 206-7; in Austria, 188 n.; in West Indies, 48

MEDICAL PROFESSION
problems of, in health schemes, 174-7; payments to, 175, 179

Mendelsohn, Dr Ronald, 88 n.; 218 n.

Merriman, Mrs Ida C., 11

MINING
high accident rates in, 65; data of workers of retirement age (Britain), 108 n.; National Coal Board and National Union of Miners' contributory scheme for workmen's compensation, 197-8

Morgan, Prof John S., 10, 235 n., 241

Murchison, C. A. L., 11

Myer, Robert J., 11

National assistance: See Public assistance

NATIONAL INCOME
proportion of social security payments to, 85-97; and social security in underdeveloped countries, 213-14; average percentage of social security costs to, 242

NATIONAL INSURANCE Fund (Britain)
share of health service costs, 66

NATIONAL SUPERANNUATION
British Labour party's recommendations for, 122

NATIONALISED INDUSTRIES
position of schemes for workers in, 30

NETHERLANDS
family allowances costs borne by employers, 65; percentage distribution of receipts for social insurance and family allowances, 67 (table), 68; expenditure as percentage of national income, 87 (table); percentage distribution of expenditure, 94 (table); life-expectation, 114 *n.*; doctors' payments, 175; unemployment insurance, 187

New Deal Social Security Act, 1935 (U.S.A.), 9

NEW ZEALAND
world's first complete social security system, 10; means tests, 50, 117-18, 206-7; co-ordination measures, 53; grading of contributions, 60 *n.*; percentage distribution of receipts for social insurance and family allowances, 67 (table), 88 (and table); percentage distribution of expenditure, 94 (table); and of income maintenance payments, 95 (table); official pensionable age, 114; life-expectation, 114 *n.*; distinction between 'superannuation' and 'age benefit', 117-18; distinction between age and invalidity for pension, 118; financing by taxes, 129; family allowances, 145-51 (*passim*); as proportion of social security benefits, 154 (table); health services, 158; doctors' payments, 175; aid for disabled and blind persons, 206-7; provision for widows and orphans, 207, 208; maternity benefits scheme, 209; responsibility of central government, 226; greatest progress in social security, 235; relation of benefits and incomes, 241 *n.*

NORWAY
waiting period for sickness benefits, 39 *n.*; financing old age pensions, 66; percentage distribution of receipts for social insurance and family allowances, 67 (table), 68; expenditure as percentage of national income, 87 (table); percentage distribution of expenditure, 94 (table); life-expectation, 114 *n.*; unemployment insurance, 187

Occupational diseases insurance: *See* Workmen's compensation

Occupational pensions
132-6; Canada, 132-3; U.S.A., 133; Britain, 133-4; equalisation fund system for, 144

OLD AGE, provision for, 111-13: *See also* Old age pensions; Occupational pensions

OLD AGE PENSIONS 98-138; Canada, 34-5, 36, 41, 74-5, 98, 130-2, 208, 226, 238; and living standards, 38-9, 124-5; financing methods, 57, 66, 66 *n.*, 68, 70, 126-30; actuarial system of calculation for, 71, 75; assessing needs, 82; hypothetical expenditure, 90-3; percentage distribution of income maintenance payments, 95 (table); percentage of social security costs in Britain, 98; proportion of costs to national income, 98; amendments and alternatives to schemes, 115; relation of wages to, 121, 123-4, 126; supplementary schemes, 122, 240; as economic stabiliser, 215; effects of inflation on, 222; financing of, in U.S.A., 226, 238; fixing of pensionable age, 244. *See also* Occupational pensions

OLD AGE, Survivors and Disability Insurance Program (U.S.A.), 22; no state contributions to, 59; contributions scheme for, 60; financing of, 74, 75 *n.*; extension of, 87

Orphans: *See* Widows and orphans

Parish relief system (Britain), 225

'Pay-as-you-go' system, 24, 25; versus accumulation-of-funds system; in wage-related pensions scheme, 124; in old age pensions schemes, 130, 243; unsuited to unemployment insurance

Pay-roll tax (U.S.A.), 34, 189, 190

Peacock, Alan T., 55 *n.*

Pensions, regulations for contributions period, 57; effect of inflation on, 79-80, 223-4; in workmen's compensation schemes, 201-4; for long-term disability, 206; seamen's pensions, 229, 230. *See also* Occupational pensions; Old age pensions

Pensions and National Insurance, Ministry of (Britain), 28

PERU percentage distribution of receipts for social insurance and family allowances, 67 (table), 68; expenditure as percentage of national income, 87 (table); percentage distribution of expenditure, 94 (table)

Phair, Dr J. T., 11

Pigou, A. C., 219 *n.*

Poland, family allowances in, 65

Poll taxes, 46, 61

Pooled contributions system, in financing of pensions, 127, 128; for health services, 157

Poor law system (Britain), 225

Poor relief: *See* Public assistance

Population increases, as factor in social security, 84

Portugal, 66

Poverty, causes of, 30-1, 111, 139, 157, 160, 245

Private insurance schemes: *See* Voluntary insurance schemes

PRIVATE SAVING
71-2, 221; social insurance as incentive to, 61; problems of, for old age, 111-13; in fixing of assistance rates, 120, 222

Productivity,
effects of, on social security, 38, 78-80; and wages of pension-age workers, 101-2; role of elderly persons in, 106-11; effect of, on incomes, 152; reduction of, by sickness and disability, 220-1

PROMOTION
as factor in early retirement, 105-6; and British civil service pensions scheme, 125 *n.*

Provident funds, 126-8

PUBLIC ASSISTANCE
40; I.L.O. standards, 45; function, operation and inequalities of, 46-51; financing systems, 70, 73, 188, 225-8; distinction from unemployment insurance, 70; effect of unemployment on, 89; percentage distribution of expenditure on, 94 (table); as supplement to old age pensions, 117; in U.S.A., 161 *n.*, 166-7, 206-8; for farmers, 192; for widows and orphans, 207-8; for disability in Canada, 206; as economic stabiliser, 217; limitation policy, 222. *See also* Parish relief system

PUBLIC AUTHORITIES
contributions by, 63; and unemployment insurance, 66

PUBLIC EMPLOYEES
percentage distribution of expenditure for, 94 (table). *See also* Civil service

Public opinion, effects of, 237

Rathbone, Eleanor, 139

Reciprocal agreements, international, 245-6

Rehabilitation services, 65, 221, 222

Rent,
as factor in public assistance, 50

RETIREMENT
98-138; disadvantages of compulsory and early retirement, 99-102, 104-5; automation as factor in, 104; promotion as factor in, 105-6; efficiency of persons of retirement age, 106-11; British statistics for persons of retirement age, and potential earnings, 109-10; estimating retirement age, 113-19; I.L.O. recommendations on pensions for, 118-19; British Labour party's proposals for supplementary pensions for, 122. *See also* Occupational pensions; Old age pensions

Rhys-Williams, Lady, 241 *n.*

Roosevelt, Franklin D., 233 *n.*

St Lawrence Seaway,
as factor in social security, 81, 83, 234

SCHOOL-LEAVING AGE
as factor in social security, 83; effect of extension of, 104; effect on family allowances in Britain, 154

Schottland, Charles I., 11

SEAMEN
I.L.O. recommendations on pensions for, 118, 121; injuries insurance in U.S.A., 199; pensions convention, 229, 230

Severance pay (in unemployment insurance), 192

SICKNESS BENEFITS
limitation and reduction of, 34, 57; in Denmark and Norway, 39 n.; anomalies in, 52; financing of, 66; hypothetical expenditure, 90-3; in U.S.A., 159-60, 166-7; employers' payments, 160; occupational and compulsory insurance for, 161-2; in South American systems, 204

SOCIAL INSURANCE
distinctions from social security and private insurance, 55-7; and workers' contributions, 59-62; percentage distribution of receipts for, 67 (table), 68; percentage distribution of expenditure, 94 (table); as economic stabiliser, 215-18; evolution and review of, 234-46

Somers, Anne Ramsay, 198-9

Somers, Herman Miles, 198-9

SOVIET COUNTRIES
employers' share of social insurance, 64; financing of unemployment insurance, 188

SOVIET UNION
family allowances' costs borne by state, 65; financing of old age pensions, 66 n.

SOUTH AFRICA, UNION OF
percentage distribution of receipts for social insurance and family allowances, 67 (table), 68; expenditure as percentage of national income, 87 (table)

SOUTH AMERICA
trade unions' pension demands, 114; workmen's compensation, 204. See also Peru; Venezuela

Sparrow, E. E., 11

STATE, THE
responsibilities of, 19, 37, 56, 79, 226, 243; and inflation effects, 57-8, 79; policy of contribution to social insurance, 63; and living standards, 64; and industrial injuries' costs, 65; and health service costs, 66, 177; and pensions, 122-6, 129, 130, 134-5; measures to alleviate effects of depressions, 184-5; and unemployment insurance costs, 187-9; and workmen's compensation, 196 n., 197; role of, in schemes by democracies, 239. See also Governmental financing

Strakhovsky, Florence, 10

SWEDEN
flat-rate benefits, 45; pensions, 45, 66, 224; sickness, maternity and unemployment insurance, 66, 188; expenditure as percentage of national income, 87 (table); percentage distribution of expenditure, 94 (table); life-expectation, 114 n.; cost-of-living adjustments to pensions, 224

SWITZERLAND
family allowances' costs distribution, 65 n.; financing sick-

ness and maternity benefits, 66; percentage distribution of receipts for social insurance and family allowances, 67 (table), 68; expenditure as percentage of national income, 87 (table); percentage distribution of expenditure, 94 (table); health service beneficiaries' payments, 180; financing of unemployment insurance, 188

Tallon, R. J., 11

TAXES
in financing social security, 34, 55, 57; and contributions, 58-9, 61; and governmental financing, 73; in old age pensions schemes, 129-30; for Canadian old age pensions and health services, 75, 130-1, 171, 173; in New Zealand, 75; and repayment of government bonds, 77; effect of inflation on, 78; income tax allowances for dependent children, 141, 152-4; in family allowances schemes, 147; in health schemes, 130-1, 177-9 (*passim*); in unemployment insurance schemes, in U.S.A., 189-90; effects on social security systems, 218-20; and powers of central governments, 226, 228; income-tax relief proposals, 241 *n.*; role of 'earmarked' taxes, 243

Taylor, Prof Malcolm G., 11
Trade recessions: *See* Depressions

TRADE UNIONS
18; and contributory methods, 131; early attitude to family allowances schemes, 144-5; proportion of members to workers in U.S.A., 163; and health service in U.S.A., 163

Training schemes, 193-4

Transport industry,
accident rates in, 65

TUNISIA
percentage distribution of receipts for social insurance and family allowances, 67 (table), 68

TURKEY
financing of benefits and pensions, 66; percentage distribution of receipts for social insurance and family allowances, 67 (table), 68; expenditure as percentage of national income, 87

Underdeveloped countries,
problems of social security in, 213-15, 236, 238-9

UNEMPLOYMENT INSURANCE
9, 182-94; fluctuating costs, 25 *n.*; limitation and reduction of benefits, 34, 57; measures to combat unemployment, 48; public assistance and, 50; fluctuations in unemployment, 70; financing methods, 34, 66, 70, 74; relation of, to national income, 89; in depression periods, 48, 216-17; hypothetical expenditure on, 90-3; percentage distribution of income maintenance payments in, 95 (table); effect of unemployment on mobility of labour, 221-2, administrative systems, 226-7; waiting periods for, 243-4

United Kingdom: *See* Britain

UNITED STATES OF AMERICA
21-2; unemployment insurance, 34, 66, 74, 96, 186-92 (*passim*); voluntary schemes statistics, 35; strong sense of individual responsibility, 37, 211; means tests, 37, 161 *n.*; wages as factor in schemes, 40, 42, 74, 121, 230, 236 *n.*; no state contribution to costs, 43, 59, 63; variable benefits, 43; public assistance, 50-1; difficulties of co-ordination, 53; contributions reductions, 56; pensions schemes contributory system, 60 *n.*; percentage distribution of receipts for social insurance, 67 (table), 68; old age pensions, 66, 71, 116 *n.*; expenditure as percentage of national income, 87 (table), 88; percentage distribution of expenditure, 94 (table); percentage distribution of income maintenance payments, 95 (table); war veterans costs, 94-5; no family allowances, 95-6, 146-7; compulsory and voluntary retirement, 105; accident rates, 108 *n.*; median incomes of families, 111; pensionable and retirement ages, 114; life-expectation, 114 *n.*; occupational pensions, 133; health services, 158-81 (*passim*); disability benefits, 183, 205-6; measures to offset depression effects, 184; assistance to farmers, 192; employment exchanges, 193; workmen's compensation, 198-202; provision for widows and orphans, 207-8; maternity schemes, 209; responsibility of local, federal and state governments, 226-9; variations in living standards, 227-8; complex problems, 235; public opinion on principles, 236-7; variations in benefits and contributions, 238: *See also* Old-age, Survivors and Disability Insurance Program.

UNIVERSITIES
superannuation scheme for, 125 *n.*; 135

VENEZUELA
early scheme, 33; grading system for workers, 45; financing of benefits, 66; wages as factor in sickness insurance, 74; medical care and benefits, 161; contributory schemes introduced, 215

Voluntary insurance schemes, 29; guarding soundness of, 34; in U.S.A., 35, 167-70; state's contributions, 43; skilled and unskilled workers in, 45; comparison with social insurance, 55-7, 239; effects of changes in money values, 58; effects of inflation, 79 *n.*; for medical care, 161, 163; in Canadian health service, 167-70; for part costs of health services, 180; views on, in Canada and U.S.A., 237. *See also* Occupational pensions

WAGES
as factor in relation to benefits and contributions, 40, 42-5, 57, 59-62, 74, 120-7, 143-5, 178, 187, 190-1, 203-4, 217, 224, 230, 238, 241; as factor in employ-

ment of elderly persons, 102; estimated loss of, in depressions, 216

WAR VICTIMS AND VETERANS percentage distribution of expenditure for, 94 (table); and of income maintenance payments for, 95 (table)

WEST INDIES poor relief, 48-9; proportion of elderly poor in Barbados, 112 n.; individual saving, 127

WIDOWS AND ORPHANS 16-17; financing of pensions, 69; percentage distribution of income maintenance payments to, 95 (table); retirement benefits in U.S.A., 114 n.; provision for, 207-8; allowances as economic stabiliser, 215

Willard, Dr Jo W., 11, 150

WOMEN retirement statistics, 108 n.; and part-time work, 109; British government's employment of older women in civil service,

110; pensionable ages, 114; in occupational pensions schemes, 134

WORKERS' CONTRIBUTIONS 59-62, 65, 66, 80-3, 123, 135, 178, 187-9, 197

WORKMEN'S COMPENSATION 194-205; early lack of, 17; present systems, 28; in Canada and U.S.A., 28, 56, 159-60, 206-7; costs distribution, 65; financing systems, 69, 74 n.; as economic stabiliser, 215; and rehabilitation and retraining, 221; effects of inflation, 223; pensions preferable to lump-sum benefits, 245. See also Disability

YUGOSLAVIA percentage distribution of receipts for social insurance and family allowances, 67 (table), 68; expenditure as percentage of national income, 87 (table)

Zelenka, Antoine, 231 n.